D1568350

WORDSWORTH'S PHILOSOPHIC SONG

Wordsworth wrote that he longed to compose 'some philosophic Song / Of Truth that cherishes our daily life.' Yet he never finished *The Recluse*, his long philosophical poem. Simon Jarvis argues that Wordsworth's aspiration to 'philosophic song' is central to his greatness, and changed the way English poetry was written. Some critics see Wordsworth as a systematic thinker, while for others, he is a poet first, and a thinker only (if at all) second. Jarvis shows instead how essential both philosophy and the 'song' of poetry were to Wordsworth's achievement. Drawing on advanced work in continental philosophy and social theory to address the ideological attacks which have dominated much recent commentary, Jarvis reads Wordsworth's writing both critically and philosophically, to show how Wordsworth thinks through and in verse. This study rethinks the relation between poetry and society itself by analysing the tensions between thinking philosophically and writing poetry.

SIMON JARVIS is Gorley Putt Reader in Poetry and Poetics at the University of Cambridge. He is the author of *Scholars and Gentlemen: Shakespearian Textual Criticism and Representations of Scholarly Labour, 1725–1765* (1995) and *Adorno: A Critical Introduction* (1998).

CAMBRIDGE STUDIES IN ROMANTICISM

This series aims to foster the best new work in one of the most challenging fields within English literary studies. From the early 1780s to the early 1830s a formidable array of talented men and women took to literary composition, not just in poetry, which some of them famously transformed, but in many modes of writing. The expansion of publishing created new opportunities for writers, and the political stakes of what they wrote were raised again by what Wordsworth called those 'great national events' that were 'almost daily taking place': the French Revolution, the Napoleonic and American wars, urbanization, industrialization, religious revival, an expanded empire abroad and the reform movement at home. This was an enormous ambition, even when it pretended otherwise. The relations between science, philosophy, religion, and literature were reworked in texts such as *Frankenstein* and *Biographia Literaria*; gender relations in *A Vindication of the Rights of Woman* and *Don Juan*; journalism by Cobbett and Hazlitt; poetic form, content and style by the Lake School and the Cockney School. Outside Shakespeare studies, probably no body of writing has produced such a wealth of response or done so much to shape the responses of modern criticism. This indeed is the period that saw the emergence of those notions of 'literature' and of literary history, especially national literary history, on which modern scholarship in English has been founded.

The categories produced by Romanticism have also been challenged by recent historicist arguments. The task of the series is to engage both with a challenging corpus of Romantic writings and with the changing field of criticism they have helped to shape. As with other literary series published by Cambridge, this one will represent the work of both younger and more established scholars, on either side of the Atlantic and elsewhere.

For a complete list of titles published see end of book.

WORDSWORTH'S PHILOSOPHIC SONG

SIMON JARVIS

CAMBRIDGE
UNIVERSITY PRESS

CAMBRIDGE UNIVERSITY PRESS
Cambridge, New York, Melbourne, Madrid, Cape Town, Singapore, São Paulo

Cambridge University Press
The Edinburgh Building, Cambridge CB2 2RU, UK

Published in the United States of America by Cambridge University Press, New York

www.cambridge.org
Information on this title: www.cambridge.org/9780521862684

First published 2007

Printed in the United Kingdom at the University Press, Cambridge

A catalogue record for this publication is available from the British Library

Library of Congress Cataloging-in-Publication data

Jarvis, Simon.
Wordsworth's philosophic song / Simon Jarvis.
p. cm. – (Cambridge studies in Romanticism; 67)
Includes bibliographical references and index.
ISBN-13 978-0-521-86268-4 (hardback)
ISBN-10 0-521-86268-X (hardback)

1. Wordsworth, William, 1770–1850–Philosophy. 2. Wordsworth,
William, 1770–1850–Criticism and interpretation. 3. Self (Philosopy) in literature.
4. Philosophy in literature. I. Title. II. Series.
PR5892.P5J37 2006
821'.7–dc22
2006025231

It is the possible, never the immediately actual, that blocks off utopia.

Contents

Acknowledgements

For help, advice, information and inspiration of various kinds over a number of years I thank the following: Ruth Abbott, Jay Bernstein, Phillip Blond, the British Academy, Marilyn Butler, Fenella Cannell, Cathy Caruth, Howard Caygill, Jim Chandler, Stefan Collini, Peter De Bolla, Haydn Downey, Elizabeth Edwards, Howard Erskine-Hill, Frances Ferguson, Yoram Gorlizki, Sarah Haggarty, Wayne Hankey, Neil Hertz, Neil Hitchen, Roger Howard, Mary Jacobus, Gillian Jarvis, Michael Jarvis, Tim Jarvis, John Kerrigan, Dominick LaCapra, Nigel Leask, Nigel Mapp, Charles Martindale, John Milbank, Drew Milne, Reeve Parker, Ian Patterson, Roland Polastro, J. H. Prynne, John and Gayle Richards, the late Gillian Rose, the Warden and Fellows of Robinson College, Cambridge, Michael Rossington, Jim Siegel, James Simpson, the Society for the Humanities at Cornell University, Keston Sutherland, Peter Swaab, Gordon Teskey, Nick Walker, Nigel Wheale, and Ross Wilson. Mark Offord's extensive comments on the whole manuscript were of the highest value. The book is dedicated to Tim Jarvis.

Abbreviations

Borderers	William Wordsworth, *The Borderers*, ed. Robert Osborn (Ithaca, N.Y.: Cornell University Press, 1982)
DC MS	Dove Cottage manuscript
EY	*The Letters of William and Dorothy Wordsworth. The Early Years, 1787–1805*, arranged and ed. Ernest De Selincourt (2nd edn, rev. Chester L. Shaver, Oxford: Clarendon Press, 1967)
Fourteen-Book Prelude	W. J. B. Owen, ed., *The Fourteen-Book Prelude* (Ithaca, N.Y.: Cornell University Press, 1985)
Home at Grasmere	*Home at Grasmere. Part First, Book First of 'The Recluse'*, ed. Beth Darlington (Ithaca, N.Y.: Cornell University Press, 1977)
Last Poems	*Last Poems, 1821–1850*, ed. Jared Curtis with Apryl Lea Denny-Ferris and Jillian Heydt-Stevenson (Ithaca, N.Y.: Cornell University Press, 1999)
Lyrical Ballads	*"Lyrical Ballads", and Other Poems, 1797–1800*, ed. James Butler and Karen Green (Ithaca, N.Y.: Cornell University Press, 1992)
OED	*The Oxford English Dictionary, Second Edition*, prepared by J. A. Simpson and E. S. C. Weiner (20 vols., Oxford: Clarendon Press, 1989)
Poems, in Two Volumes	*'Poems, in Two Volumes' and Other Poems, 1800–1807*, ed. Jared Curtis (Ithaca, N.Y.: Cornell University Press, 1983)

Reed, *Early Years*	Mark L. Reed, *Wordsworth: The Chronology of the Early Years, 1770–1799* (Cambridge, Mass.: Harvard University Press, 1967)
Reed, *Middle Years*	Mark. L. Reed, *Wordsworth: The Chronology of the Middle Years* (Cambridge, Mass.: Harvard University Press, 1975)
Reiman	Donald Reiman, ed., *The Romantics Reviewed. Part A. The Lake Poets* (2 vols., New York and London: Garland, 1972)
Ruined Cottage	Wordsworth, *The Ruined Cottage and the Pedlar*, ed. James Butler (Ithaca, N.Y.: Cornell University Press, 1979)
Shorter Poems 1807–1820	*Shorter Poems 1807–1820*, ed. Carl H. Ketcham (Ithaca, N.Y.: Cornell University Press, 1989)
Salisbury Plain	Stephen Gill, ed., *The Salisbury Plain Poems of William Wordsworth* (Ithaca, N.Y.: Cornell University Press, 1975)
Thirteen-Book Prelude	*The Thirteen-Book Prelude*, ed. Mark L. Reed (2 vols., Ithaca, N.Y.: Cornell University Press, 1991)
Tuft of Primroses	Joseph S. Kishel, ed., *The Tuft of Primroses, with Other Late Poems for The Recluse* (Ithaca, N.Y.: Cornell University Press, 1986)
Wu, *1770–1799*	Duncan Wu, *Wordsworth's Reading, 1770–1799* (Cambridge: Cambridge University Press, 1993)
Wu, *1800–1815*	Duncan Wu, *Wordsworth's Reading, 1800–1815* (Cambridge: Cambridge Univeristy Press, 1995)

Introduction: poetic thinking

When Wordsworth is trying to get started on his projected long poem, 'The Recluse', he reviews the fantasies of major poetic achievements which he has at various times entertained. The catalogue culminates in this:

> Then, last wish,
> My last and favourite aspiration! then
> I yearn towards some philosophic Song
> Of Truth that cherishes our daily life;
> With meditations passionate from deep
> Recesses in man's heart, immortal verse
> Thoughtfully fitted to the Orphean lyre;
> But from this awful burthen I full soon
> Take refuge, and beguile myself with trust
> That mellower years will bring a riper mind
> And clearer insight.
>
> (i. 229–39)[1]

How important, and in what ways, was this 'favourite aspiration' to what Wordsworth actually did in the end write? For one of the most illuminating among recent readings of Wordsworth, it was not very important at all. Or rather: not only was it important only in so far as it was harmful, but it was not even fully Wordsworth's *own* aspiration:

Coleridge wanted to believe for reasons of his own, and he persuaded Wordsworth also to believe, that a young poet's gradual development toward self-consciousness was his major theme, and that its truth for morals was gratitude to nature for having made him what he was. With that description of the poet's work came the burden of a special project, of which Wordsworth was the destined executor – a theodicy, both metaphysical and historical in scope, whose leading evidences would come from the receptive and infinitely associable mind of the poet. ... But his friend's ambitions were mismatched to his own talents. When you have

I

disposed of the philosophy of *The Prelude*, you have not disposed of Wordsworth but only of a notion someone once had of him, which he unfortunately came to share. The long poem he withheld for most of his life is a record of accidents, to which the author hoped to give coherence.[2]

It is easy to go along with these remarks when we read what Coleridge himself later said about the matter. Coleridge remembered that in the poem envisaged by them together, Wordsworth

should assume the station of a man in repose, whose mind was made up, and so prepared to deliver upon authority a system of philosophy. He was to treat man as man – a subject of eye, ear, touch, and taste, in contact with external nature – informing the senses from the mind and not compounding a mind out of the senses – then the pastoral and other states, assuming a satiric or Juvenalian spirit as he approached the high civilization of cities and towns, and then opening a melancholy picture of the present state of degeneracy and vice – thence revealing the necessity for and proof of the whole state of man and society being subject to and illustrative of a redemptive process in operation – showing how this Idea reconciled all the anomalies, and how it promised future glory and restoration. Something of this sort I suggested – and it was agreed on. It is what in substance I have been all my life doing in my system of philosophy.[3]

We should indeed be grateful that Wordsworth never completed any such pandect. The poet's mind is to be 'made up'. He is to deliver ('upon authority'!) a 'system of philosophy'. And, in the end, everything is to come out right. All the 'anomalies' are to be reconciled. Here, just as Bromwich says, is an entire theodicy. Worse, it is *Coleridge's* theodicy. Wordsworth, it appears, is to do little more than just add verse.

This in turn may raise doubts about the way Wordsworth writes about his 'last and favourite aspiration' at the beginning of *The Prelude*. Perhaps this aspiration was an 'awful burthen' just because it was not really his own? And perhaps he kept taking refuge from it just because of the inadequately imagined relationship between thinking and versifying which surfaces in the very expression of that aspiration?

This line of thought is attractive for a number of reasons. Bromwich feels keenly that some recent Wordsworth criticism traces a path of misrecognition – in which, he implies, an over-philosophized conception of Wordsworth has been an important instrument in turning his writing into an object suitable to the purposes of suspicion. If the systematic or metaphysical or epistemological aspects of Wordsworth's writing can be regarded as in large part an alien growth, then it will be harder for the systematizing or metaphysical or epistemological readings which have so dominated Wordsworth criticism to take reductive purchase on his authorship. Whether such philosophizing readings are concerned with leading Wordsworth back to some set of epistemological or metaphysical sources, or whether they wish to see him as anticipating or violating some more recent set of epistemological or metaphysical ideas, any such approach would risk at once disqualifying itself from primary interest, because it would take Wordsworth to be interesting chiefly in so far as he thinks or writes like someone else. In such a case whatever might be singular in Wordsworth's writing must be overlooked.

But perhaps Wordsworth's aspiration to 'philosophic Song' was not quite the same as Coleridge's later picture of a verse theodicy? Curiously, impatience with Wordsworth's philosophizing can *also* find a Coleridgean point of departure. Stanley Cavell has seen in Coleridge's treatment of the 'best Philosopher' passage of the great Ode a moment at which the critic's insight falters: 'It is this sudden', for Cavell, '– when Wordsworth flies his philosophical colours, then Coleridge's seemingly limitless capacity for sympathetic understanding toward other writers he thought genuine is stripped away, his tolerance for mysticism and his contempt for reductive empiricisms forgotten, and he starts firing at will.'[4] Bromwich draws a sharp distinction between the interesting accidents and the tedious generalities in Wordsworth's writing, and we can all think of passages in the poet's work of general reflection lacking vital interest. Yet what Wordsworth writes when he talks about his aspiration to philosophic song seems to suggest that he does not think of the relationship between singular experience and general truth in quite that way. What is yearnt towards is a song 'Of Truth that cherishes our daily life'. It appears not to be the kind of aspiration which seeks to shake off 'the accidents of nature, time, and place' (x. 822) but the opposite: one which can 'incorporate itself with the blood and vital juices of our minds'.[5] The question at issue is whether, as Bromwich suggests, the philosophical aspirations in Wordsworth's writing are adventitious, superimposed upon a steady look at the subject which already contains all that is of vital interest; or whether that steady look at the subject itself developed as it did partly because of, rather than in spite of, Wordsworth's aspiration to be a philosophical poet.

If that last possibility were true, what could be meant by 'philosophic Song' might be something quite different from a system, a method, a theodicy, or any other kind of philosophical edifice from which '[a]ll the anomalies' would have been removed. It might mean, not that philosophy gets fitted into a song – where all the thinking is done by philosophy and only the handiwork by verse – but that the song itself, *as song*, is philosophic. It might mean that a different kind of thinking happens in verse – that instead of being a sort of thoughtless ornament or reliquary for thinking, verse is itself a kind of cognition, with its own resistances and difficulties. If that were so, Wordsworth's verse would not be 'philosophic Song' chiefly in so far as it exemplified or anticipated some already existing or future philosophical system or authorship. Quite the reverse: it would be philosophic *song* precisely in so far as driven – by the felt need to give utterance to non-replicable singular experiences in the collectively and historically cognitive form of verse – to obstruct, displace or otherwise change the syntax and the lexicons currently available for the articulation of such experience. Driven to truth, that is, less by top-quality ratiocination than by attention to problems of poetic *making*: provided that such making be understood not as sheer craft, but as itself already a cognitive matter.[6] And, in this, it would, after all, rejoin at least in part another Coleridge: not the one who wanted all the anomalies to be reconciled, but the one who understood that 'in Shakespeare's poems, the creative power and the intellectual energy wrestle as in a war embrace. Each in its excess of strength seems to threaten the extinction of the other.'[7]

This book attempts to explore this last possibility. The remainder of this introduction investigates what Wordsworth himself understood by the phrase 'philosophical Poet', and where we might find elements of such philosophical poetry in his verse.

The structure of the main body of the book requires a word of explanation, because its two parts pursue very different kinds of enquiry, and with very different methods. The first part, 'Counter-spirits', constitutes a kind of extended philosophical introduction, but one which continually returns, at varying intervals, to Wordsworth himself. In it, I argue that it is mistaken to assume that poetic thinking and materialist thinking must be opposites. I proceed by scrutinizing some of the reasons which have been or might be given for discounting the possibility of philosophic song: scrutinizing, that is, both the reasons for discounting the possibility that any poetry might bear truth, and the reasons for arguing that Wordsworth's in particular does not. The chapters in this part of the book therefore range widely, both across Wordsworth's authorships and across other authorships anterior to, contemporary with, and post-dating his. They are concerned not only with literary and aesthetic material, but also with fundamental arguments in the sphere of social theory.

I begin this attempt sideways on, by looking at a motif which might at first sight appear to be of marginal importance both to this author and to this period: the motif of idolatry and of idol-breaking. Wordsworth comes to feel that these apparent opposites are mutually dependent. His verse and prose trace this dependence steadily and subtly. This matters more broadly, I then suggest in the second chapter, because of the way in which our ubiquitous social-scientific concept of 'ideology' has developed out of the older Christian concept of 'idolatry'. I show that this is not merely a matter of ancient history but very vitally concerns weaknesses in the concepts of 'ideology' and 'ideology-critique' as they are applied today. Here I defend Marx against some of his admirers. I contrast Marx's comic and restricted conception of 'ideology' with some of the literal and generalized ones prevalent today. Marx's conception was not primarily an assault on mystifying ideals. It was an assault on the idea that assaulting mystifying ideals would make you free. Its subsequent extension to domains such as poetry is therefore in need of consideration, rather than self-evidently legitimate. Smashing up an idol is not necessarily a less superstitious act than venerating it. What we now call 'ideology-critique' is what Marx meant by 'ideology'; essential to what I am tempted to call Marx's *romantic materialism* is an emphatic and unbridgeable distinction between the living and the non-living which would now in most quarters figure as 'romantic ideology' or as 'metaphysics' (chapter 3).

If, then, we are not free to draw upon a polar opposition between a supposedly disenchanted 'materialism' and a supposedly deluded 'ideology', we are free to reconsider the range of questions brought up by the idea of materialism in relation to Wordsworth's writing. In the following chapter I suggest that would-be 'materialism' has too often relied upon an economistic framework for thinking about the experience and social organization of need, desire and pleasure: a framework, that is, which generalizes to all experience the common sense associated with a particular mode of production, distribution and consumption. I argue that Wordsworth was able to attend to experiences of need, desire and pleasure which could not be properly described or understood according to an economistic framework. The idea that these acts of attention are 'ideological' can be sustained only if a historically particular notion of an opposition between disinterested giving and interested exchange is converted into a universal economic anthropology.

In these chapters which make up the first part, I am attempting to call into question a number of philosophical, historiographical and social-theoretical assumptions familiar from some recent approaches to

Wordsworth's poetry, as well as from some other contexts; but I am not mainly interested in the question of whether some group or other of critics might be right or wrong. Instead I am attempting to limit the powers of some large and imposing conceptual arrays which are sometimes applied as if they required no philosophical scrutiny. I am attempting to do this in the first place on the basis of my own arguments and evidence; and, in the second place, on the basis of my argument that Wordsworth's own writing provides resources for truer apprehensions of some of the problems which these assumptions concern. I am also suggesting that the 'historical' 'contexts' necessary to a consideration of any modern poetry extend back through centuries, and even millennia, rather than decades.

Having thus, as I hope, shown that the possibility that Wordsworth's poetry might bear truth cannot, at least, be ruled out in advance, I turn in the second main part of the book, 'Common day', to attempt an interpretation of some aspects of the truth-content which I hope to find in it. These four chapters each take a narrower and more consecutive form than their predecessors. Each is principally concerned with a single reading, around which readings of other work and sources are in each case clustered.

A recent work of subtle phenomenology sets as its goal a quality of attention which 'might cease to rule out of court the appearing of those phenomena which exceed us, which surprise us, and which most closely affect us'.[8] There could be worse analogies for the wish animating Wordsworth's acts of poetic attention. His writing is always breaking through to some experience for which the available lexicons fail to allow. Each of these chapters, then, attempts to bring to light the way in which the experience of attending closely to some poem or passage of a poem in Wordsworth's authorship leaves inoperable the series of philosophical or commonsensical *idées reçues* by means of which the experiences concerned are usually suppressed, obliviated, or ruled out of court. Each thus moves gradually towards opening up some of the meanings in Wordsworth's poetic thinking of some central concept or concepts. This is more and less than a philological task, because it is concerned with exceptional rather than with typical or unexceptional moments in Wordsworth's authorship. Instead it is a task for philosophical poetics.[9] These chapters deliberately concern themselves with conceptual constellations which seem to be amongst the most rebarbative and least redeemable for many contemporary readers: those around *happiness* ('The Tuft of Primroses'), *infinity* (books 7 and 8 of the 1804–5 *Prelude*), *life* (book 5 of *The Prelude*) and *light* (Ode ('There was a time')); and they deliberately seek 'philosophic Song' not only in reflective or speculative poems and passages, but also in those where the poet collides with or cherishes quotidian particularities. In their course, some other fundamental concepts of Wordsworth's poetic thinking are also interpreted: *human, gift, thinking, glory, bliss*, in particular. Together, these chapters lead to a conclusion in which a possible reinterpretation of Wordsworth's Imagination is suggested.

A word is needed here about the practice adopted in this book in relation to proper names. As would be expected, all quotations are attributed, and given precise references.[10] But on a few occasions, and especially when I quote from the works of authors not contemporary with Wordsworth, the author's proper name is given only in the accompanying note, and is not mentioned in the main text. The reason for this is as follows. One serious obstacle to the vitally necessary exchange between philosophy and literary criticism – an obstacle which has made many good literary critics wish that the exchange would cease altogether – has been the unphilosophical practice of allowing the name of an authorship to usurp the consideration which should be given to the thoughts contained in it. The reliance on the proper names of the philosophers or of the star theorists creates a situation in which their thoughts are 'always already read', in the sense that as soon as we see those names a pre-interpreted series of 'positions' tends to be marshalled. In these circumstances, readers' eyes readily slip from the words quoted to the proper name taken to be in possession of them. The name is read *instead of* the thoughts. The proper names are not suppressed here – all may be found in the relevant notes – but they are sometimes deprived of prominence where it is judged that such prominence might tend to divert attention from the thoughts themselves.

It is also necessary to say why substantial passages of this book, and especially of Part I, are devoted not only to authors other than Wordsworth, but, in many instances, to authors whose works he could not have read. Much of what we think of as simple common sense is yesterday's unintelligibly avant-garde social science, or metaphysics or epistemology. Primary discussions of concepts determined by those fields are essential, not so that we shall have a new set of tools to apply to Wordsworth, nor (still worse) so that Wordsworth can be made to fit in with some contemporary or social-scientific position – but simply in order to have a chance of recovering some of what is peculiar to Wordsworth from the frameworks used to contain him. All the humanities are philosophical through and through – except where they expect some other discipline to do their thinking for them. In this sense it is my contention that no book which does not renew epistemological, metaphysical, aesthetic, social-scientific and other ideas for itself is likely to be able to hope to interpret Wordsworth's *singularity* at all.

'According to Democritus, truth lies hidden at the bottom of a well; and, according to Schopenhauer, it gets a rap on the knuckles when it tries to come out.'[1] The aphorism is comic and faintly sinister. Personified, but only enough so to have knuckles, truth looks less like a goddess than like the half-human monster everyone is trying to push back into the well. Here 'truth' may be, not what is arrived at when all error shall have been deleted, but what gets *blurted out* when the usual defences are down.

This sense of the word 'truth' as something which is blurted out might seem to be at the furthest remove from the kind of truth-effect which, if any, is to be found in Wordsworth's poetry. Schopenhauer's idea relies on a sense of puncturing, of the material breaking in upon the ideal. So its most comfortable element, if anywhere in verse, might seem to be in satire: in a medium which allows for or indeed may even be structured around the kind of bathos exemplified in Schopenhauer's aphorism. In particular, much critical attention to Wordsworth over the last two decades has understood what is happening in his poetry as the very *reverse* of any such process: as the concealment, sublimation, occlusion or efface-ment of minute socio-historical-material specificity in an idealizing or aestheticizing 'ideology'. It is then reserved to materialist or historicist criticism to perform the kind of truth-effect imagined by Schopenhauer: to bring to light the inconvenient particularities which an idealizing poetry has been shoving back into the well. If, however, the reader can (as I hope he or she later may) be persuaded that the description of Wordsworth as an idealist has limitations, then it may be that this sense for truth is not closed to his poetry either. What that blurting-out might mean in poetry could be, for example, a moment at which a loss of control over a language which it is precisely the poet's art to master, to turn into an instrument, appears to testify to some specific emotional or intellectual (and necessarily and quite trivially material, historical and particular) pressure which makes that instrumentalism break down.

It could be this kind of moment:

> Stern Lawgiver! yet thou dost wear
> The Godhead's most benignant grace;

Nor know we anything so fair
As is the smile upon thy face:
Flowers laugh before thee on their beds;
And Fragrance in thy footing treads;
Thou dost preserve the Stars from wrong;
And the most ancient Heavens through Thee are fresh and strong.[12]

The connection between stars and duty had been made more famously, and in a rather different way, before:

Two things fill the mind with ever new and increasing admiration and reverence, the more often and more steadily one reflects on them: *the starry heavens above me and the moral law within me.* I do not need to search for them and merely conjecture them as though they were veiled in obscurity or in the transcendent region [*im Überschwenglichen*] beyond my horizon; I see them before me and connect them immediately with the consciousness of my existence.[13]

This passage has the power that it does partly because its suddenly concrete evocation of wonder and amazement comes at the end of a closely reasoned and difficult account of the a priori grounds of moral theory. Yet there is more to it than this. Perhaps the power which the passage has had for readers of Kant partly results from the faint hint of a transgression which this phrase contains of Kant's prohibition upon 'stray[ing] [*ausschweifen*] into intelligible worlds', a prohibition obedience to which, in Kant's mind, critically distinguishes his thought from dogmatic metaphysics.[14] By saying in passing that he sees the moral law before him, it feels as though Kant is treating the reality of the moral law as known not merely by practical but also by theoretical reason. When he says that he sees the stars before him it is as though what we know to be true of cognition from the first critique – that the manifold of intuition presented by sensibility to the understanding has no determinacy until determinacy is bestowed by the categories – is momentarily bypassed, and we just are really seeing the stars: *I see them before me.* It is as though, then, in this phrase, 'I see them before me', we experience the temptation of getting our hands on a continually re-prohibited immediacy of experience. Yet at the same time, the passage testifies to an irreparably split life. The moral law is inside, the stars are outside. What creates a wondrous effect here is the vertiginous contrast which is compressed into the single emphatic phrase: *the starry heavens above me and the moral law within me.* It is vertiginous not because it is a contrast in scale: because, for example, we pass from something infinitely large to something infinitesimally small; but because it is a contrast between 'two things' which cannot in fact be compared with each other at all. Each is immeasurable; both are mutually incommensurable. Yet here our perception of both is represented as absolutely immediate.

Wordsworth's lines were first received in print not as wondrous but as ridiculous. 'The two last lines seem to be utterly without meaning; at least we have no sort of conception in what sense *Duty* can be said to keep the old skies *fresh*, and the stars from wrong.'[15] Whatever we might think of Jeffrey's implied valuation, he has put his finger on an important part of what it is like to read these lines. It really is hard to know what is meant by them. Before rushing to defend them by supplying such a meaning, and perhaps in the process rushing to destroy just what is interesting about them, I want to consider some of the metrico-rhythmic questions they raise, not with the foolish hope of reasoning the reader into finding them beautiful, but rather, starting from my singular and perhaps non-universalizable experience of their pathos, to search in the manner of reflective judgement for the possible concepts which they may require.[16]

There is a suggestion of hypermetricality about that last line: 'And the most ancient Heavens through Thee are fresh and strong.' The stanza shape adopted by Wordsworth, in fact, produces of itself the sense of an excess or overspill since, in each, seven four-foot lines culminate in a closing hexameter. All of these final closing hexameters, except this and the last line of the first stanza, have twelve syllables. In the closing line of the first stanza and in this line the syllable count is uncertain:

> From strife and from despair; a glorious ministry.
> And the most ancient Heavens through Thee are fresh and strong.

Standard practice in the century before Wordsworth would have removed any ambivalence by reading with a clear elision on 'glorious' ('glor-yus') in the first instance and 'Heavens' ('Heav'ns') in the latter, so as to make both of these words into disyllables rather than trisyllables. In a penetrating recent study of Wordsworth's metrical practice, Brennan O'Donnell has shown the importance of such words.[17] O'Donnell shows that much of Wordsworth's thinking about metre implies the importance of keeping open a separation between rhythm and metre which much prosodic thinking of the period wished to close in favour of the former. Whereas John Thelwall, for example, developed a theory of prosody based on musical categories, in which syllable counting and the concept of abstract metrical feet were both rejected, Wordsworth's statements about prosody and practice of versification instead depend upon a difference between the metrical set, an abstract norm which can never perfectly be realized, and the singular specificity of any given rhythmic utterance. It is in this tension between norm and fact, as it were, that the life of verse-reading is conceived to lie. Neither a sing-song reading which uses the metrical set to override variations which may be syntactically required, nor a 'prosaic' reading in which metrical expectations are simply overridden, is satisfactory. In a letter to Thelwall written in mid-January 1804, close to the time at which Wordsworth was writing the 'Ode to Duty',[18] Wordsworth agreed with him that 'the art of verse should not compell you to read in ... emphasis etc that violates the nature of prose', but also warned against the opposite vice:

This rule should be taken with limitations for not to speak of other reasons as long as verse shall have the marked termination that rhyme gives it and as long as blank verse shall be printed in lines, it will be Physically impossible to pronounce the last words or syllables of the lines with the same indifference, as the others, i.e., not to give them an intonation of one kind or an other, or to follow them with a pause, not called out for by the passion of the subject, but by the passion of metre merely.[19]

In the preface to the 1815 *Poems* Wordsworth put the problem in these terms: 'the law of long syllable and short must not be so inflexible, – the letter of metre must not be so impassive to the spirit of versification, – as to deprive the Reader of all voluntary power to modulate, in subordination to the sense, the music of the poem'.[20] The two passages are full of suggestive connections with Wordsworth's broader habits of feeling and reflection. If we consider for now, though, what they might mean for the case before us, we can develop an answer by analogy. For both Wordsworth and Thelwall 'Heav'ns' and 'glor-yus' would be readings that would 'violate the nature of prose', but for Wordsworth a clearly trisyllabic 'glo-ri-ous' and disyllabic 'Hea-vens' would also risk ignoring 'the passion of metre'. The reading indicated, then, would seem to be one which would preserve the syllabic ambiguity of the words. This would leave us in both cases, not with clearly hypermetrical lines, but with lines in which there is a trace, a suggestion or a potential for hypermetricality.

This may be one of several reasons why the atmosphere of this poem feels so different from that of the poem which Wordsworth later described as its model, Gray's 'Ode to Adversity'. The stanza pattern is

what is called the 'same' as that in Wordsworth's poem, and O'Donnell
notes that the introduction of a closing hexameter to ode stanzas was
widely popularized by Prior's 'Ode, Humbly Inscrib'd to the Queen. On
the Glorious Succession of Her Majesty's Arms, 1706. Written in Imitation of Spenser's Stile'.[21] There the ode stanza is a Spenserian one
enlarged by the addition of a further pentameter before the final
hexameter. In that poem, and in Gray's, however, none of the closing
hexameters at all risks hypermetricality. In Gray's ode, the final lines may
still produce a sense of a swell of feeling at the close of each stanza,
especially in the polysyndetonic (and most Spenserian and proto-
Wordsworthian of all the hexameters here) 'Despair and fell Disease and
ghastly Poverty';[22] but at no point does the sense of near loss of control
which belongs (as I shall argue) to Wordsworth's ode surface. In Prior's
ode the possibility is at one point explicitly excluded by typographical
direction of reading: 'To find the vent'rous Foe, and Battel him again.'[23]
And, unless we are arbitrarily and artificially to abstract from our
experience of these works, it is relevant to note that this line, 'And the
most ancient Heavens through Thee are fresh and strong', is by some
distance also typographically the longest in the poem.

   The line's excess may be part of what makes it feel like a key point in or
climax to the poem. What is going on in this excess, if we return to the
passages of prosodic theory quoted above, is that the letter of metre and
the spirit of rhythm are in a relationship of mutual correction. The
scriptural opposition between spirit and letter is notoriously a trope
which Wordsworth can deploy to elevate living spirit and to deprecate the
dead letter;[24] yet here the implication, if we read both passages together,
is slightly different: the letter must accommodate the spirit, but the spirit
must also measure itself against the letter. (This figure from *philologia
sacra* has the advantage over, say, Kant's figure of prosody as a
'mechanism', that both aspects are in a partially flexible tension: a
mechanism's shape, barring a miracle, remains the same irrespective of
what is put inside it.)[25]

   If we reflect on this, it does not take long to see that the problem which
the poem is discussing has important consequences for the way we read
the metrical-rhythmic relation in it. One remarkable fact about the poem,
and what makes it surprisingly generous and involving for a poem so
explicitly about duty, is the extent to which the poet, instead of writing
from a vantage point at which the moral law would have been fully
secured, writes instead almost an apology for the weakness which makes
him need to obey it. Whether or not it was written with knowledge of

Schiller's *Letters on the Aesthetic Education of Humanity*, the poem precisely demarcates the *in*sufficiency of what may, if anything may, properly be called 'aesthetic ideology': of the idea that there is an 'aesthetic state' which represents a *harmony* between duty and inclination.[26] The poet wishes well to any for whom this still works (ll. 9–16), while none the less asking duty to help them out when it should stop working (16); but he bluntly regards it in his own case as having diminished to an alibi: 'I shoved unwelcome tasks away' (30). What is remarkable is that even though the poem is explicitly presenting a case for the bindingness of duty *instead of* any possible harmony of duty and inclination, the motive for this very case is nevertheless represented, not as the eventual emergence of a sincere disinterestedness, but as in its turn a new form of desire:

> Through no disturbance of my soul,
> Or strong compunction in me wrought,
> I supplicate for thy controul;
> But in the quietness of thought:
> Me this uncharter'd freedom tires;
> I feel the weight of chance desires:
> My hopes no more must change their name,
> I long for a repose which ever is the same.

The reason given here for rejecting 'Uncharter'd' – or what we might possibly call, with a borrowing of idiom, 'abstract' freedom – is not that such freedom is irresponsible, but that it does not in the event feel very free. The contrast seems almost designed with what we might think of as the *sortilege of landscape* with which the 'Poem / Title not yet fixed upon' opens – 'should the guide I chuse Be nothing better than a wandering cloud / I cannot miss my way. . . . Or shall a twig or any floating thing / Upon the river, point me out my course?'[27] Duty is supplicated because, it is *almost* admitted, of a laziness, a longing for a repose which can never be disturbed.

It is this *longing* which can be felt in the ambiguous or potential hypermetricality of the line 'And the most ancient Heavens through Thee are fresh and strong.' The equivocal or possible hypermetricality arises just because one kind of abstract freedom (the freedom to speak the lines exactly as you ordinarily would like to) and one kind of abstract rigorism (the demand to speak the lines just as the metrician supposed to know would have you) have been rejected: yet not in favour of some actually existing harmonious state, a perfect balance between the duty to metre and the inclination to prose, but in favour of a tense or, better, *living* recognition of difference – that [sense of] 'similitude in dissimilitude' which Wordsworth thought so vital as to offer an explanation for the pleasures of sex and prosody alike.[28]

If metrical-rhythmic features help this line come to seem as though it is a climax to the poem, this sense is if anything increased rather than diminished by the difficulty that, as Jeffrey straightaway remarked, it is so hard to see what it means. It was perhaps because Wordsworth felt this difficulty that he wrote thus of this part of his poem in his 'Reply to Mathetes':

When in his character of Philosophical Poet, having thought of Morality as implying in its essence voluntary obedience, and producing the effect of order, he transfers, in the transport of imagination, the law of Moral to physical Natures and, having contemplated, through the medium of that order, all modes of existence as subservient to one spirit, concludes his address to the power of Duty in the following words . . . [29]

The explanation is especially significant for us because of what it implies about Wordsworth's idea of philosophical poetry. Wordsworth, perhaps conscious of the apparent absurdity in having said that duty keeps the stars and skies working, none the less, by describing this moment as happening 'in the transport of imagination', confers on it the highest possible status within his authorship. And still more significantly, he associates this transport of imagination with the 'character of Philosophical Poet'. A much less surprising way to have put this would have been to say that while the philosopher knows that it is not duty that keeps the stars going, the poet, in his transport of imagination, nevertheless imagines that it does. It is striking that Wordsworth, by contrast, feels that it especially belongs to the philosophical poet to have such a transport of imagination: to say, in fact, just what a philosopher never would. The explanation nevertheless has the effect of stilling this transport of imagination even as it describes it: it identifies the separation between the law of moral and physical natures as the literal truth, and the transfer of the former to the latter as a poetic transport of imagination (even if one performed by a philosophical poet). The effect of the verse, by contrast, comes precisely from there being no such caveat in it, from its being asserted, as directly and naïvely as could be, that duty stops the skies from falling in. Wordsworth from time to time did resort to the kind of self-defence which says that something in a poem was not meant literally but poetically; and whenever he does, what readers at once notice is that something critical goes missing from our sense of the verse if we believe the explanation. For at such moments the critic has partial or temporary recourse to an alibi which it is essential to the strength of the verse to deny itself: since all the life of this philosophic song lies precisely in the refusal of the bad choice between versified theory and cognitively empty autonomy.

We can see this if we consider what Wordsworth later said about his Ode ('There was a time'). The title given to the Ode from 1815 onwards already looks suspiciously convenient in providing an answer to early criticisms that the poem appeared to lack a clear subject. 'This is the subject: Intimations of Immortality from Recollections of Early Child-hood.' Equally convenient appears the remark to Isabella Fenwick in which Wordsworth displaces one of the poem's central thematic interests to the myth-kitty:

Archimedes said that he could move the world if he had a point whereon to rest his machine. Who has not felt the same aspirations as regards the world of his own mind? Having to [yield *rev to*] wield some of its elements when I was impelled to write this Poem on the 'Immortality of the Soul' I took hold of the notion of pre-existence as having sufficient foundation in humanity for authorizing me to make for my purpose the best use of it I could as a Poet.[30]

The heterodoxy, we are to think, is not believed, but only made use of. It is debited to the professional persona of the poet. In such an account, the autonomous or cognitively empty character of poetry risks looking like a fairly straightforward alibi. Yet this explanation is more elaborate than that simple purpose would need it to be. It relies on a peculiar leap from a founding proposition of physics to the creative exigencies of the poet. Moving the world of one's own mind is not very much like moving the world, so it is hard to see why Archimedes had to be introduced. Presumably one has 'to wield some of [the mind's] elements' when writing any poem. The explanation confers a peculiar arbitrariness on the use made of the doctrine of pre-existence. It suggests that it has been chosen because a pivot of *some* kind is wanted, and all that was required was for the chosen notion to have a 'sufficent foundation in humanity'. It suggests that the impulse to write the poem came first and then the subject was chosen later.

Is it possible that Wordsworth's poetic thinking takes much of its force just from a resistance to any simple separation of the character of the poet from the character of the philosopher? It is worth remembering that there is more than one way of overlooking minute historical specificity: certainly, this may easily be done by imposing some over-philosophical framework on the verse; yet it may just as easily be done by misreading back into poetic theory and practice of the late eighteenth and early nineteenth centuries a theory of the naturalized and perfected separation between philosophy and poetry which is in fact much more characteristic of the presumptions dominant in our own era. There were many at this earlier date who were entirely willing to think philosophy and poetry not merely connected, but vitally so. George Dyer's important 'Prefatory Essay. On Lyric Poetry' to his *Poems* (1800) praises 'the Greek lyrists' for 'a taste . . . philosophically beautiful'.[31] Dyer's description belongs to an austerely anti-mercantile tradition of reflection on the arts in which their central political and cognitive significance is held to have gradually been forfeited by the conversion of arts of all kind into mere luxuries and amusements, a tradition in which Gianvincenzo Gravina's often-cited *Della ragione poetica* (1731) is an especially important point.[32] John Brown's *Dissertation on Poetry and Music* (whose work Dyer cites) provides an especially clear instance of this tradition. In that work a speculative analogy is drawn between the poetry of ancient Greece and that of present-day American Indians. Did elements of civilization arrive amongst the latter, '[t]heir *Songs* would be of a *legislative* Cast; and being drawn chiefly from the Fables or History of their own Country, would contain the essential Parts of their *religious, moral,* and *political* systems.'[33]

Wordsworth does not in any simple way belong to this tradition; but its presence warns us against assuming that the idea of poetry as vitally connected to philosophy and to cognition more broadly is a late invention. In one of Wordsworth's most extended prose considerations of immortality, the character of 'philosophic Poet' plays a significant part:

Simonides, it is related, upon landing in a strange country, found the corse of an unknown person lying by the sea-side; he buried it, and was honoured throughout Greece for the piety of that act. Another ancient Philosopher, chancing to fix his eyes upon a dead body, regarded the same with slight, if not with contempt; saying 'See the shell of the flown bird!' But it is not to be supposed that the moral and tender-hearted Simonides was incapable of the lofty movements of thought, to which that other Sage gave way at the moment while his soul was intent only upon the indestructible being; nor, on the other hand, that he, in whose sight a lifeless human body was of no more value than the worthless shell from which the living fowl had departed, would not, in a different mood of mind, have been affected by those earthly considerations which had incited the philosophic Poet to the performance of that pious duty. And with regard to this latter we may be assured that, if he had been destitute of the capability of communing with the more exalted thoughts that appertain to human nature, he would have cared no more for the corse of the stranger than for the dead body of a seal or porpoise which might have been cast up by the waves. We respect the corporeal frame of Man, not merely because it is the habitation of a rational, but of an immortal Soul. Each of these Sages was in sympathy with the best feelings of our nature; feelings which, though they seem opposite to each other, have another and a finer connection than that of contrast.[34]

The passage moves in open paradox. It admires Simonides for caring for a corpse; it admires 'another Philosopher' for slighting one. '*Each* of these Sages was in sympathy with the best feelings of our nature.' How can that be? Because these feelings 'have another and finer connection than that of contrast'. The 'finer connection' is provided by the hope of or faith in immortality. Yet it seems that whatever one does, one testifies to it. Bury the corpse or do not bury it: your action will in any case witness a hope for immortality. Wordsworth assures us that if Simonides had not had any intimations of immortality, he should certainly have treated the corpse like the dead body of, say, a sea-mammal. But just such treatment – 'see the shell of the flown bird!' – by the other sage is what shows that *he* respects the immortal soul. What makes the finer connection, then, can hardly be action, if opposite actions alike witness it; yet nor is it really correctness of opinion either. The words suggest instead that this hope is something which is not quite in our control. Wordsworth's interest in the hope of immortality, at its most vital, does not circulate around its possible dogmatic demonstrability but rather around the extent to which this hope is not in our power, not to be wilfully got rid of like any old superstitious opinion, but rather recurring as an involuntary implication of apparently quite disenchanted thoughts and behaviours – and even when these seem to be quite opposed to each other. (It is significant that Wordsworth has just been arguing that total deletion of the hope for individual immortality, were it conceivable, would make 'social affections' themselves inconceivable.) The wish to live for ever is in this sense 'a Presence which is not to be put by', bespoken by your acts whether you tenderly bury the corpse or loftily leave it to rot. What was once remarked of Kant, that his thought is animated by *die Unausdenkbarkeit der Verzweiflung*, the impossibility of fully conceiving despair, also fluctuates through Wordsworth's philosophic song, but in a way which, if it is less rigorous, is also less superstitious, in that it does not believe that the only way to arrive at justified hope is to make the experiment of despairing to the maximum possible extent.[35] That is one difference between Kant's *misère ouverte* and Wordsworth's open grief.

Yet this is not all. Not only must both these opposite ways of behaving testify to the best in our nature; each must also be capable of the opposite kind of excellence. Wordsworth insists not only that Simonides would have been perfectly capable of the 'loftiness' which caused the other philosopher to slight a dead body; but also that the other philosopher would in another mood have behaved just as Simonides did. How does he know? He hopes so, and so he believes it. But why should he hope it? Perhaps because the passage is no less centrally, if less explicitly, concerned with the relation between philosopher and poet than it is with immortality and its relation to commemoration of the dead. At the phrase 'another Philosopher' we see that Wordsworth must regard Simonides as a philosopher too. This is then confirmed by his description as 'the philosophic Poet'. He is the philosophic poet who, while in the event acting tenderly, could equally have acted loftily; the other sage, while acting loftily, could equally have acted tenderly. The poet Simonides could on another occasion have acted just like the philosopher. The philosopher could on another occasion have acted like the poet. For the philosopher's loftiness to be lofty, it matters that he 'gave way' to it, that he surrendered to loftiness in a generous fluctuation of feeling rather than occupying it as his stratum by right. For the poet's tenderness to be tender, it matters that he be capable also of communing with exalted thoughts. Yet when we remember that these are not harmoniously complementary but directly opposed stances (bury the body: slight the body) we see the extent to which 'the character of philosophical poet' cannot at any rate be one of placidly co-operative addition, as it is when lofty philosophy is tenderly versified, producing neither loftiness nor tenderness. It is instead one of simultaneous affinity and antagonism between two characters which are themselves internally in productive conflict.

Is it conceivable that Wordsworth's characterization of Simonides as a 'philosophic Poet' was seriously meant, and important for his sense of what philosophical poetry was? The analysis above suggests that more is meant than simply that 'Simonides was by trade a poet, and in this instance behaved philosophically.' Although, then, if we wish to explain the power of these lines, 'Thou dost preserve the Stars from wrong, / And the most ancient Heavens through Thee are fresh and strong', we might find it useful not to close down the interpretation in accordance with the

'Reply to Mathetes', it is worth taking seriously its implication that this is a moment especially important for understanding what is meant by philosophical poetry. Let us reflect upon Jeffrey's, or our, certainty that it is unmeaning to transfer the law of moral to physical natures. That certainty rests on a long history of the purification of fact from value which is still not perfect and which may not be perfectible. It has not always been the characteristic even of western philosophy to regard it as obvious that 'moral' and 'physical' natures are evidently separate territories with separate laws governing them. Indeed it may be observed that the continuing currency of the term 'law' to describe what goes on in 'nature' exemplifies the difficulty of perfectly discontaminating a discourse of nature from moral or political concepts sedimented with historical experience.

The very first extant text of the western philosophical tradition says that successive heavens 'pay penalty and retribution to each other for their injustice'.[36] Cosmology, the description of what there is in the universe, is elaborated here through the language of legal and/or moral obligation.[37] The language is of recompense for the taking of a life. When Theophrastus quotes these remarks several centuries later, he says that Anaximander is speaking 'in rather poetical terms' here.[38] That is to say, in Theophrastus' opinion it is not that Anaximander literally thinks that the heavens pay penalties to each other. This is just a metaphor drawn from the juridical sphere and applied to the natural. For Theophrastus it is just what Anaximander is doing to 'transfer' (whether in the transport of imagination or not) 'the law of moral to physical natures', and quite as self-consciously. We may wonder, though, whether this interpretation does not retrospectively project a clean cut between political and cosmological thought back on to an epoch which did not draw the boundary in this way. And we may also note that – thanks to the ineliminably speculative character of language itself, the inconceivability of a perfect deletion of all its normative, evaluative, legislative, or other supradescriptive elements – the neat solution offered by Theophrastus has in the event never been adequate to the question. It can hardly now be determined which comes 'first', but it can be determined that metaphysics, ontology and epistemology have never succeeded in getting rid of the language of exchange, right down to Kant's use of the word 'reciprocity' to explain one of his twelve logical categories.[39] Epistemology's expressions for what there is are these: 'the given', 'data', that is, things given, gifts. We 'collect' these gifts of data, we 'work' on them, and we 'produce' results. These expressions are not in themselves figurative, but have been represented as figurative as epistemology has separated itself, as a knowing of knowing, from particular disciplines. In this light Wordsworth's insistence that it is in the 'character of Philosophical Poet' that the properties of moral nature are in the 'Ode to Duty' transferred to physical nature looks especially significant. The idea that moral and physical natures simply are separate realms relies in part for its establishment on a theory about poetry, about the 'poetical' nature of transferring the properties of one to the other. It can thus be seen that the disenchanting or enlightening work of separating one from the other proceeds in tandem with the disenchanting or enlightening work of separating literal cognition from poetical figure.

The line, and Wordsworth's defence of it, raise again the question of poetry's relationship to truth. In an important study, Marcel Detienne has traced the way in which one historical society thought about this relationship. He examines the function of poetic performance as magically efficacious speech in archaic Greek lyric. Detienne shows that such performances were not, say, an occasion for heightened sensation, lying alongside and separate from language which would be soberly true description. Rather the sense given to 'truth' in archaic Greek society was fundamentally characterized by performative efficacity.

Whether as an official of the sovereign or as one who praised the warrior nobility, the poet was always a master of truth. His 'truth' was a performative truth, never challenged or demonstrated, and fundamentally different from our own traditional concept of truth. Early *Alētheia* meant neither agreement between a proposition and its object nor agreement between judgements [i.e. neither correspondence nor coherence]. It was not the opposite of 'lies' or 'falsehood'. The only meaningful opposition involved *Alētheia* and *Lēthē*. If the poet was truly inspired, if what he had to say was based on his gift of second sight, then his speech tended to be identified with 'truth'.[40]

Such a sense for truth was unable to coexist with classical democracy, in which truth was to be established through dialogue. In this light the poet could no longer be understood as a master of truth, but only as a parasitic flatterer. Theophrastus' certainty that transferring the properties of moral to physical nature is 'poetical' already implies a world in which 'poetical' is what has no truth. Norms are separate from facts. Poems are separate from knowledge.

To blurt out 'Thou dost preserve the Stars from wrong' violates both separations at once. So far as any enlightened understanding is concerned, it is just wishful thinking. Duty does not preserve the stars from wrong. It is as though the line hopes that by saying that it does the poet might make it true. The pathos of the line comes from its open failure to do anything of the kind. It requires a voice strong enough to utter its naïvest wish. The alternative would be to wish for something more readily intelligible and so more polite, and which was not actually wished for. This line participates, I want to suggest, in a *speculative element* of Wordsworth's verse. Its mood is indicative. Yet beneath the indicative syntax sounds an implied optative. And perhaps this line can help us to understand something of the affective power of this kind of 'speculative' moment. The speculative element in Wordsworth's verse can be thought of as a kind of cognitive hypermetricality. It exactly overflows the measure, that is: as a 'spontaneous overflow of powerful feelings' in which poetry blurts out its wish to have back everything which has been taken away by (what is now) sheer common sense. It is an echo of poetry as efficacious magic, but an echo which knows that there is no such thing as magic. The following line places this cosmology in a temporal context: 'And the most ancient Heavens through Thee are fresh and strong.' The line is bewildering, in that it seems to imply that the heavens are so old as to be almost obsolete. If they were not kept going by duty, they might fall apart. Is there not the cognitive equivalent of a transferred epithet at work here? It is lyric poetry that is ancient, so old as to be almost obsolete, in danger of falling in. Once it could be met with on every side. Now it appears almost dead. What is blurted out here is a wish believed at the moment of utterance, that poetry may still speak truth: not in the sense of describing or explaining the truth, but in the sense that this utterance be the living event of truth.

THE SPECULATIVE ELEMENT OF WORDSWORTH'S VERSE

'I do not know how without being culpably particular I can give my Reader a more exact notion of the style in which I wished these poems to be written than by informing him that I have at all times endeavoured to look steadily at my subject.'[41] The problem with moral theories, as Wordsworth thought of it, was not only that they were not trying to look steadily at their subject (or indeed, in the worst case, precisely trying *not* to look steadily at the subject) but that they did not have a subject to look steadily at. 'They *describe* nothing.'[42] But as a matter of technique, it became clear that describing nothing was as likely to happen by saying too much as by saying too little. One important shock of the kind of poetry which Wordsworth begins to write in 1797 is its repeated refusal to offer the reader the consoling pay-off of a point. The striking out of the final stanza of an early version of *Salisbury Plain*, 'Heroes of truth . . . ' becomes a model.[43]

But what resulted was not, in the event, sheer description either. Just because it was determined to excise bald and naked reasonings, the poetry discovered, rather than pre-empted, the limits of absolute descriptiveness. We can see Wordsworth attempting to get to grips with this achievement in some of the letters which he writes to admiring correspondents, or to insufficiently admiring correspondents, or to those who admire enough but in the wrong way. The letters do not provide anything like a theory or a manifesto for his writing. They are, rather, attempts after the fact to come to terms with the novelty of the way of writing which he has discovered – if the phrase did not underestimate the force of the internal and external pressures which have driven him to it, one could almost say, which he has *happened* upon – in what Alan Bewell has aptly called 'the experimental poetry'.[44] What they circle around is just this relation of prescription and description:

You have given me praise for having reflected faithfully in my poems the feelings of human nature I would fain hope that I have done so. But a great Poet ought to do more than this he ought to a certain degree to rectify men's feelings, to give them new compositions of feeling, to render their feelings more sane pure and permanent, in short, more consonant to nature, that is, to eternal nature, and the great moving spirit of things. He ought to travel before men occasionally as well as at their sides.[45]

We might expect a poet who has offered it as his goal to try to look steadily at his subject, who has complained of the emptiness of a moral theory which describes nothing, which presents no picture of human life, to respond with delight to the praise that he has 'reflected faithfully in his poems the feelings of human nature'. Wouldn't this count as success? When the praise is offered, though, Wordsworth finds himself feeling dissatisfied with it. To have *reflected faithfully the feelings of human nature*: just to have given back to human nature what it already in any case has in its possession, its feelings. He is groping here for what more it is that he would want to have done: to rectify men's feelings, to give them new compositions of feeling. How then might this be done, if the poems are not to become bald and naked reasonings themselves?

The difficulty persists through the whole authorship wherever it is alive. It is not a 'contradiction' which primarily needs to be harmonized into a state of non-contradictoriness, whether by 'fantasized and illusory cultural solutions' or by anything else, but a difficulty which needs to be kept open, because it is the condition of vitality of Wordsworth's great writing. I am not sure that it is right to think of the systematic (or, better, the architectonic) impulse in Wordsworth – that element in the authorship which David Bromwich associates with what he thinks of as the damagingly intellectualistic influence of Coleridge – as a source of poetical decline. Wordsworth had the historical instinct both to plan a grand philosophical poem and not to be able to complete it. As Hugh Sykes Davies put it, 'Both greatness and originality were forced on Wordsworth because he wished to be both a Teacher and a Poet, and because of the inherent tensions between these two aims, between the kinds of teaching and the kind of poetry established in the time upon which he fell.'[46] So he came to understand, not as opinion, but at the level of poetic technique, what Friedrich Schlegel formulated as a maxim: that 'it is equally fatal to spirit both to have a system and not to have a system, and that it will therefore simply have to decide to combine the two'.[47] 'At the level of technique', because the problem did not present itself (for all the certainty of some contemporary reviewers that Wordsworth was the proud owner of a 'system')[48] primarily at the level of theory, but in the poet's own dissatisfaction with any of his own efforts which did not do more than merely report a feeling or clothe a theory. When the reviewer for the *Monthly Repository* comments of Wordsworth in 1835 that '[t]he division of labour is not rightly kept up between the picture gallery of his imagination, and the logical workshop of his understanding', this hostile complaint contains a truth: the failure or refusal to keep up a division of labour between imagination and understanding (to say nothing of a refusal to treat the imagination as a gallery and the understanding as a workshop) indeed distinctively characterizes Wordsworth's way of writing philosophic song.[49] So much can be seen even from so admittedly 'compressed' an account of his procedure as Crabb Robinson's:

I stated as a compression of Wordsworth's rather obscure account of poetic abstraction the following as the operation. The poet first conceives the essential nature of his object and strips it of all its casualties and accidental individual dress, and in this he is a philosopher; but to exhibit his abstraction nakedly would be the work of a mere philosopher; therefore he reclothes his *idea* in an individual dress which expresses the essential quality, and has also the spirit and life of a sensual object, and this transmutes the philosophic into a poetic exhibition.[50]

Put like this, the procedure sounds almost comically mechanical, and it is hardly to be imagined that any one of Wordsworth's poems was actually written according to such a recipe. 'Comically', because of the redundance of the various filtrations and supplementations performed. First the accidental and casual is removed so that the poem shall not be merely idiosyncratic, but then it has to be put back in again so that it shall not be emptily philosophical. None the less, what it clearly indicates is Wordsworth's reluctance that his work should be either merely casual and accidental or 'the work of a mere philosopher'. We may admire the fervour with which, for example, Julius Hare could insist upon the abstract identity between the two, that 'Poetry is philosophy, philosophy is poetry';[51] but a better hint towards the relation operative between the two in Wordsworth's poetry is given by Coleridge's 'war embrace'.

In my view what is at work from, say, 1797 onwards in Wordsworth's poetry is a still more subtle and more speculative wager than Robinson's redaction of Wordsworth's *post hoc* legitimation of it suggests: not a willed exemplification of the universal by the particular, nor an inductive generalization from the particular to the universal, but rather a risk taken: that provided that one look steadily *enough* at anything really experienced it will turn out to be, not accidental, but meaningful. One of our finest contemporary poets has written that 'our nature is my greatest privacy, and this is the sustaining and silly paradox, that the most idiosyncratic and inadmissible is the most deeply shared'.[52] The early reception indicates the extent to which this risk was a risk, because in it Wordsworth can be reproached within the same review for being *both* a reductive systematizer *and* someone who gave a quite inappropriate weight to the merely idiosyncratic details of his own life. Jeffrey introduces his suspicions of the 1807 volumes on the grounds that they are 'written avowedly for the purposes of exalting a system',[53] and goes on to hope that a poor reception will lead to the abandonment of the system. Later in the same review, however, it appears that it is not merely systematicity, but also singularity, which is exceptionable in these productions:

Their peculiarities of diction alone, are enough, perhaps, to render them ridiculous; but the author before us really seems anxious to court this literary martyrdom by a device still more infallible, — we mean, that of connecting his most lofty, tender, or impassioned conceptions, with objects and accidents, which the greater part of his readers will probably persist in thinking low, silly, or uninteresting. Whether this is done from affectation and conceit alone, or whether it may not arise, in some measure, from the self-illusion of a mind of extraordinary sensibility, habituated to solitary meditation, we cannot undertake to determine. It is possible enough, we allow, that the sight of a friend's garden-spade, or a sparrow's nest, or a man gathering leeches, might really have suggested to such a mind a train of powerful impressions and interesting reflections; but it is certain, that, to most minds, such associations will always appear forced, strained, and unnatural; and that the composition in which it is attempted to exhibit them, will always have the air of parody, or ludicrous and affected singularity.[54]

For Jeffrey, of course, there is no contradiction here: Wordsworth's perverse attachment to system *is* his 'affected singularity'. Yet the passage instructively illustrates how vulnerable was Wordsworth's verse to being ground up by a critical machinery for which the risk of bathos was an ever-present test of taste. The 'singularity' of Wordsworth's willingness to find meaning even in the meanest flower that blows is interpreted merely as a failure of taste, comparable to writing 'Pindarics on gooseberry-pye'.[55] At stake here is not merely lowness, to which so much attention has been given, but also the risk of unassimilable singularity, a verse 'silly' precisely in the sense alluded to by Wilkinson, of a maladaptive attachment to what are apparently the mere 'accidents' of singular experience, and the conviction that such accidents will in the end turn out to be more than accidental.

The long, disabling division of Wordsworth scholarship between the systematizers and the anti-intellectuals, to label parties too neatly and quickly, a division which continues to repeat itself in more complicated ways in the current reception, misses the fact that as soon as the persisting tension between these two impulses – which in the end is also the tension between the disenchanting attempt to look steadily at a subject, and the nostalgic and utopian wish for efficacious magic, the wish actually to change this world with poetic writing – is lost, everything that makes Wordsworth's poetry his own is lost with it. Wherever it reappears, so does that excellence: and this may be one reason why amidst the detritus of versified reminiscence we may still encounter, especially wherever the hope to complete the philosophic poem is rekindled, verses of power. This is where the notion that the philosophical aspects of Wordsworth's poetry are all somebody else's idea goes badly wrong. If that were the case only academics would be interested in them. For every reader who is drawn by expressive immediacy, there is another (often the same one) who is drawn by the hope which shines in poetic thinking. Large regions and long stretches of twentieth-century intellectual life were dominated by a lazily contented suppression of fundamental questions about human experience, a suppression often legitimated by some smart tricks which were supposed to show that those questions were, say, 'poorly formed'.[56] Some of what popular appeal remains to Wordsworth's poetry in our day comes from the fact that he kept on and on thinking about the experience of such questions, which he could never be persuaded to treat as a subject proper only for the ratiocinations of professionals.

How much depends upon the open wound between the desire for efficacious magic and the disenchanting steady look can be seen in the prospectus to 'The Recluse'.

> Beauty – a living Presence of the earth
> Surpassing the most fair ideal Forms
> Which craft of delicate Spirits hath composed
> From earth's materials – waits upon my steps;
> Pitches her tents before me as I move,
> An hourly neighbour. Paradise, and groves
> Elysian, Fortunate Fields – like those of old
> Sought in the Atlantic Main – why should they be
> A history only of departed things,
> Or a mere fiction of what never was?
> For the discerning intellect of Man,
> When wedded to this goodly universe
> In love and holy passion, shall find these
> A simple produce of the common day.
> I, long before the blissful hour arrives,
> Would chant, in lonely peace, the spousal verse
> Of this great consummation: – and, by words
> Which speak of nothing more than what we are,
> Would I arouse the sensual from their sleep
> Of Death. . . .[57]

It is hard not to be struck by an apparent contradiction here. The poet seems at first to say that paradise is already here. To emphasize this point, he protests against thinking of paradise only as a mythical 'history' or as a utopian 'fiction'. Then, however, he tells us that he is singing 'long before the blissful hour arrives'. Doesn't this mean that his own song must be 'a mere fiction of what never was'? Wordsworth's description of the method of his song contains an answer to such a question. The description is a pointed one. The 'sensual' are to be woken from their 'sleep Of Death' not by being upbraided, nor by being seduced into other pleasures, but 'by words / Which speak of nothing more than what we are'. The line recalls Wordsworth's insistence upon looking steadily at his subject. Determined and alert description is to find out that bliss which is not adventitious to our lives, but their condition of possibility. This is what makes of this prospectus one which does not merely look forward to a philosophical scope which is never delivered, but which rather seizes the hope and the achievement which *already* animates Wordsworth's poetry. The lineaments of paradise shall be found a simple produce of the common day. Yet they can *only* be found so upon condition that the poet look steadily at his subject. Only that enchantment which we find in the world when we turn our steadiest, our most penetrating, gaze upon it, the look most really freed both of superstition and of superstitious intellectualism: only such enchantment may be admitted in 'the blissful hour'.

This animating paradox, or, if one wishes, this contradiction, is not at all a question merely of the architectonic of Wordsworth's authorship. It sounds in the peculiar force which the most inconspicuous words take on in his poetry. The most eminently inconspicuous of all words, what modern anti-metaphysical metaphysics understands as the 'copula': 'is' and its cognates, that verb which is thought to add no property, agency or other peculiarity to its subject or predicate other than to affirm their bare existence; words which everyone knows how to use without knowing what they mean, and upon enquiring into whose meaning a long series of strident prohibitions has been imposed, prohibitions which are the condition of the possibility of modern anti-metaphysical metaphysics:[58] these words not only take on an unprecedented force in Wordsworth's poetry but are occasionally even the explicit topic of his reflection:

I consider the manner in which I was rescued from my dejection and despair almost as an interposition of Providence. 'Now whether it was by peculiar grace A leading from above'. A Person reading this Poem with feelings like mine will have been awed and controuled, expecting almost something spiritual or supernatural – What is brought forward? 'A lonely place, a Pond' 'by which an old man *was*, far from all house or home' – not stood, not sat, but '*was*' – the figure presented in the most naked simplicity possible. This feeling of spirituality or of supernaturalness is again referred to as being strong in my mind in this passage – '*How came he here* thought I or what can he be doing?'[59]

Words which speak of nothing more than what we are: words, for example, such as '*was*'. What emerges in this remarkable self-interpretation is the emphatic weight placed on that word, an emphasis which would surely have appeared barely comprehensible to most of Wordsworth's contemporaries. How may *this* word carry the force of the description, the force, even, of the poem, when it tells us nothing about the man? The way in which it bears that force is strange indeed, because it does so, for Wordsworth, by a kind of flatness. The reader who is in the right frame of mind will be 'expecting something almost spiritual or supernatural'. What the reader gets is the bare copula, '*was*'. Yet the reader has not, for all that, been given something which is *not* spiritual or supernatural. Immediately after explaining that 'was' represents the figure in the most naked simplicity possible, Wordsworth then speaks of '[t]his feeling of spirituality or of supernaturalness'. It is this disappointment, this near-bathos *itself*, the order of Wordsworth's explanation invites us to consider, which confers this feeling of something more than natural. The word *was* has the power that it does have primarily because of what it deprives the reader of: 'not stood, not sat, but *was*'. Yet it is in this very privation that the word takes on a more than natural force: that it seems to do something more than provide the mere logical cement joining subject to predicate. Words which speak of nothing more than what we are, when they speak of what we emphatically *are*, must nevertheless speak of more.

Wordsworth was led to think so hard about the word *was*, I think, less by a process of epistemological or historico-philosophical reflection, than because he was unhappy with the way someone else had described his poem, and because that unhappiness led him to reflect on what had been missed in that description. One thing which can be seen in the letter he wrote to Sara Hutchinson is the extent to which he understood the power of his poetry as resting on subtraction. The removal of extraneous commentary – of uplifting or upbraiding *pointing* of a description – migrates into the poetry's most fundamental words. Much of its power is to depend on privation, on the removal of those props of familiarity which stop readers reading and which allow them to substitute for reading a train of associations which have become habitual. It is this mechanism of substitution which Wordsworth has in mind when he complains of readers who read, as it were, under an alien personification; who like a poem well enough for themselves but who complain that 'to such and such classes of people it will appear mean or ludicrous'.[60] '*Was*', in Wordsworth's mind, will not permit this self-disowning to be operated: it perhaps illustrates what Coleridge meant when he noted harshly of 'Wordsworth's enemies' that 'his works make them restless by forcing them in on their own worthless Selves – and they recoil from the Heart, or rather from the place where the Heart ought to be, with a true *Horror Vacui*.'[61] '*Was*' forces the reader inwards because it deprives him or her of any ontic information. So that it is precisely through this deprivation that substance is discovered. But this substance turns out not to be a rump of sheer literalness. The stripping down of poetry, the removal of everything which is adventitious to a description, all this does not in the end leave us with the impossible dead letter, with perfected literalness, but rather forces us right up against that in language which will not be made absolutely literal: the way in which under the steadiest description still sounds a prescription, the way in which a norm, or a value, or a meaning, echoes in what is apparently the most naked and simple 'is'.

When Wordsworth makes clear, then, that his idea of philosophic song is not a versified system, but a song 'Of truth which cherishes our daily life', this may mean, less that large metaphysical or epistemological principles are to be illustrated with reference to quotidian examples, than that philosophic *song*, because it is not a system, is able to hear as emphatic, as bearing a weight of significance which needs to be patiently uncovered, what are thought of as the most straightforward and transparent and empty linguistic building blocks of our experience: 'is' or 'was' or 'being', for examples. It has not been sufficiently noticed how strange many of Wordsworth's employments of these words are. The words which first appear in *The Pedlar*, and which are then applied to the poet himself in the two-part *Prelude* – 'I felt the sentiment of being spread / O'er all that moves, and all that seemeth still' have most often been read with an emphasis on 'all': on that *unity* which has so often, and, as I hope to show, so mistakenly, governed interpretation of the philosophical aspects of Wordsworth's verse; it has less often been reflected upon how strange, to any thinking accustomed to regard 'being' as adding nothing to that of which it is predicated, it must seem to write of a 'sentiment of being' spread over anything. What else can this mean but that before this feeling a sentiment of *nothing* was spread over all that moves and all that seemeth still: that nothing, precisely, which goes under the name of 'being', whenever being is understood as no more than the bare predicative cement in a proposition? When we hear of a time in which '[t]he pulse of Being everywhere was felt' we can only conclude that it was not felt everywhere before, and consequently that something more is meant by saying that the pulse of being everywhere was felt than merely the tautology that everything that was existed. 'Being', in such passages, like the copula in Wordsworth's explication of 'Resolution and Independence', takes on a more than merely descriptive or predicative force; it is implied that something unspecified which has otherwise been lost to experience is, in such moments or passages of a life, now felt.

> There is an active principle alive in all things:
> In all things, in all natures, in the flowers
> And in the trees, in every pebbly stone
> That paves the brooks, the stationary rocks
> The moving waters, and the invisible air.
> All beings have their properties which spread
> Beyond themselves, a power by which they make
> Some other being conscious of their life;
> Spirit that knows no insulated spot,
> No chasm, no solitude, – from link to link
> It circulates, the soul of all the worlds.[62]

It has been fatally easy to read this passage only for its apparent sum result: for the 'all' which resounds in its first line, in its last line, and at many points in between, and to see in it a confirmation of Wordsworth's supposed doctrine of pantheism; to read this passage, as it were, for the resultant *one* life rather than to ask what that *life* might be. But the active principle which is alive in all things, and which is presumably to bring oneness to them, is strangely multiple. The ways in which it is described do not fit together. At last it 'circulates'. By implication, that is, it bestows life, in its activity, on beings originally bereft of it: as blood is thought of as animating a body, or as capital 'animates' an economy. Yet the beginning of the sentence says something quite different. There this aliveness has no unity: it originates multiply, in a barely graspable surplus of each being over itself. The 'spirit' which is at last arrived at is at first only this surplus by which beings are somehow, as it were, more than what they are. The model is not one of chiasmic exchange, but of an original proliferating excess.

But what could be meant by saying that all beings have their properties which spread beyond themselves? To many of Wordsworth's contemporaries it could doubtless have meant very little, and might have been ranked amongst those passages which readers often found inappropriately speculative in a poem of any kind. We could none the less begin to see what kind of meaning it might have if we think about the way the relationship between properties and beings was thought of in the common sense resulting from the defeat of scholastic philosophy. The result of this would only be to show us what Wordsworth's paradox does not fit in with. It does not fit with any thinking in which the problems raised by fundamental concepts such as being, or life, or nature are solved by saying what each of those concepts separately means.[63] This is almost to say that it does not fit in with philosophy itself. The passage does not attempt to define the 'beings' which supposedly have properties which spread beyond themselves; yet it clearly does not permit, either, the conclusion that the meaning of a word such as 'being' is so evident to all as to require no further discussion. What we are partly discovering here is the difference which philosophic song's being *song* makes. It is characteristic of Wordworth's verse thinking to sound apparently sheerly descriptive or constative fundamental words in a way which shows that they are irresolvably *emphatic*: that is to say, that they are haunted by a desire, or a need, or a wish, which makes of them more than can be exhausted in adequation to a state of affairs.

That may seem like wishful thinking. What it means can be seen if we consider the question of the mood of some of Wordsworth's apparently unequivocal assertions, those lines in which some large principle is being declared: *there is one great community alive on earth: there is one only liberty; there is an active principle alive in all things.* In none of these declarations does the mood of the verb pose problems of interpretation. It is indicative. Yet the mood of the passages over which these declarations stand is not so straightforwardly indicative. They possess, I want to suggest, an undecidability of mood which is constitutive for what is peculiar to Wordsworth's poetic language, yet which is easy to miss or inadvertently to delete, because it falls between what we have come to think of as an exhaustive array of alternatives for interpretation. The first line of the present fragment well illustrates this. It is a generously hypermetrical overstatement which is at once partially checked by the following line: 'In all things, in all natures'. The use suggests either a qualification to, or a gloss upon, the statement of the opening line. It suggests either that 'things' is not quite right, because an active principle might not be alive in all things, only in all natures, or, alternatively, it glosses 'things' as 'natures', suggesting that any thing which deserves the name must have its own nature, that it may not be merely some nominal entity. It becomes clear, then, that a normative force is hidden behind the opening line's apparently purely indicative mood. The line is only true if we understand 'things' to be a valuation as well as a description: there is an active principle alive in all things that deserve the name. 'There is an active principle alive in all things' requires that we read it, neither as a sheerly constative statement of fact, nor as the merely fanciful application of a figure to facts. It rather carries the force of a credal declaration, a profession of faith.

When Wordsworth, disappointed, asks his correspondent to understand how much affectivity can inhabit a word like 'was', he is not merely setting straight the interpretation of a particular poem, but arriving retrospectively at a critical insight into the texture of his own writing: in *is, was, being, nature, life* sound wishes, desires, hopes. One peculiar characteristic of the mood of the poetry is its frequent undecidability between the indicative and the optative. The desire that Wordsworth felt so strongly once he had been disappointed by the wrong kind of praise, by praise which he felt had not attentively described what was happening in his poems: that his poetry should look steadily at its subject, that it should above all describe something, but that it should do more than merely reflect back or abstractly edify its subjects; this desire is not treated as a purely architectonic or generic question, but migrates into the grain of the verse itself. We might think of this as the speculative element of Wordsworth's verse: 'of', not 'in', because it is not only an element which sits in the authorship alongside others, but rather what appears to bear the writing up. It is constellated across the falsely naturalized separation between *is* and *ought*. Yet the horizon which makes this speculative element possible, or towards which it aims, is not a totality – such as, for example, the concrete identity of the actual and the rational; nor is it an opposition, a doctrine of their infinite incommensurability; but a series of near-indiscriminable differences: between idolatry and veneration; between revenge and justice; between fantasy and imagination. Keeping open the concrete possibility of bliss, despite the resentful or sentimental apriorisms which would close it, requires the repeated attempt, case by case, to open these differences. To look steadily at the subject.

PART I

Counter-spirits

The two main principles of the so-called historical criticism are the Postulate of Vulgarity and the Axiom of the Average. The Postulate of Vulgarity: everything great, good and beautiful is improbable because it is extraordinary and, at the very least, suspicious. The Axiom of the Average: as we and our surroundings are, so must it have been always and everywhere, because that, after all, is so very natural.

CHAPTER I

Old idolatry

What am I doing if I break an idol? Am I showing that I do not believe in its supposed powers? Or am I, instead, doing just the reverse: demonstrating, in fact, that I believe in the idol's powers so much that I think it needs to be smashed up?

Wordsworth's 'poem to Coleridge' ends with an address to Coleridge himself, and with a figure drawn from sacred history:

> Oh! yet a few short years of useful life,
> And all will be complete, thy race be run,
> Thy monument of glory will be raised;
> Then, though, too weak to tread the ways of truth
> This Age fall back to old idolatry,
> Though men return to servitude as fast
> As the tide ebbs, to ignominy and shame
> By Nations sink together, we shall still
> Find solace in the knowledge which we have,
> Bless'd with true happiness if we may be
> United helpers forward of a day
> Of firmer trust, joint-labourers in the work,
> (Should Providence such grace to us vouchsafe)
> Of their redemption, surely yet to come.
> Prophets of Nature, we to them will speak
> A lasting inspiration, sanctified
> By reason and by truth: what we have loved
> Others will love; and we may teach them how,
> Instruct them how the mind of man becomes
> A thousand times more beautiful than the earth
> On which he dwells, above this Frame of things
> (Which 'mid all revolutions in the hopes
> And fears of men doth still remain unchanged)
> In beauty exalted, as it is itself
> Of substance and of fabric more divine.[1]

The friends are compared to 'Prophets of Nature' who, though the nations 'fall back to old idolatry', a lapse here connected with a 'return to servitude', will jointly build a lasting inspiration able to counteract such idol-worship. The central opposition here is between idolators and prophets. The nations are liable to fall back into idolatry. The poets are prophets who, like the old Hebrew prophets, will guard against this lapse.

Yet several facts cloud this clear picture. (1) The first scourges of idolatry were not prophets 'of Nature', but of God. And indeed, part of what the prophets in this passage are supposed to teach the nations is that the mind of man becomes a thousand times more beautiful than the earth. The clear implication is that anyone who values the earth as highly as they value the mind of man is an idolator. He or she wrongly places a transcendent value upon an object unworthy of it. If this is the case, in what sense are Wordsworth and Coleridge prophets 'of Nature'? It would appear that they must be prophets of a (divinely) *human* nature, the nature of the mind of man. This aspect of the confidence in the ending of the poem thus feels a little strained. In emphasizing the value of mind over earth, it forces a note which, elsewhere, has been only one amongst others. (2) Although these are prophets foreseeing only a few short years of useful life, they are none the less to expect a lasting inspiration. This implies that their work will be done not in person, but by proxy: by this poem and, perhaps, by the 'monument of glory' which Coleridge is to leave. These prophets, then, are not only idoloclasts. They also set up monuments of their own: prophetic monuments, which, it is implied, are to be standing prophylactics against idols. This aspect of the ending, therefore, complicates the confidence of its tone. It suggests that the difference between prophet and idolator may not be a gulf but a nuance. Both construct sacred monuments, but one makes a true work of glory (perhaps a 'shrine'[2]) where the other makes an idol.

What we are to do and feel about idols looks still more complicated if we consider an earlier passage from the poem.

> Thus strangely did I war against myself;
> A Bigot to a new Idolatry
> Did like a Monk who hath forsworn the world
> Zealously labour to cut off my heart
> From all the sources of her former strength;
> And, as by simple waving of a wand
> The wizard instantaneously dissolves
> Palace or grove, even so, did I unsoul
> As readily by syllogistic words,

Some Charm of Logic, ever within reach,
Those mysteries of passion which have made
And shall continue evermore to make,
(In spite of all that Reason hath perform'd,
And shall perform to exalt and to refine)
One brotherhood of all the human race
Through all the habitations of past years
And those to come, and hence an emptiness
Fell on the Historian's Page, and even on that
Of Poets, pregnant with more absolute truth.[3]

At the poem's conclusion, old idolatry: here, a new idolatry. This *new* idolatry consists, in fact, of indiscriminate idol-*breaking*. Thus – in a way which is wholly characteristic of Wordsworth's approach to this question – one familiar trope in rational thinking's picture of itself is inverted. The supposed disenchanter, logician or political philosopher or moralist, is the *en*chanter: a 'wizard' whose power of dissolution is not made any less of a mystifying spell by the fact that it is 'dissolving' something rather than making something. The 'Bigot' or 'Monk' who thinks of himself as renouncing or breaking idols worships an idol of his own: the idol of his own renunciation.

These two contrasting epithets for idolatry, 'old' and 'new', and these two contrasting passages, well indicate what an ambivalent motif the motif of idol-worship is in Wordsworth's writing. And not only the motif of idol-worship, but also all those which come to cluster around it in association with it or opposition to it: prophet, bigot, monk, sage, enthusiast, zealot, to name only a few. These motifs are ambivalent, I want to suggest, because Wordsworth comes to see how closely idolatry and idol-breaking are connected. These apparently sworn foes are intimate friends. An understanding of this kind, I shall suggest, is not merely, as it were, an opinion held by Wordsworth. It is undergone at the level of technique. It is central to the revolution in Wordsworth's way of writing poetry and thinking about poetry which takes place in the late 1790s. Its ambivalence, I shall argue, can not only take us into the heart of Wordsworth's poetical thinking, but also show in what respects that thinking is truer and more subtle than some of the influential arrays of thoughts and tropes which have been used to contain it.

'STOCKS AND STONES'

The manuscript of the poem now known as 'The Baker's Cart', as James Butler indicates in his edition of *The Ruined Cottage and the Pedlar*,

occupies two columns of a single side of paper.[4] The left-hand column
gives the lines which make up Butler's 'reading text'; the right-hand
column gives these lines beginning opposite line 12 of the right-hand
column:[5]

> forget
> my eyes were turned nor can I well
> With what a low and fearful voice [?she] [?s]aid
> The low   with which she said
> by misery and rumination deep
> Tied to dead things and seeking sympathy
> In stocks and stones

When the poem was printed in the first volume of de Selincourt's
edition, some attempt was made to work some of this material into the
edited text, presumably on the principle, commonplace until recently,
that as much material as possible is to be recruited and incorporated into
a conflated text. In de Selincourt, then, and also in John O. Hayden's
Penguin text, lines 14–16 of the Cornell 'reading text' are expanded thus:

> she saw what way my eyes
> Were turned, and in a low and fearful voice
> By misery and rumination deep
> Tied to dead things, and seeking sympathy
> She said: 'that waggon does not care for us'[6]

The result, of course, is a conflator's catachresis, in which the woman's
'voice' is represented as '[t]ied to dead things'. The last half-line, however,
despite apparently representing the latest stage, the last words of the poem
to have been written, is the only part of the poem which (although, of
course, printed in Butler's volume) has not made it into any final reading
text of the poem as a whole. In its local context, the force of this last half-
line is apparently clear: under the weight of her distress, the woman
attributes or misattributes voluntary agency to the stocks and stones
which make up the waggon, as though it were the waggon's own hard-
heartedness which had denied her family bread. But the words also call up
another register, a biblical one. 'Stocks and stones' recall the recurrent
lapses of the ancient Hebrews into idolatry:

As the thief is ashamed when he is found, so is the house of Israel ashamed; they,
their kings, their princes, and their priests, and their prophets.

Saying to a stock, Thou art my father; and to a stone, Thou hast brought me forth: for they have turned their back unto me, and not their face: but in the time of their trouble they will say, Arise, and save us. (Jeremiah 2.26–7)

This aspect of that last half-line is more surprising. Why should Wordsworth summon up these apparently pejorative connotations in the course of a piece part of whose object, we perhaps assume, is to awaken our sympathy for its heroine? The allusion might even appear to suggest that to seek sympathy in dead things is not simply a pitiable effect of extreme distress but rather active impiety, 'sick' not merely in a descriptive but also in a normative sense. The apparently pejorative emphasis of the last half-line is only made more surprising when we look for analogues elsewhere in Wordsworth's oeuvre. Even if we temporarily exclude mountains, lakes, rivers, trees, and clouds, and restrict ourselves to stones – which might be thought of as a kind of limit case for seeking sympathy in dead things – there appears to be little doubt that the ability to find such sympathy is a test of imaginative power. It is said of the pedlar in MS. B of the *Ruined Cottage* that 'Even the loose stones which cover the highway' were given 'a moral life' by him, in lines which are later, tellingly, applied to the poet himself in the 1805 *Prelude*.[7] The woman's pitiable search for sympathy in stocks and stones risks idolatry, whilst the pedlar's looks more like a prophetic bestowal of sacred meaning upon objects initially devoid of it.

Idolatry perhaps appears to be a dead issue, something about which people may once have been exercised but which now disturbs nobody. Yet it has long been understood that Wordsworth regarded the Hebrew prophet-poets, the first scourges of idolatry, as, in part, models for his own poetic practice. The note to 'The Thorn' explaining the possible sublimity of tautology with reference to Deborah's elegy in Judges testifies to the influence of Robert Lowth's admiration for the language of ancient Hebrew poetry upon the *Lyrical Ballads*.[8] In the preface to his 1815 volume, Wordsworth explicitly connected his admiration for Hebrew poetry to the Hebrews' dislike of idols:

The grand store-houses of enthusiastic and meditative Imagination, of poetical, as contradistinguished from human and dramatic Imagination, are the prophetic and lyrical parts of the Holy Scriptures, and the works of Milton, to which I cannot forbear to add those of Spenser. I select these writers in preference to those of ancient Greece and Rome because the anthropomorphitism of the Pagan religion subjected the minds of the greatest poets in those countries too much to the bondage of definite form; from which the Hebrews were preserved by their abhorrence of idolatry.[9]

Amongst Lowth's most admired prophets was Isaiah. His annotated translation of that prophet prompted Benjamin Blayney to produce an almost equally impressive version of Jeremiah shortly afterwards.[10] The two prophets most closely associated with trenchant denunciations of idol-worship, then, had both, at the time when Wordsworth began writing poetry, recently been the subject of English-language versions and commentaries expressly concerned with their poetic as well as their prophetic merits.[11]

Before dismissing 'stocks and stones' as a chance turn of phrase, then, it may be worth recovering something of the contextual significance of 'idolatry' in the era in which 'The Baker's Cart' was written. This may be especially pertinent in view of the extremely intimate connection between the Christian notion of 'idolatry', especially in its application not merely by radical Protestants but also, as we shall see, by deists and atheists, and a concept which has become pivotal over the last twenty years to readings of Wordsworth, and, indeed, of Romanticism in general: that of 'ideology'. It is not simply that there are a set of rough formal similarities in the way in which the two concepts are used at different times and in different places by different people. It is, rather, a question of a decisive feature of the genealogy of the concept of ideology itself: a feature which continues to determine the way the concept is used, but which often does so unconsciously, not simply because this connection has not been given the attention which it deserves, but also because certain acute problems in the theory of ideology itself would come to light were the intimate connection of the two concepts more extensively considered. In what follows I first examine some key theoretical problems in the discourse of ideology and try to show how they are illuminated by a study of the connection between 'ideology' and 'idolatry'. In particular I argue that the opposition between 'ideology' and 'materialism' may be a problematic one in so far as it is premised upon a materialism conceived of as absolute disenchantment. This is because, despite the ways in which it is often understood, ideology is itself a form of disenchantment.

The 1793–4 text of *Salisbury Plain*, like Coleridge's *Moral and Political Lecture* of 1795, links political despotism to idol-worship and with human sacrifice:

Though from huge wickers paled with circling fire
No longer horrid shrieks and dying cries
To ears of Daemon-Gods in peals aspire,
To Daemon-Gods a human sacrifice;
Though Treachery her sword no longer dyes
In the cold blood of Truce, still, reason's ray,
What does it more than while the tempests rise,
With starless glooms and sounds of loud dismay,
Reveal with still-born glimpse the terrors of our way?[12]

Modern despotism may no longer rely on literal human sacrifice, but the consequences of war between nation-states are hardly less bloody. Wordsworth left a memorandum headed 'Druids' listing a number of classical and modern sources, many of which – unlike the most celebrated account, William Stukeley's *Stonehenge* (1740), which attempts to argue that the Druids followed the religion of Abraham[13] – emphasize human sacrifice as a central component of Druid religion.[14] In one instance a passage from Lucan not directly about Druids is listed by Wordsworth apparently solely because of its association between idolatry and human sacrifice: 'the altars were heaped with hideous offerings, and every tree was sprinkled with human gore'.[15] Of course other contemporary writers, notably Blake and Daniel Eaton, also represented Druidism both as a practice of human sacrifice and as a model for the modern impositions of priestcraft.[16] What is most of interest here is the violence of Wordsworth's proposed remedy for the continuing sacrificial reign of superstition. The poem closes with a shrill fanfare:

Heroes of Truth pursue your march, uptear
Th'Oppressor's dungeon from its deepest base;
High o'er the towers of Pride undaunted rear
Resistless in your might the herculean mace
Of Reason; let foul Error's monster race
Dragged from their dens start at the light with pain
And die; pursue your toils, till not a trace
Be left on earth of Superstition's reign,
Save that eternal pile which frowns on Sarum's plain.[17]

The stanza is startling in its power, crudity and courageous determination. It carries in itself the evidence of its own impossibility as a project. Heroic idoloclasts are not merely to dismantle the combined edifices of superstition and oppression, but utterly to liquidate them. 'Not a trace' is to remain but Stonehenge itself: it is not the literal sacrificial altar which was once 'fed / With living men' which these idoloclasts are to break, but the systematic sacrifice of living individuals which is political economy on a war footing.[18] Yet the stanza's own instruments are superstitious. Reason itself appears as a mythical fetish, a 'herculean mace', accompanied by a series of other properties: dungeons, towers and dens. Coleridge's warning, which follows immediately upon his *own* comparison of modern despotism to the Mexican temple built of human skulls, comes to mind: 'Let us beware . . . lest when we erect the temple of Freedom we but vary the stile of architecture, not change the materials.'[19]

The stanza, significantly, disappears from the later version of the poem, *Adventures on Salisbury Plain* (1795–9). This chapter begins by focussing on the part which motifs of idol-worship and idol-breaking, and, more broadly, of enchantment and disenchantment, play at the crucial juncture in his work which marks the beginning of the Wordsworth with which this study is concerned. It argues that the 'turn' in Wordsworth's writing to which so many critics have drawn attention needs careful handling if its significance is not to be too hastily decided upon. In particular, it confirms the view of those critics who have argued that this turn cannot adequately be understood as a turn 'away' from enlightenment. Indeed, the term 'enlightenment' is too global to be of much help here. Instead, I want to suggest, the turn arises from an insight which from 1797 onwards becomes quite central to Wordsworth's authorship, an insight into the intimate *connections* between superstition and rationality, illusion and disenchantment, idol-worship and idol-breaking. He becomes especially interested in the kinds of irrationality which stick to apparently rational behaviours, thoughts, theories like a second skin or like the 'poisoned vestments' mentioned in his prose on epitaphs.[20]

It does not need to be denied that there are certain affinities in this turn with that taken by critics of enlightenment political, moral and epistemological thought, critics who were often politically conservative. But the nuances make all the difference. In particular, Wordsworth is interested in understanding the ways in which abstract rationality fails, precisely, to be rational *enough*. It is not 'too rational', but rational in theory only. Wordsworth's turn does not present us with a preference for superstition over rationality, but with an attempt to understand the connection between them – a connection which rationalism, irrationally, tends to suppress.

THE PERSISTENCE OF IDOLATRY

For the whole of the eighteenth century attacks on idolatry had offered a means for dissenters and also for deists to mount criticisms of the established church from a position with scriptural support.[21] Tom Paine's writings, as so often, put the issue at its starkest. The potential political implications of discussion of the topic of idolatry in the Old Testament are already clear in his *Common Sense* of 1776. In that work Paine argued that there was a close connection between idolatry and monarchy, because the excessive respect paid to temporal monarchs was itself a species of idolatry. Paine argued that monarchy was originally a heathen invention imported by the Jewish people and that 'Monarchy is ranked in scripture as one of the sins of the Jews ... '.[22] 'Government by kings was first introduced into the world by the heathens, from whom the children of Israel copied the custom. It was the most prosperous invention the Devil ever set on foot for the promotion of idolatry.'[23] But Paine's later position was rather differently argued. Whereas in *Common Sense* Paine had appealed to Samuel's authority to argue that monarchy had no biblical justification, in *The Age of Reason* he attacked the whole edifice of revealed religion as, in effect, idolatrous, as a ruse of a mediator-class of priests who had managed to monopolize what should be a universal and natu- rally evident relation between human beings and the supreme being.[24] The veneration of scripture was itself idolatrous, on this account, because the authenticity of scripture could be disproved.[25] Here Paine was partly helping himself at second hand to such philosophic attacks on revealed religion as d'Holbach's *Inquiry into St. Paul.*[26] D'Holbach's approach was later developed by figures such as Volney and Condorcet. Both writers thought that idolatry had arisen through a conspiracy of interest on the part of astrologer-priests, who had supposedly presented rudimentary natural-scientific information in a deliberately mystifying form so as to protect their own monopoly of expertise.[27] Idolatry was thus the common basis of all revealed religion.[28]

Of course there was no shortage of responses to this kind of view.[29] Many who had in other respects been admirers of Paine, particularly Unitarians such as Gilbert Wakefield and Joseph Priestley, were also drawn to attack Paine's 'natural religion'.[30] A key topic in all these arguments was the destruction of the Canaanites. For Paine it was impossible to credit the notion that a beneficent deity would expressly command the slaughter of an entire people, especially when it was borne in mind that many of those slaughtered had been children and so could not be held responsible for the sins of their parents.[31] Defences of the destruction of the Canaanites usually also mentioned idolatry, but like Watson, did not place any particular emphasis on this point.[32]

When Samuel Taylor Coleridge came to defend revealed religion, however, the idolatry of the Canaanites took on a central role in legitimating their destruction. In his *Lectures on Revealed Religion* the ancient Hebrew polity was presented as the type of an egalitarian republic rivalled only by Sparta,[33] in which land was originally equally distributed and this equal distribution preserved by a prohibition on usury, periodical debt amnesties and a jubilee every fifty years in which any inequalities which had none the less crept in could be eliminated. Coleridge was drawing closely here, as his editors indicate and as Nigel Leask has re-emphasized, on Moses Lowman's neo-Harringtonian accounts of the ancient Hebrew state and religion, *A Dissertation on the Civil Government of the Hebrews* (1740) and *A Rational of the Ritual of the Hebrew Worship* (1748).[34] His conception, indeed, was potentially more unsettling than Lowman's because he insisted that the Hebrew polity rested ultimately not only on an equal distribution of property but on an awareness that the very notion of permanent human property rights over land was impious. Leviticus 25.23 took on central importance: 'The land shall not be sold for ever, for the land is mine; for ye are strangers and sojourners with me.'[35]

In these early lectures idolatry is taken as indissolubly associated with the practice of human sacrifice and with political inequality and despotism. The extirpation of the Canaanites was essential not only because '[i]t was a common and meritorious rite of Religion among them to burn their children as sacrifices to Moloch'[36] but in particular so as to keep one people at least free from idolatry and the political inequality which, like Paine, Coleridge associated with idolatry. In his *Moral and Political Lecture* of 1795 Coleridge made this link explicit, using an image of the temple of tyranny which he may have been given by Southey: 'Like the fane of Tescalipoca the Mexican deity; it is erected with human skulls and cemented with human blood.'[37] The relatively minor place given to preservation from idolatry in previous defences of revealed religion is here replaced by a vision in which the central function of the Mosaic dispensation is '[t]he preserving one people free from Idolatry in order that they might [be] a safe Receptacle of the necessary precursive Evidences of Christianity!'[38]

The result of this defence of revealed religion, however, is a curious paradox. Coleridge sets his defence of those aspects of ancient Hebrew ritual which deist and free-thinking critics had regarded as risibly particularist firmly on the ground of the need to preserve the Hebrews from idolatry. Thus the often-mocked injunctions that 'Thou shalt not round the Corner of your Heads, neither shalt thou mar the Corner of thy Beard – Neither shall a Garment of Linen and Woollen come upon Thee'[39] are given a historical defence drawn from Lowman: 'the first of these Customs was a pretended Magical Ceremony of the idolatrous priests, and the second – mixed garments of Woolen and Linen were their peculiar dresses – to prohibit these therefore is but another mode of prohibiting Idolatry and all things that may lead to it.'[40] Religious practices which themselves look idolatrous to writers like Paine are defended, as Lowman defends them, on the grounds that they were essential to preserve the Jews from idolatry.[41] Thus the existence of an established priesthood is justified on the grounds that 'Teachers were absolutely necessary to prevent them from idolatry'[42] even though Coleridge is well aware of the risk that such an argument will abet the contemporary established priesthood of which he remains scarcely less sceptical than Paine: as Coleridge himself goes on to comment in Priestleian fashion: 'whatever Idolatry there may be among us, it is all orthodox'.[43] We are presented with the further paradox that the ancient Hebrew constitution is a model of political and personal virtue, but that the Jews themselves were, for all this, 'too ignorant a People' and 'too deeply leavened with the Vices of Aegypt'[44] not to need some compensatory substitute for the idolatry which had been prohibited them, and which, in Coleridge's view, they were continually liable to long for.

What is illustrated here is a structural difficulty which one kind of sceptical account can find in articulating the relation between concept and image, spirit and matter, universal and particular, in religion. D'Holbach wants to portray idolatry as a harmless-enough worship of local deities, but still finds himself fulminating against revealed religion as a species of – idolatry. Conversely, Coleridge wants to portray idolatry as the evil which must be defended against at all costs but finds himself arguing that in order to secure this, elements of ritual which had often themselves been regarded as a species of idolatry must needs be legitimated. The meeting point between d'Holbach and the early Coleridge is that they both want to get rid of false mediations: of the particular object, image, or priest who or which falsely claims to represent the universal concept of the deity.

IDOLATRY AND IDOLOCLASM

The remarkable 'Essay on the Character of Rivers' prefixed to the 1797 version of *The Borderers* is only partly an attempt to justify the obscurity of this character, which had led to the play's rejection. Wordsworth later insisted to Isabella Fenwick that it was written 'still more to preserve in my distinct remembrance what I had observed of transition in character & the reflections I had been led to make during the time I was a witness of the changes through which the French Revolution passed'.[45] Rivers is an idoloclast, to himself a 'hero of Truth', who refuses to take truth upon authority and who insists upon subjecting all supposed truths to the scrutiny of reason: 'he nourishes a contempt for the world the more dangerous because he has been led to it by reflexion'.[46] The essay offers a diagnosis of the condition of enlightened moral despair in which a figure like Rivers finds himself: 'He looks at society through an optical glass of a peculiar tint: something of the forms of objects he takes from objects, but their colour is exclusively what he gives them, it is one, and it is his own.'[47]

The problem is not that Rivers is insufficiently willing to endow social objects with imaginative meaning of his own, but that he is too willing so to do. Inattentive to the complexity of what the objects might be in themselves, he is a kind of idealist whose mistake, rather than whose virtue, it is in this instance to spread the tone of the ideal world around the objects he considers. Once again we have a pejorative counterpart to the laudable bestowal of moral meaning: as when we give a moral life even to loose stones on the highway. Rivers is not too rational, but rational in theory only. His reason has become tinged with superstition because it must necessarily, relying upon its ethos of total independence of judgement, become solipsistic. It is by this path, Wordsworth is suggesting, that apriorists come to venerate their dead systems as idols: 'a Block / Or waxen image which yourselves have made, / And ye adore', as he later puts the matter in the 1804–5 *Prelude*.[48] Wordsworth's essay aims at showing how superstitious the ratiocination of a man like Rivers still remains:

Benefits conferred on a man like this will be the seeds of a worse feeling than ingratitude. They will give birth to positive hatred. Let him be deprived of power, though by means which he despises, and he will never forgive ... Having shaken off the obligations of religion and morality in a dark and tempestuous age, it is probable that such a character will be infected with a tinge of superstition. The period in which he lives teems with great events which he feels he cannot controul.[49]

Moral and political apriorism has an internalized pseudo-aristocratic character, an independence all the more ferociously asserted because it is in this case theoretical and not real. Like Coriolanus, Rivers cannot bear to be obligated. He is unable to accept either literal or cognitive and moral 'benefits', because they tie him to reciprocate. He wanted, as it were, '*not* to love, wanted to be free by not loving'.[50] His character thus exemplifies the paradox that this will to be absolutely free from super- stition, to shake off the accidents of nature, time and place, is what itself infects him with superstition. Rivers must live in an illusory world because his fantasized independence brings him to misrecognize his own dependence, and with it to misrecognize the character of society as such. He can paint society only one colour: 'it is one, and it is his own'.

The superstitious character of Rivers's idoloclasm is confirmed by the terms in which, in the play itself, he justifies the murder of Herbert. 'We recognize in this old man a victim / Prepared already for the sacrifice', he declares. This sacrifice is to be a sacrifice to reason, one relying on a '[g]enuine courage' which is not 'an accidental quality' but rationally grounded.[51] These are terms which Lacy echoes shortly afterwards when he suggests, in the 1797 text, that 'in open day / He shall be sacrificed': '*here*, / Where Reason has an eye that she can use, / And men alone are umpires'.[52] But Rivers distinguishes himself by resisting bringing Herbert to a public trial, and preferring secretive murder. In Rivers the notion of the sufficiency of the independent intellect has become – as Words- worth's prefatory essay suggests that it has an inherent tendency to become – a despairing rhetoric of disinterestedness which cannot but serve particular and interested ends.

The last additions to 'The Baker's Cart' are not the only lines in which the language of Jeremiah appears in Wordsworth's work at around this date. In the lines latterly known as 'Nutting', Wordsworth describes how as a boy he wrought destruction on a hazel tree. Before this act of violence to nature, he is described in a rather different mood:

> In that sweet mood when pleasure loves to pay
> Tribute to ease, and, of its joy secure,
> The heart luxuriates with indifferent things,
> Wasting its kindliness on stocks and stones,
> And on the vacant air. Then up I rose,
> And dragg'd to earth both branch and bough, with crash
> And merciless ravage, and the shady nook
> Of hazels, and the green and mossy bower,
> Deform'd and sullied, patiently gave up
> Their quiet spirit ... [53]

The act of the boy Wordsworth, smashing the trees, bears startling resemblances to the destructive idoloclasm of Rivers. In the essay on that character Wordsworth recalls Rousseau's aphorism that a child will destroy fifty toys before making one, and then implicitly compares this infantile destructiveness with Rivers's apriorism: '[h]e is the Orlando of Ariosto, the Cardenio of Cervantes, who lays waste the groves that should shelter him'.[54] In 'Nutting', the allusion to Jeremiah suggests a troubling undercurrent to the apparent approval of the boy Wordsworth's bene-ficent mood, 'Wasting its kindliness on stocks and stones'.[55] For all its kindliness, there is also a delusive aspect to this mood, it is implied; a mood in which, as in idolatry, fantasies are projected upon stocks and stones. Immediately afterwards the boy appears as a furious idol-breaker: 'Then up [he] rose', an infant prophet, mercilessly ravaging the same stocks on which he has earlier been dispensing his spiritual largesse. 'In the time of their trouble they will say, Arise, and save us.' The passage implies that these two personae, fantasist and destructive exploiter, idolator and idol-breaker, are not in fact polar opposites but are deeply connected in their violent misrecognition of the 'quiet spirit' of the bower.

This complex approach cannot be regarded as a retreat either from reason or from universalism. At the end of the *Prelude* – in 1832 as in 1805 – Wordsworth is still conceiving of himself and Coleridge as 'Prophets of Nature' who will remind an age 'too weak to tread the ways of truth' and consequently liable to 'fall back to old idolatry' of the advent of a 'redemption, surely yet to come'.[56] If we look forward to Wordsworth's middle and later work we can find him still using the figure of the idol with parallel implications. Gross national product is identified in *The Excursion* as 'the Master Idol of the Realm', to which political economy readies human sacrifice, whilst in the late poem 'Humanity' Wordsworth refers to 'an Idol, falsely called "the Wealth / Of Nations"', again with the explicit link to human sacrifice.[57] But he begins to imagine a reason alive to the shapes of illusion from which it emerges, shapes from which it can no more walk free than from its own history. The work from now on is looking to discriminate amongst these shapes of illusion, not as amongst discrete objects from which the poet's own position could somehow be quite separate, but as shapes in which the work itself participates and from which it emerges. I want to turn at this point to think about the way in which this relationship between reason and illusion is approached in the manuscripts written towards the turn of the century which at various different stages gave rise to the poems known as *The Ruined Cottage* and *The Pedlar*, although whether the latter was ever a separate poem in its own right is a matter of some dispute.[58]

Once again, I want to understand this question from the slightly unfamiliar angle of the motif of idolatry, and to notice in particular how often moral-aesthetic acts and responses which are often regarded as uncomplicatedly beneficent border on idolatrous delusion. *The Ruined Cottage* is as much concerned with the damage wrought by delusive fantasy as with the beneficence of imagination. It does not seek to separate these out from each other like sheep from goats, however, so as to demarcate a spiritual aristocracy. Instead, it lays bare how powers and capacities which might be as common as the air we breathe are in the event laid waste. When Robert loses his job he takes to hobbies: he

> whistled many a snatch of merry tunes
> That had no mirth in them, or with his knife
> Carved uncouth figures on the heads of sticks ... [59]

The mirthless whistling and the idle carving are a form of mechanical activity, mouthing a letter void of spirit. Robert's uncouth carvings are the fetishes of compulsory free time. But whereas a literal idol is invested with the most powerful fantasized meanings, these uncouth figures would be devoid of meaning. They are there to kill time, not to render it sacred. The period in which Robert, no less than that in which Rivers lives, 'teems with great events which he feels he cannot controul'. For Wordsworth, these graven images are a kind of despairing secular idolatry. The measure of the depth of this despair is that it does not know what it is trying to propitiate. Yet Robert's impulses are separated from the pedlar's less by a hierarchy of spirit than by a personal and social history. Even this lowest ebb of the spirit, this apparently spiritless whittling, bespeaks those impulses to which a manuscript fragment of around this date appeals as the necessary basis of any social ontology:

> Why is it we feel
> So little for each other but for this
> That we with nature have no sympathy
> things
> Or with such ~~idle objects~~ as have no
> power to hold
> Articulate language[60]

Whereas for Condorcet and Volney, social progress depends on removing the idle objects – fetishes, crowns, titles, crosses, hieroglyphic writing, idols – which interrupt and distort human exchange, for

Wordsworth real social exchange could only happen if we could understand the material world, even down to the stick which we whittle, as
composed of more than 'idle objects', and our dependence upon it as
more than humiliating servitude.[61] Even idle objects, the line implies,
speak an inarticulate language – like 'the language of the senseless stone'
in the *Essays upon Epitaphs*.[62] Benjamin Blayney, retranslating the King
James version of Jeremiah – 'The stock is a doctrine of vanities' to read
'The very wood itself being a rebuker of vanities' – comments thus:

> The very wood itself being a rebuker of vanities] The true meaning and force of
> this passage seems to have escaped the notice of all our Commentators. מוסר
> properly signifies *rectifying* or *correcting* a false notion by just reproof; and by
> vanities are meant *idols*, so called from their being of no real use or advantage to
> those who had recourse to their assistance. And this unprofitableness of the idol
> the very dull and senseless matter, says the prophet, out of which it was formed,
> is capable of demonstrating. But the 'rebuke', strictly speaking, is not directed to
> the idol, but to those who had not sense to perceive, that all the efforts of human
> art could never change an inanimate log of wood into an animated being,
> possessed of power and intelligence far surpassing the person, from whom its
> origin was derived. There is therefore an energy and pointedness in this short
> sentence at least equal, in my opinion, to whatever has been said upon the same
> subject by the most spirited writer, sacred or profane.[63]

The pointedness admired by Blayney is paradoxical. Jeremiah's bold
figure – that the wood itself rebukes those who turn it into an idol – is
'pointed' because it needs itself to personify the wood in order to work; so
that a rhetorical mock-idolatry, the wood as a speaking rebuker, is used to
rebuke the real idolatry. This 'senseless matter', like the 'senseless stone',
turns out to be not wholly senseless, not simply 'an inanimate log of
wood', but to speak an inarticulate language. There are *no* objects which
are sheerly indifferent in and of themselves. The idea of sheer matter,
devoid of all idolatrous projection whatever, is itself a chimera, an idol. It
may be that we can only be 'human' if we understand that meaning and
value are not conferred by human labour – mental or manual – alone.
Only in this complex sense could Wordsworth be understood as a
'humanist': a humanism, not of the empire of spirit over matter, nor of
the self-sufficiency of spirit, but of a capacity to receive and depend upon
the non-human.[64]
    The double-sidedness of Wordsworth's reflection on this point is
confirmed if we look at the pedlar himself. From one point of view, of
course, he is a kind of antithesis to Rivers, a figure who shows what the

powers which make up Rivers can accomplish when they are not misdirected into idoloclastic despair. It is just this point which should alert us to the deep kinship between some of the language used to describe Rivers in the 'Essay' and the language used to describe the pedlar; here what are apparently differences of nuance are what make all the difference between moral despair and a moral aesthetic. A sense of the close connection between the pedlar and the later narrator of *The Prelude* should not blind us to the fineness of this distinction. When we are told, for example, that

> He had a world about him – 'twas his own,
> He made it – for it only lived to him
> And to the God who looked into his mind[65]

these lines are divided from Rivers's solipsism not by a gulf but by a nuance. The suggestion that this world 'was his own' echoes Rivers's monochromatic view of the social world – 'It is one, and it is his own' – especially when we are told that this world, alive to him, is dead to all other humans, 'for it only lived to him' and to the transcendent deity who is here evoked with startling confidence and suddenness. The picture appears to suggest a deluded fantasist, and this is a possibility which Wordsworth carefully countenances: this made world, he acknowledges, would have come close to madness

> But that he had an eye which evermore
> Looked deep into the shades of difference
> As they lie hid in all exterior forms,
> Which from a stone, a tree, a withered leaf,
> To the broad ocean and the azure heavens
> Spangled with kindred multitudes of stars,
> Could find no surface where its power might sleep,
> Which spake perpetual logic to his soul,
> And by an unrelenting agency
> Did bind his feelings even as in a chain.[66]

The pedlar is distinguished from a madman not by his ability to perceive an essential and universal unity underneath apparent and particular differences, but rather the reverse: it is the 'shades of *difference*' which are said to 'lie hid in all exterior forms'. The earlier claim that ''twas his own, He made it' is implicitly qualified. What saves the pedlar from madness is the element of compulsion within this apparently unlimited freedom of the eye. The possibility of undeludedly sensing meaning in things or idle objects depends on seeing the distinctness of what is not our 'own', on not understanding meaning as a form of spiritualized property right. It would mean knowing the right exit from Rivers's furious and despairing claim to self-sufficiency; would mean being able to receive gifts, to acknowledge our debt to the object. Rivers cannot bear to be ob-ligated, to be tied: the pedlar's feelings, conversely, are bound even as in a chain. But as Robert's case shows, the conditions for this willingness are external as well as internal. The ability to find our feelings bound to things even as in a chain is not the inalienable possession of a spiritual aristocracy. It is a capacity which all may claim, yet of which each may very well be deprived by material distress.

AFTER IDOLATRY

Wordsworth wrote in the fragment now known as the 'Essay on Morals' composed between late 1798 and early 1799 that the problem with aprioristic moral theories was their contentlessness: 'They contain no picture of human life; they *describe* nothing.' Moral theories like Godwin's, hyperbolically put, are not *about* anything. It is almost as though Wordsworth had at around this date made a conscious decision to excise from his work any passages of which the same complaint could be made – not to the end of replacing empty prescription with sheer replication, but rather to the end of finding a kind of philosophic writing 'written with sufficient power to melt into our affections, to incorporate itself with the blood and vital juices of our minds'.[67]

The state of extreme distress in which the woman finds herself in 'The Baker's Cart' is one which leads her to delusive imaginings, imaginings which in the latest draft are implicitly compared to those which stand behind idolatry. We might expect the rest of the poem to represent her as pitiably in thrall to superstition. Yet the terms in which her mental state is described again testify to the way in which Wordsworth at this date understands idolatry and idol-breaking as deeply entangled with each other. She is driven to 'that state / In which all past experience melts away / And the rebellious heart to its own will / Fashions the laws of nature.' On a literal level, of course, the laws of nature which she is fashioning to her own will are physical laws: her figure of speech, hardly so bold, transfers the baker's unfeelingness to the waggon, thereby refashioning the laws of nature by implying that stocks and stones can feel. Yet there is also a strong connection here to the way in which Wordsworth understands moral and political apriorism. 'All past experience melts away': as though the woman were shaking off the accidents of nature, time and place. Wordsworth is also, implicitly, offering us a social psychology of revolution here. There is a deep and historically significant affinity between the distress which melts all past experience in refashioning the physical laws of nature, and the despair which melts all past experience in deducing natural social law. Wordsworth is neither celebrating nor lamenting this affinity between distressed superstition and despairing apriorism. He seeks to understand its emergence from the world of which it is one shape.

By this point it should no longer seem so surprising, if it ever did, that the last words Wordsworth added to his draft of 'The Baker's Cart' allude so prominently to biblical accounts of idolatry. Poems are themselves a kind of fetish or idol. They are historical objects which often claim a more than historical truth; particular objects which often claim a universal meaning; they are things which almost claim the dignity of persons, things which claim to have not just a fixed price but an unmeasurable worth. This offers a perspective for understanding the tendency of recent work which has focussed on Wordsworth's poetics as a form of 'aesthetic ideology' or 'romantic ideology'. The connection between idoloclasm and demythologization goes at least as far back as Bacon's 'idols of learning'.[68] When Destutt de Tracy coins the term 'ideo-logy', the science of ideas, it is with the drastically materialist intention, developing out of the tradition of Helvétius and d'Holbach, and later of Condorcet and Volney, of offering a natural history of ideas in which 'ideology is an aspect of zoology'.[69] De Tracy's science of ideas was intended to liquidate false ideas by exposing their causes as material ones. The school of ideo-logists thus holds true, for all its materialism, to a belief that its own consciousness can nevertheless determine being. The programme of a totalized materialism leads back to idealism. Actually managing to think as a materialist proves to be much harder than appropriating the label.

In Wordsworth's patient attempts to understand the subterranean connections between idolatry and idol-breaking, we already have something like a genealogy of the intellectual approach which later turns into ideology-critique. James Chandler has plausibly suggested that Wordsworth could have heard about the work of the ideologists in early issues of the *Monthly Magazine*, although there is no need to suggest that de Tracy *rather than* Godwin is the central target of *The Borderers* and the 'Essay on the Character of Rivers': in his short fragment on moral philosophy, after all, Wordsworth is capable of coupling such dissimilar thinkers as Godwin and Paley.[70] Whenever Wordsworth is understood as idealistically occluding, 'subliming',[71] displacing, or mystifying a reality which is taken to be 'fundamentally' material, historical and political, the real demand, whether acknowledged or not, is for the idol of the aesthetic to be broken – or dismantled. But we already have the record of what can be achieved when the demands of this Romanticist ideolatry are met. It is there in much of the right-thinking magazine and newspaper verse of the 1790s, the kind of poems printed in Benjamin Flower's *Cambridge Intelligencer*, for example, where few poets can refuse themselves the luxury of extended moral comment or political instruction rather in the vein, although often much less powerful, of Wordsworth's own closing stanza to the first version of *Salisbury Plain*: 'Heroes of Truth'. This kind of verse puts its author in the right, but at the cost of blocking an understanding of the work's own entanglement in what it is describing or judging.

These issues, I want to suggest, have implications for the way in which we need to understand Wordsworth's lifelong project to write a philosophic song. The failure of the universalist ambitions of 'The Recluse' need not be discussed with any element of *Schadenfreude*. It certainly is the case that the vision which Coleridge recalled in 1832 is thoroughly unWordsworthian in some important ways. Yet the main reason why that idea for a poem was so bad, I want to suggest, has less to do with its universality of ambition – signalled by Wordsworth himself on the first recorded occasion when he mentioned 'The Recluse', writing to James Webbe Tobin in 1798 that 'I know not anything which will not come within the scope of my plan'[72] – than to do with the relation between truth and error which is there understood by Coleridge, there at least, as proper to a system of philosophy. The system-deliverer is to have his mind made up, to be in repose; he is to stand and deliver his correct opinions, and presumably to put incorrect ones right along the way. The poet, as Coleridge there understands it, is to put himself in the right. He is to look out from an undeluded vantage-point over a world of error. As I understand the earliest efforts towards 'The Recluse', its very genesis was bound up with a recognition that reason emerges only out of and in connection with illusions. The writing on London in the poem to Coleridge, the antechamber to 'The Recluse', is less a satire on urban degeneracy than a phenomenology of urban feeling. The poem would understand the ineliminable entanglement of all our shapes of feeling and cognition with things, with 'idle objects' and with 'great and permanent objects' alike. In this sense we might understand Wordsworth's poetry as, in the event, more really materialist than his materialist critics – on condition we understand materialism, not as a 'position', nor as a method, but as thinking's attempt to do justice, both ethically and cognitively, to the qualitative complexity of experience.[73] What we can read in the earliest essays towards 'The Recluse' is the record of this attempt: an attempt for which it cannot be sufficient to abandon the worship of false gods, but which needs also to understand what kinds of idols idoloclasm itself sets up and leaves behind.

CHAPTER 2

From idolatry to ideology

In the last chapter, I considered Wordsworth's thinking about idolatry and idol-breaking in relation to the century preceding his poetic activity. This, however, is insufficient. The motif has a history of millennia, all of which is part, however inconvenient this might be, of what is called the socio-historical material specificity relevant to Wordsworth's long poem. For this reason, this chapter steps back from Wordsworth's poetry to take a broader view of the aporias of ideology and idolatry.

The opening lines of *The German Ideology* have often been quoted but have sometimes been read too quickly.

Until now human beings have always formed false ideas about themselves, and about what they are or should be. They have ordered their own relations according to their ideas of God, of normal human beings, etc. The progeny of their heads have got out of control. They, the creators, have bowed down before their own creations. Let us free them from the chimeras, the ideas, the dogmas, the insane imaginations under whose yoke they are wasting away. Let us rebel against this dominion of thoughts. Let us teach them to exchange these imaginations for thoughts which correspond to the real nature of humanity, says one; to conduct themselves critically towards them, says another; to get them out of their heads, says another, and – existing actuality will collapse. These innocent and childish fantasies form the core of recent young-Hegelian philosophy, which is not only received by the German public with horror and awe, but which is also proclaimed by the *philosophical heroes* themselves with a solemn consciousness of its world-shattering danger and criminal ruthlessness. The first volume of this publication aims to unmask these sheep in wolves' clothing ...[1]

'They, the creators, have bowed down before their own creations.' This sounds rather like what is often taken to be Marx's own view. Human beings misrecognize their own products as though they had an autonomous life of their own. They worship as 'natural' social relations which they themselves have produced. But here the words are a citation. They offer, not

Marx's views, but those of the thinkers who are to be 'unmasked' in the coming text as the German ideo-logists: the German successors to the French ideologists led by Destutt de Tracy. These ideologists are stigmatized not as idol-worshippers but as idol-breakers. Or rather: idol-breaking is *itself* to be unmasked as a form of superstition. Ideo-logy is a form of disenchantment – but a mystifying one. The idol-breaker is superstitious in so far as he thinks that breaking the idol will dispel the worship of it. In breaking the idol, he himself superstitiously attributes to it a power over its worshippers. It is worth remembering that in the patristic origins of the discourse on idolatry, the idols are by no means denied to have supernatural powers. They are thought to have many such powers, powers conferred on them by demons.[2] Just so, for Marx, the ideo-logists – Feuerbach, Bauer, Max Stirner – are in fact ideolators.[3] In so far as they think that breaking the *ideas* of transcendence will produce demystified social relations, they superstitiously attribute to those ideas a power of their own, a kind of power which in truth belongs, for Marx, only to living human individuals.

What is thus produced in ideo-logy is something like what was later diagnosed as a 'dialectic of enlightenment'.[4] Disenchantment is perennially liable superstitiously to confer powers on just what it would expose as devoid of them. It is a dialectic whose 'beginning' can hardly be known, whose 'end' is hardly in sight, and in which Marx, with his talk of 'unmasking', also knows himself to be entangled. I want to return to this question of disenchantment later. For now, though, what I want to focus on is the strictness of the sense in which Marx uses the term 'ideology'. It still means for him what it meant to its inventor, Destutt de Tracy: 'the science of ideas'. This is a point which is often, understandably, lost sight of, because Marx goes on to apply the concept of ideology so very widely, to a variety of kinds of illusion which are hardly at first sight cognate with whatever illusions de Tracy's 'science of ideas' might be guilty of. Yet this gap, I want to suggest, is quite deliberate. It is not meant to indicate that we can forget about the old, literal sense of 'ideology' as the 'science of ideas' and accustom ourselves to a new sense in which this term is arbitrarily co-opted to mean something like 'systematic social illusion', or however we want to interpret it. Rather, we are intended constantly to be jolted, by this very gap, into a realization that social illusion *always* takes the form, not of mere mystification, but of *disenchantment as mystification*. This can be illustrated by a use of the term 'ideologists' which crops up later in Marx's text:

Division of labour only actually becomes a division from the moment when a division of mental and manual labour appears.* From this moment onwards consciousness *can* really flatter itself that it is something other than consciousness of existing practice, that it *really* represents something without representing something real; from now on consciousness is in a position to emancipate itself from the world and to proceed to the formation of 'pure' theory, theology, philosophy, etc.

* [Marginal comment by Marx:] The first form of ideologists, *priests*, is concurrent.[5]

Marx's reference to '[t]he first form of ideologists, *priests*' sounds rather unsurprising if we simply take ideology to mean 'mystification'. When we remember that Marx has at no stage explicitly distinguished his use of the term 'ideology' from de Tracy's, it becomes more startling. Priests are not simply mystifiers, the term insists, but would-be demystifiers. Their mystification takes the form of disenchantment: as, for example, in providing supernatural *explanations* for natural phenomena. The comparison of priests to ideologists is a deliberate contrast in registers which works both ways. The supposed 'scientists' of ideas are compared to a priesthood, superstitious in the powers which they attribute to the ideas whose hold they intend to break. Yet the priest, conversely, is compared to a scientist of ideas. His monopoly on ideas is achieved not through sheer mystification, but through mystifying *de*mystification. Thus is illustrated what becomes for Marx the central point, that it is not mystifying *theories* that cause systematic social illusion. 'Demystification', then, may not be the solution to such illusion; indeed, 'demystification' may very easily be the preferred activity of its beneficiaries.

The idea that ideology is a form of disenchantment is not a result produced merely by a passing reading of this single text, *The German Ideology*. We can see it at work in so central a passage of *Capital* as the discussion of 'the fetishism of the commodity and its secret'. The way in which illusions *arise from* disenchantment is well illustrated in the analysis of the actions of partners in commodity exchange. At first sight, there could hardly be a less undeceived form of action. It is no part of Marx's analysis here to show that partners in exchange are acting in the service of illusory higher values, of which they would need to be disabused. Rather they are acting in the most disabused way known to them: a calculation of their own rational interests. The point of the analysis is to show how what Marx thinks of as the central illusion of capitalist society – the apparent naturalness and self-determiningness of social relations and 'laws' of the market, etc., relations and laws which would in fact be nothing at all without the labour of the living individuals who then understand themselves as bound by these relations and laws as by laws of nature – is produced, not by fidelity to mystifying higher values, but by the most disenchanted behaviour available. Through this behaviour relations between people come to appear as though they were properties of things. The chapter is trying to explain how it happens that human beings can live in the grip of a particular systematic social illusion, an illusion which not only appears dismayingly resistant to mass disenchantment, but which operates precisely by means of that disenchantment. It is then central to *Capital* to undertake the paradoxical and aporetic task of disenchanting us about our veneration for disenchantment.

As with so many other central motifs of Marx's thought, it has been the unfortunate fate of 'ideology' to be taken for a technical term in the imaginary pseudo-science of 'Marxism'.[6] Of course it is true to say that Marx uses the term in a much wider set of contexts than, say, de Tracy. He does this, not because he has invented a new meaning for the word, which would henceforth have some esoterically 'Marxist' signification, but as a continual corrective: wherever we would be tempted to set *our* scientists against *their* priesthood, *our* secular reason against *their* superstition, the very use of the word 'ideology' as a name for social illusion reminds us that this is, precisely, the kind of illusion that cannot be obviated by having the correct opinions. The name 'ideology' keeps reminding us that escaping from social illusion can never be merely a matter of specifying the correct method for thinking — including Marx's own materialist method. This does not mean that Marx does not think that his own account is true. It means that the truth of his account would not of itself suffice to dispel social illusion.

Two important consequences follow from this. Firstly, what passes today for 'ideology-critique' is what Marx understood as 'ideology'. Feuerbach was *already* undertaking what is now called 'ideology-critique'. Secondly, straight oppositions between 'science' and 'ideology', or between 'materialism' and 'ideology' are necessarily misconceived, because it is not the truth or falsity of ideas that decides whether they form part of 'ideology', but their relation to monopolies over whatever is needed for life. Both these points are important when we come to think about the place of the concept of 'ideology' in the study of Romantic poetry. What happens when the task of the ideology-critic is understood as a deciphering of the way in which socio-historical specificity is sublimed, occluded, displaced, etc. in Romantic poems is *ideology* in its most straightforward sense. The 'materialist' would unmask or decode the way in which an illusory transcendence conceals its own material history. What he or she is doing when he or she does this is much more like what Feuerbach does than it is like what Marx does. The critique of the 'ideology of the aesthetic' is ideo-logy no less than Feuerbach's critique of religion.

This is not merely the banal and untrue point that, say, critics of ideology must themselves be ideologues. It concerns the whole way in which the criticism of aesthetic artefacts is understood as salutary demystification. If it is the case that ideology is itself a form of demystification, but a mystifying one, scepticism is called for about the emancipatory effects of an assault on ideas of the beautiful. Marx spots the way in which the ruthless critics of religion and their horrified opponents in the Germany of the 1840s actually live rather contentedly together. The idolaters resist the idol-breakers but console themselves that they are at least in possession of something which is thought to be worth smashing up. *The German Ideology*, as Robert Kaufman has so well shown, is a text full of plays on and allusions to *Don Quixote*.[7] Its comic mode is essential, not a rhetorical ornament. It is not disgraceful criminals who are here to be unmasked, but sheep in wolves' clothing.

For this reason it could not be my hope here to unveil (yet another) recipe for final disenchantment; to say, as though it had not been said sufficiently and indeed tediously often, that critics ought to stop being like Feuerbach and start being like Marx. As it happens, I think neither that Marx ever solved the problems which he discovered in writing the book, nor that 'ideology' is a rubric under which they can be solved. His use of the term is a cunning lexical warning to anyone who thinks that they can exit from systematic illusion by *fiat*, but it is not usefully thought of as the inaugural term of a special domain of social science. In particular, whenever a materialism, 'Marxist' or otherwise, sets to work to dismantle an ideology, there we have ideo-logy in its classical form. What Marx's text puts its finger on is how he, and we, are caught up in the illusions which are to be dispelled. But as a matter of fact Marx's own farewell to philosophy has a good deal in common with the essential character of ideology in both its de Tracyan and Feuerbachian shapes, as a unilateral farewell to metaphysics. It has been one achievement of a number of different philosophical authorships in this century to show in differing ways how much more difficult it is really to achieve such a farewell than it is to announce it.

In my view, then, the resources provided by the term 'ideology' for thinking about cultural artefacts have been overestimated. The unfortunate idea that the word is a special or technical term has detached it from its long prehistory in patristic and, later, enlightenment discourse about idolatry. It is useful to reconsider this prehistory when we are thinking about current applications of the term 'ideology'; useful because it can show us that the problems addressed in Marx's book and its battered after-life are not a special wisdom but are instead very closely connected to the debate out of which they emerge: the enlightenment account of the origins and function of 'religion', and its ancestors, the deist attack on revealed religion and, ultimately, the patristic attack on idol-worship. That we could here go back still further to consider, for example, Xenophanes' attack on religious anthropomorphism is much more than a game of genealogies: what it indicates is that the problems which Marx raises in *The German Ideology* are not in fact problems which can be detached from a very lengthy philosophical and cosmological tradition, as though they concerned a special offshore zone in which social theorists had been granted a dispensation from considering any too bewildering difficulties, but are rather problems which can *only* be understood if social (or 'human', or 'cultural') 'science' is not too hastily detached from what is called metaphysics. Ideo-logy, now in the guise of 'ideology-critique', continues to perform the manoeuvre for which it was invented: the separation of sciences of society, later of humanities or human sciences, from 'metaphysics' and, in the end, from philosophy *tout court*. This is a separation which has been profoundly damaging, as well as locally enabling, to the disciplines in question. The next parts of the chapter resist this damage in two ways: firstly, by investigating some of the contours of the link between 'idolatry' and 'ideology' in the enlightenment, deist and patristic traditions; secondly, by reconsidering the relationship between ideology and disenchantment in the work of two leading ideologists. Both centrally concern Wordsworth: the first in so far as it might allow us to reconsider what have sometimes seemed rather inflexible views about what is conservative and what is progressive in his relationship to enchantment and disenchantment; the second in so far as it addresses two of the most powerful sources for currently favoured ways of thinking about poetry in this period.

DEMONOLOGIES

The aporias of ideology and idolatry have a long history. Shaped as their eighteenth-century form undoubtedly was by locally and temporally specific pressures, their fundamental shape emerges far earlier, with the very notion of idolatry itself. An attempt to understand them solely in relation to the 1790s, or even the eighteenth century, would drastically foreshorten the real scope of the problem and would risk representing it as wholly comprehensible within the horizon of, say, revolutionary politics. It would allow us a much cheaper exit from the history of enlightenment than is really available. Two especially important moments in the longer *durée* which would instead be necessary are represented by those apparently diametrically opposed book-polities, Augustine's *City of God* and Hobbes's *Leviathan*. The latter (not accidentally, given his significance for a figure such as Volney)[8] offers an especially acute case of what Marx was later to call ideology. The third book of the *Leviathan*, 'Of a Christian Commonwealth', has recourse to the notion of idolatry in order to press home Hobbes's contention that incorporeal substances are chimerical, that is "*Substance incorporeall*" are words which, when they are joined together, destroy one another'.[9] Hobbes separates the scriptural references to spirits from this patristic and scholastic chimera by arguing that the term spirit is often used to refer merely to non-solid substances: '*Aire*, and *aeriall substances*, use not to be taken for *Bodies*, but (as often as men are sensible of their effects) are called *Wind*, or *Breath*, or (because the same are called in the Latine *Spiritus*) *Spirits*; as when they call that aeriall substance, which in the body of any living creature, gives it life and motion, *Vital* and *Animall spirits*.' Such references to spirits are to be distinguished from patristic and scholastic notions of incorporeal substance: 'But for those Idols of the brain, which represent Bodies to us, where they are not, as in a Looking-glasse, in a Dream, or to a Distempered brain waking, they are (as the Apostle saith generally of all Idols) nothing; Nothing at all, I say, there where they seem to bee.'[10]

Spirit in the sense of incorporeal substance is expelled from Hobbes's cosmos. But there is a symptomatic over-driving here. Hobbes does not merely say that the idols are inefficacious, but that they are 'nothing; Nothing at all'. If idols are nothing, how are they to be broken? It might, of course, be suspected that to raise such difficulties is merely to muddy Hobbes's own very clear distinction between the literal and the figurative.[11] That there is more at stake here is confirmed by the course of Hobbes's argument in the final book, 'Of the Kingdome of Darknesse'. Here Hobbes, having explained the necessary laws of political nature, attempts to explain how it has nevertheless come about that these laws have not been recognized as such. The problem, he argues, has been a widespread worship of (non-existent) idols. Although conducted in a very different philosophical idiom, the book well illustrates the pattern later detected by Marx in Feuerbach's work. The language of idol-breaking is perennially liable to slip into overestimating the powers of what is to be broken. An instance of this kind of difficulty arises late in the fourth book. Hobbes is reluctant to think of what he takes to be the worship of images in the post-apostolic church as having been the result of mis-understandings of Scripture, because this would imply that Scripture itself might be dangerously unclear on this point. Instead, Hobbes offers this startling explanation. Image-worship was the result of

not destroying the Images themselves, in the conversion of the Gentiles that worshipped them ... The cause whereof, was the immoderate esteem, and prices set upon the workmanship of them, which made the owners (though converted, from worshipping them as they had done Religiously for Daemons) to retain them still in their houses, upon pretence of doing it in the honor of *Christ*, of the *Virgin Mary*, and of the *Apostles*, and others the Pastors of the Primitive Church; as being easie, by giving them new names, to make that an Image of the *Virgin Mary*, and of her *Sonne* our Saviour, which before perhaps was called the Image of *Venus*, and *Cupid*; and so of a *Jupiter* to make a *Barnabas*, and of a *Mercury* a *Paul*, and the like.[12]

This powerful image of the survival of the pagan gods conceals an important difficulty, because the apparently sober explanation is in fact, when one follows the claims through, not devoid of superstition. The persistence of idolatry is explained from 'not destroying the Images themselves'. Because they remain in place, so does idolatry. It is hard to escape the implication (most unlikely to have been intended by Hobbes) that they have a power of their own, because although the esteem set upon them can explain why they were not destroyed when paganism gave way to Christianity, it is powerless to explain how pagan gods could become Christian saints.

This is hardly an accidental slip. It is the trace of a central problem for Hobbes's political science: that of explaining why irrational misrecogni-tions of the natural laws of politics and religion should have become so widespread, given the supposed self-evidence of such laws. Hobbes argues that the true faith of Scripture, as taught in the apostolic church, has become corrupted in a number of ways during the patristic period. It was at this time that pagan mythology and pagan philosophy became grafted on to the scriptures, producing what later came to be regarded by many enlightenment historians of religion as an inseparable couple, idolatrous superstition and priestly monopoly on access to the deity. In doing so, he has recourse to a very un-secular hypothesis indeed: that of demonic interference.

> The Enemy has been here in the Night of our naturall Ignorance, and sown the tares of Spirituall Errors; and that, first, by abusing, and putting out the light of the Scriptures: For we erre, not knowing the Scriptures. Secondly, by introducing the Daemonology of the Heathen Poets, that is to say, their fabulous Doctrine concerning Daemons, which are but Idols, or Phantasms of the braine, without any reall nature of their own, distinct from human fancy; such as are dead mens Ghosts, and Fairies, and other matter of old Wives tales. Thirdly, by mixing with the Scriptures divers relics of the Religion, and much of the vain and erroneous Philosophy of the Greeks, especially of Aristotle. Fourthly, by mingling with both these false, or uncertain Traditions, and fained, or uncertain History. And so we come to erre, by giving heed to seducing Spirits, and the Daemonology of such *as speak lies in Hypocrisie*, (or as it is in the Originall, 1 *Tim.* 4. 1, 2 *of those that play the part of lyars*) *with a seared conscience*, that is, contrary to their own knowledge.[13]

The patristic period is the era in which scriptural faith has become corrupted, both by the mingling of what Hobbes thinks of as a primarily Aristotelian philosophy with the Christian faith – 'these noisy Sophists strive in vain / God's Sacred Word, by *Grecian* Cant, t'explain', as a doggerel translation of Hobbes's verse *Ecclesiastical History* put the matter – and, coevally, by the syncretic grafting of pagan superstition on to an originally more austere religion.[14] Hobbes later spells out just what he means by this point in an extended argument that a series of central features of medieval worship are of pagan, not apostolic, origin.[15] The doctrine of the real presence is regarded as idolatrous. None of this is unfamiliar.[16] What is striking is the origin alleged for these effects. 'The Enemy' has been among us: the adulteration of apostolic truth with pagan philosophy and superstition alike is the work of the devil. Indeed, it is the work of presumably demonic *spirits*: 'we come to erre, by giving heed to seducing Spirits, and the Daemonology of such *as speak lies in Hypocrisie*'. These words are significant, because the explanation given for our belief in spirits is that spirits have led us to believe in them. The first demonology, that of the Fathers, is in the event supplemented by a second demonology, Hobbes's own.

Patristic philosophizing and early medieval 'idolatry' are thus not in the event given a merely diffusionist explanation, but rather a particular kind of Christian explanation. They are given an explanation which is itself, ultimately, patristic in origin. Unlike Hobbes, and with better philological grounds, the Fathers did not regard the notions of demons and spirits (or the witches or mediums who could raise them) as unscriptural. Their view of pagan religion was not that it entirely lacked the access which it claimed to supernatural powers, but rather that the power attributed to their deities by the pagans was in fact a power exercised by demons and granted to those demons by the devil. The power in idols is real enough, but it belongs in reality to demons: as Augustine notes in his *City of God*, 'although man was the creator of his gods, he was not, their very maker, any the less possessed by them when he was delivered by his worship into their fellowship; a fellowship, I mean, not with stupid idols, but with wily demons'.[17] It becomes important both to understand that the power associated with idols is real, and that it is not really exercised by the idols. Hence the value of 1 Corinthians 10.19–20: 'What say I then? that the idol is any thing, or that which is offered in sacrifice to idols is any thing? But I say, that the things which the Gentiles sacrifice, they sacrifice to devils, and not to God: and I would not that you have fellowship with devils.' The demons derived their own power from Lucifer, who, ultimately, derived his from God. For this reason scriptural passages in which mediums appeared successfully to raise spirits could become acutely sensitive areas. The Old Testament narrative of the raising of Samuel's spirit at Saul's behest by the 'witch' or rather medium of Endor (1 Samuel 28) makes no mention of Satan. The medium is herself implied to have the ability to raise spirits. In patristic exegesis the medium's powers are transferred to Lucifer, who is declared to have produced either the real Samuel or a diabolical illusion of him.[18]

Just as Hobbes's demystification of the patristic demonology leads him into a further demonology of his own, so that patristic demonology itself is founded on a demystification: that of the anthropomorphic 'pagan' deities. Just so, for Marx, Feuerbach will later superstitiously attribute a power to the ideas he would break. Nor is this the only significant homology between Hobbes and Augustine. For both, idolatry is inseparably bound up with social non-transparency, an imposition by one class upon another: with Hobbes, the papist priesthood, with Augustine, the pagan rulers.

[M]en who posed as prudent and wise made it their business to deceive the people in matters of religion. In this they not only worship, but also imitate the demons, whose greatest desire is to deceive. For just as demons can only possess those whom they have treacherously deceived, so also the rulers – certainly not honest men, but men like the demons – taught the people as true in matters of religion what they knew to be false. In this way they bound them with tighter chains, as it were, to the civil society, in order that they might possess men similarly enthralled.[19]

Such an association between idolatry and the interests of an elite sustained by imposture was to remain central in various forms in the critique of religion from Hobbes to de Tracy. The deist Charles Blount's theory that '[t]he Primitive Institution of Idolatry receiv'd its Birth from Princes, at whose charge it was afterwards Educated by Ecclesiasticks; the one made the Idol, and the other ordain'd the worship of it'[20] could later be extended by Paine to Christianity itself: 'The Christian theory is little else than the idolatry of the ancient mythologists, accommodated to the purposes of power and revenue; and it yet remains to reason and philosophy to abolish the amphibious fraud.'[21]

These correlations are significant, not because they could (implausibly) show that Hobbes's thought is rather like Augustine's or has little new to add on the topic of political illusion, but, instead, precisely *because* Hobbes was a thinker who set himself so vigorously against patristic and scholastic thought, which he tended to regard as a unified continuum. Seventeenth-century exponents of natural and rational religion play a crucial role in handing over the concept of idolatry invented in patristic theology and exegesis to the 'science' of ideo-logy when it is born. The discourse of idolatry has the outstanding advantage of being both pious and philosophical. It could be turned not merely against obvious targets, such as the Roman church, but also, at need, against more surprising ones. Henry More understood even Calvinism (which he called 'Super-lapsarianism') as a form of idolatry: 'For the object of their Worship is a God-Idol of their own framing, that acts merely according to *Will* and *Power*, sequestered from all respect to either *Justice* or *Goodness* . . . which is the genuine *Idea* of a *Devil.*'[22] The extension of the concept to refer not merely to the worship of non-scriptural deities but also to a wide range of kinds of perceived irrationality is certainly anticipated by the Fathers but becomes far more systematic with the scientific and epistemological revolutions of the seventeenth century.

An illustration of the very wide range of referents which the concept of idolatry could be made to take – and one with special resonance for Wordsworth – is provided by a figure who often found himself in disagreement with Hobbes, Robert Boyle. His *Free Enquiry into the Vulgarly Received Notion of Nature* regarded, for example, the scholastic notion that *Natura est sapientissima* not merely as mistaken but as a form of 'idolatry':

> According to the foregoing hypothesis, I consider the frame of the world already made as a great and, if I may so speak, pregnant automaton, that like a woman with twins in her womb, or a ship furnished with pumps, ordnance, etc. is such an engine as comprises or consists of several lesser engines. And this compounded machine, in conjunction with the laws of motion freely established and still maintained by God among its parts, I look upon as a complex principle, whence results the settled order or course of things corporeal ... To manifest therefore the malevolent aspect that the vulgar notion of nature has had, and therefore possibly may have, on religion, I think fit in a general way to premise what things they are which seem to me to have been the fundamental errors that misled the heathen world, as well philosophers as others. For if I mistake not, the looking upon merely corporeal and oftentimes inanimate beings as if they were endowed with life, sense and understanding, and the ascribing to nature and some other beings (whether real or imaginary) things that belong but to God, have been some (if not the chief) of the grand causes of the polytheism and idolatry of the Gentiles.[23]

The demand for a wholly disenchanted concept of nature is cast as a reproof of idols. This allows the demand to be represented not merely as a scientific, but also as a religious imperative. A strict separation between the literal and the figurative plays a central part in this manoeuvre. Were any reader to object that, far from presenting us with a genuinely disenchanted concept of nature, Boyle's 'pregnant automaton' resembles a monstrous prodigy, he or she might be referred to the signal which has already been given that this is only a figure: 'if I may so speak'. What has taken place is less a demystification than the replacement of one set of anthropomorphic imaginations about nature with another, mechanical set. But this latter set of imaginations has been defended by being announced as figurative. Would we attach any sense to Boyle's concept of Nature more than that it is the sum total of existing entities, we must have recourse to just those images whose function has already been represented as figurative rather than literally descriptive.

LIFE DELETED

It is hard not to think of such monsters as Boyle's 'pregnant automaton' when considering these lines from Wordsworth's 'poem to Coleridge':

> Call ye these appearances
> Which I beheld of shepherds in my youth,

> This sanctity of Nature given to man,
> A shadow, a delusion? – ye who are fed
> By the dead letter, not the spirit of things,
> Whose truth is not a motion or a shape
> Instinct with vital functions, but a block
> Or waxen image which yourselves have made,
> And ye adore.[24]

Wordsworth here turns the rhetoric of idol-breaking against itself. Literalism like Boyle's thinks itself disenchanted. But its disenchantment is superstitious. It is in a strict sense idolatrous, for Wordsworth, in that, having disenchanted the living world, it venerates its own dead product. The attempt of the literalists is to see the world without illusions – by deleting from it all that which is taken to be merely our own fantasized projection. The notion that Nature might have any significance of its own would be such a projection. But for Wordsworth, this attempt does not have the enlightening effects for which it hopes. Meaning is expelled from the world, because the idea of a meaningful world is taken to be idolatry. The stripping of meaning from the world, on the grounds that the idea of meaning is a superstitious fiction, only promotes a rival superstition, which is that our own activity is the source of all meaning. Veneration of nature is replaced by veneration of production, and of the dead product, the system of disenchanted reason.

Wordsworth is a long way from the varieties of idealism which are sometimes attributed to him.[25] On the contrary, idealism is what he is attacking here: an idealism which is not decided by whether the thinker in question calls him- or herself an empiricist, or a rationalist, or even a materialist, but rather by what actually happens in his or her thinking. The dead-letter-men are idealists, because they can venerate only what they have themselves produced. For Wordsworth, by contrast, it is imperative that truth be 'a motion or a shape / Instinct with vital functions'. He does *not* say, 'instinct with consciousness'. Here as elsewhere, Wordsworth's founding opposition is not that between thought and being, but that between the really living and the living dead: here, between a thought inseparable from somatic affectivity – 'vital functions' – and the mock-life constructed out of components already in advance stripped of it, an affectless pure consciousness on one side and meaningless data on the other.

From such a perspective, the notion that language may be perfectly split between the literal and the figurative is a further symptom, rather than available as a legitimate defence, of this disenchanted idolatry. In a view like Boyle's the letter kills in the specific sense that any description which implies that what is real is also meaningful can only be regarded as figurative. The real is dead. It can only superstitiously be called alive, since life is only a movement of dead matters. This is a half-life 'feeding' on a grotesque anti-meal: the dead letter. But Wordsworth's general address to 'ye', the refusal to name individuals here, is no accident, because his point is not one about a specific mistaken set of tenets or opinions, as though if these were replaced with the right opinions all would be well. It is a point which applies to any thinking in which this logic of a double expulsion of life is at work: consciousness purified of affect, a world purified of meaning. It is important that the passage occurs just where Wordsworth is defending himself against an anticipated objection: that the appearances of shepherds which he beheld in his youth were a shadow or a delusion, or, as the matter would now less trenchantly be put, an 'ideology'.

What is beginning to come into view is the way in which ideology-critiques, that is, ideo-logies, as well as their ancestors, the demonologies, cannot but be at all turns intimately connected with a much broader set of ontological presuppositions. The attempt to say what an idol or an ideology is, like any attempt to dispel an illusion, always implies an account, whether explicit or not, of what there is. And in such accounts, as has been extensively demonstrated in the last century, the crucial determinants may often be answers to some obsolete and long-forgotten series of questions of which the given questioner may no longer even be aware as problems. This is why the 'science of ideas', like its descendant, the science of society, has already blocked the exit which it claims to be seeking. It is just by placing himself outside the set of illusions to be dispelled that the ideologist hands himself over to them. The philosophical problems have not actually been solved, just set aside. They have been suppressed. So they continue to inhabit just that supposedly quite undeceived 'science' which is all the time vigilantly scanning the world outside itself for idols to break, ideologies to unmask.

The debate about ideology, then, cannot properly be understood unless we operate both with some sense of this *longue durée* of the assault on anthropomorphism from Xenophanes to the present, and an awareness that the science of 'social' illusion has not in fact completed any unilateral farewell to philosophy. One of the most acute instances of these difficulties is also, indirectly, one of the most significant for applications of the concept of 'ideology' to poetry. Louis Althusser was by no means a

thinker who was naïve about the kinds of problem set out above. Indeed,
his work does much to lay them bare. Although poetry and literary
criticism are not Althusser's most frequently deployed instances of
ideology, this has formed no obstacle to the application of his thought in
this direction, because 'the formal structure of all ideology is always the
same ... the same demonstration can be produced for ethical, legal,
political, aesthetic ideology, etc.'[26] At the centre of ideology for Althusser
is the interpellated 'subject', which here denotes a compulsory illusion of
free agency: 'the individual *is interpellated as a (free) subject in order that he
shall submit freely to the commandments of the Subject, i.e. in order that he
shall (freely) accept his subjection*, i.e. in order that he shall make the
gestures and actions of his subjection "all by himself"'.[27] The same idea
has been put in less technical terms earlier in the same argument: 'every
"subject" endowed with a "consciousness", and believing in the "ideas"
that his "consciousness" inspires in him and freely accepts, must "*act
according to his ideas*", must therefore inscribe his own ideas as a free
subject in the actions of his material practice. If he does not do so, "that is
wicked".'[28] The account is of real interest for the insight which it gives us
into the nature of agency in a society in which, as Rousseau put it, we are
forced to be free. The theory of our freedom is itself taken to be the means
of our subjection. For Althusser, subjectivity, by which he means this
subjection, *is* ideology.

What is the force of the inverted commas in this last quotation? The
words and phrases insulated by them are disowned. They tell us that such
terms as subject, consciousness, ideas are not Althusser's, but those of
ideology. And with that they put a distance between ideology and the
ideology-critic. This distance is a problem. Althusser is acutely aware that
the force of Marx's text was a reminder that the idea that we are outside
illusion is itself part of the structure of ideo-logy. Yet he wishes to offer an
undeceived account of its workings. Hence such formulations as the
following:

those who are in ideology believe themselves by definition outside ideology: one
of the effects of ideology is the practical *denegation* of the ideological character of
ideology by ideology: ideology never says, 'I am ideological'. It is necessary to be
outside ideology, i.e. in scientific knowledge, to be able to say: I am in ideology
(a quite exceptional case) or (the general case): I was in ideology. As is well
known, the accusation of being in ideology applies only to others, never to
oneself (unless one really is a Spinozist or a Marxist, which, in this matter, is to
be exactly the same thing). Which amounts to saying that ideology *has no outside*

(for itself), but at the same time *that it is nothing but outside* (for science and reality).[29]

The Marxist is distinguished from the Feuerbachian by being able to admit that he is inside ideology, and has no access to a position 'outside' ideology. Yet he is also to be the scientist who is to diagnose ideology not merely as illusory, but as 'nothing but outside'. The formulations are unhappy not in any merely pejorative sense, but in that applied by Hegel to the unhappy or soteriological consciousness – whether religious, political or philosophical – which declares all truth and meaning to be outside itself at the same time as it understands itself to be entangled in a world devoid of such truth and meaning.[30] For such a consciousness the true mark of salvation is to be able to declare our own guilt: it is necessary to be outside ideology in order to be able to say 'I am in ideology'. The similarity between ideology in Althusser's account and original sin in much Christian thought is by no means introduced here as though it represented a decisive strike against Althusser, but rather as a way of indicating the powerful way in which patristic discourse continues to shape discussion of ideology and does so the more powerfully the more the latter is thought of as a technical term with its own autonomous structure, somehow separate from the question of enlightenment and disenchantment in general. The parallel becomes stronger when we read that '[b]efore its birth, the child is therefore always-already a subject', not in this case because of natural, but cultural inheritance: it is 'appointed as a subject in and by the specific familial ideological configuration in which it is "expected" once it has been conceived'.[31] Although, for science, ideology is nothing real at all; nevertheless, for us, nothing else is real. The availability of a perspective of 'science', a perspective from which, it can only be thought, Althusser's theory of ideology is written, makes of his recognition of our own entanglement in illusion something merely formal. It is not acknowledged as having adverse consequences for science, but only for the scientist, who is bifurcated rather in the manner of a Kantian moral agent.[32]

The idea that ideology is subjection introduces a key difference from Marx, but also a key determinant of ideo-logical discourse on Wordsworth. Marx, as is too rarely recognized, does not in fact make comfortable reading for collectivist social theorists. Marx's (effectively in the last analysis antinomian) hopes for human community are not for a suppression or deletion of individuality in favour of the collective good, but rather for a non-contractual reconciliation among free individuals. This is an unsurprising consequence of his social ontology, which is not at all collectivist but individualist in the specific sense that for Marx the experience of 'living human individuals' is what is real.[33] In one sense there is indeed no such *thing* as 'society' or 'history' for Marx, because society is no more than the relations between living human individuals. In Bruno Bauer's work '*history*, like *truth*, becomes a person apart, a metaphysical subject of which the real human individuals are merely the bearers'.[34] Althusser can be understood as having seen this point, but the exhaustive and literal application which he makes of Marx's ironic and restricted concept of ideology changes everything. At first Althusser acknowledges a distinction between the 'concrete individual' and the 'subject'. This door, however, then slowly swings shut:

> As ideology is eternal, I must now suppress the temporal form in which I have presented the functioning of ideology, and say: ideology has always-already interpellated individuals as subjects, which amounts to making it clear that individuals are always-already interpellated by ideology as subjects, which necessarily leads us to one last proposition: *individuals are always-already subjects*.[35]

The idea that 'ideology is eternal' is an acknowledged divergence[36] from central features of *The German Ideology*. Marx's claim that 'ideology has no history' means that ideology has no history of its own, only that created for it by living human individuals, the ideologists and their predecessors, priests and ideology-critics alike, and those who believe them. It is this divergence which here leads 'science' to speak with the voice of 'ideology'. Individuals *are* always-already subjects. The gulf is crossed as soon as the idea that 'individuals are always already interpellated by ideology as subjects' is allowed to lead into this emphatic ontological claim, that individuals just are subjects: even though there are, for science, no such things as subjects. The distance taken from Marx's 'positivism' in *The German Ideology* is crucial. Marx is supposedly 'positivist' there because he thinks he can say something about what these living human individuals are, independently of ideology.[37] The distinction which Marx always keeps open between suffering-desiring-thinking bodies, on the one hand, and the representations and personifications which such bodies are made to inhabit, on the other, is allowed to close. There is real experience, but not for us.

Such a closure – the declaration that individuals emphatically *are* always-already subjects – confirms a loss of experience, if not as absolute, then as something whose remedy remains unthinkable, short of *something turning up* in the form of millennial or lucky rescue.[38] This ratification of the loss of experience has had a powerful impact on the study of Romantic poetry, which has widely been thought to promote an ideology of the subject. I shall argue later that the most distinctive and characteristic moments of Wordsworth's poetic language are those at which the conceptions of the subject as a set of forms for processing representations begin to break down. Here I want merely to note how the discourse of ideology has been the means by which a whole series of persistent and unresolved philosophical problems have been ruled out of court. In so far as there is a 'positivism' to be complained of in Marx, it results not from his refusal to regard the idea of real human experience as an 'ideology', but rather from the idea of a unilateral farewell to philosophy; a farewell to which his work in practice only in part aspires, but which, in so far as it does, he shares with the first 'positivist', Auguste Comte. The damage of this fantasized departure is everywhere evident in the widespread assumption that the difficulties associated with such aporetic ideas as nature, subjectivity, beauty, goodness and truth can be overcome simply by suppressing, avoiding, or junking those categories, – or by subjecting them to 'ideology-critique', that is to say, to ideology.

A MATERIALISM OF THE LETTER?

It should by now be clear that I do not think that this damage can be mended simply by coming up with a better theory of ideology. Rather, the literal and exhaustive application given to that intially comic and restricted concept is itself part of the problem. A more promising path, if hardly a full remedy, lies in the reanimation of the relationship between philosophy and the 'human sciences', including literary criticism. One of the outstanding strengths of the deconstructive current in literary criticism has been its caginess about the kind of abrupt idol-breaking which I have so far been examining. The term deconstruction is itself in part a translation of Heidegger's notion of a *Destruktion* or *Abbau* of the history of previous ontology;[39] and Heidegger perhaps more than any other thinker in the last century showed just how pervasively intimate with our every thought, breath and movement are the consequences of that allegedly obsolete metaphysics from which ideo-logy thinks to be emancipated by decree. Deconstructive readers have wanted to distinguish their operations from 'ideology-critique', not because they are less critical, but because of a salutary awareness about the difficulty of saying goodbye to philosophy.

A special interest therefore attaches to the late Paul de Man's late reflections on 'aesthetic ideology'. De Man understands at once that the motif of 'ideology' can never properly be addressed if it be simply detached from philosophy in advance. He chooses, in the essay 'Phenomenality and Materiality in Kant', to approach the motif through the very promising avenue of a reflection upon transcendental thought. An early paragraph sketches the problem:

> Ideologies, to the extent that they necessarily contain empirical moments and are directed towards what lies outside the realm of pure concepts, are on the side of metaphysics rather than critical philosophy. The conditions and modalities of their occurrence are determined by critical analyses to which they have no access. The object of these analyses, on the other hand, can only be ideologies. Ideological and critical thought are interdependent and any attempt to separate them collapses ideology into mere error and critical thought into idealism. The possibility of maintaining the causal link between them is the controlling principle of rigorous philosophical discourse: philosophies that succumb to ideology lose their epistemological sense, whereas philosophies that try to by-pass or repress ideology lose all critical thrust and risk being repossessed by what they foreclose.[40]

De Man is attempting to understand the relation between criticism and 'ideologies' (a word which, although he refers briefly to de Tracy, he is here using in its looser twentieth-century sense) through an analogy with the relationship between Kant's critical thought and the metaphysical speculation upon which critical thought wishes to place a limit. The point of the analogy is an insight which admits a central feature of what is valuable in Marx's (and to an extent in Althusser's) accounts of ideology: the insight into the interdependence of criticism with the ideology criticized. The attempt finally to separate them produces idealism, even where materialism is loudly proclaimed. The effects of any final distinction between science and ideology are equally pronounced on both sides of the equation: science can no longer account for its own entanglement in ideology ('idealism'); ideology now appears as merely accidental 'error' rather than as a set of illusions occurring for reasons which may not easily be set aside.

De Man's use of Kant as a medium in which to think this problem is pertinent, because the relationship he sets out is just that between critical limitation and speculative reason set out in Kant's 'transcendental dialectic'. Although de Man's argument focusses on the third critique, this relationship as it pertains to all critical thought is most fully set out in the first. Kant's celebrated declaration of his intention to confine reason to the coastline of experience rather than allowing it to set sail in the seas of metaphysical speculation raises some of the central problems of Kantian reason, problems on which Hegel's reading, for one, was later to focus.[41] Reason's tendency to pretend to a priori knowledge of metaphysical objects, such as God, a free will, or an immortal soul, is not legitimate, for Kant, yet this tendency is more than a simple mistake. It is rather a tendency which is inherent in the nature of reason itself. Reason always will keep making these mistakes. As a result, it will always be in need of a critical limitation, 'ever and again calling for correction'.[42] Hence the force of De Man's comparison with the structure of ideology. Unlike simple error, ideological error does not disappear just because the mistake is pointed out. In the same way, Kant does not think that the *Critique of Pure Reason* is likely to put an end to reason's speculative excursions. These are illusions which are inseparable from human reason itself, the very power on which we rely for our ability to conceive of the world as in any way intelligible. Indeed, Kant's transcendental dialectic might be thought of as that revolution in our views of the relationship betwen truth and error which makes possible the understanding of ideology as a 'real illusion'. Kant has managed to find an exit from the opposition between scepticism and rationalism, an exit which allows us to think of some kinds of error as significantly related to, rather than accidentally irrelevant to, truth. It is an exit which provides a central avenue for Hegel's more all-encompassing use of the term 'dialectic'.

The counter-weight to ideology here is provided by de Man's claim to have uncovered what he calls 'Kant's materialism'; and it is here that his argument becomes both more provocative and harder to sustain. Its aim, and that of several pieces in the collection as a whole, is to detach a more austere Kantian *critique* of aesthetic judgement from the more meta-physically compromised account of aesthetic experience offered by Schiller, Hegel and numerous points downstream. The reading corrects the assumption that a vast range of what is called 'aesthetic ideology' can rapidly be labelled 'Kantian'. In a reading of Kant's analytic of the sub-lime de Man begins to uncover what he regards as a 'formal materialism' at work in that section of the *Critique of Judgement*. There is a materi-alism, de Man claims, because we arrive in the course of Kant's analytic at a moment when a sheer materiality, devoid of mediation by spirit, is invoked; indeed, de Man argues, it is for Kant essential to the effect produced that 'no mind is involved' at this stage. Kant is arguing that when we find the starry sky sublime it is essential that we do not think of astronomical laws – this would produce only a 'teleological' and hence a non-aesthetic judgement – but must regard it just as we see it; likewise

> we sometimes think of the ocean as a vast kingdom of aquatic creatures, or as the great source of those vapours that fill the air with clouds for the benefit of the land, or again as an element that, though dividing continents from each other, yet promotes the greatest communication between them; all these produce merely teleological judgements. To find the ocean nevertheless sublime we must regard it merely as poets do, merely by what the eye reveals – if it is at rest, as a clear mirror of water only bounded by the heavens; if it is stormy, as an abyss threatening to overwhelm everything.[43]

It is at this point that de Man turns to a contrast with Wordsworth, the better to illuminate Kant's materialism by contrast with Wordsworth's (implied rather than stated) idealism:

> . . . one thinks of the famous passage from 'Tintern Abbey':
>
>> And I have felt
>> A presence that disturbs me with the joy
>> Of elevated thoughts; a sense sublime
>> Of something far more deeply interfused
>> Whose dwelling is the light of setting suns,
>> And the round ocean and the living air
>> And the blue sky, and in the mind of man: . . .

The sublimity of the round ocean, horizon-bound as a vast dome, is especially reminiscent of the Kant passage. But the two invocations of sublime nature soon diverge. Wordsworth's sublime is an instance of the constant exchange between mind and nature, of the chiasmic transfer of properties between the sensory and intellectual world that characterizes his figural diction, here explicitly thematized in the 'motion and spirit that impels / All thinking things, all objects of all thoughts / And rolls through all things.' No mind is involved in the Kantian vision of ocean and heaven. To the extent that any mind, that any judgement, intervenes, it is in error – for it is not the case that heaven is a vault or that the horizon bounds the ocean like the walls of a building.[44]

This thesis of a Wordsworthian *economy*, of a continual and profitable exchange between mind and nature, is one that will be argued in this book to be only partially applicable. I shall be arguing that Wordsworth's poetry often pushes against this inherited ontological opposition, as well as against the inherited view that the grand point is dialectically or chiasmically or metaphysically or imaginatively to *overcome* opposition – as though *opposition*, in and of itself and in this abstract way, were something that Wordsworth was concerned about for its own sake.

Here, though, I want to think about some other features of de Man's account which I think are not merely arbitrarily but fatefully misleading. Both concern the point which is stretched in using this contrast to illustrate 'materialism'. In one rather restricted sense de Man is correct to say that '[n]o mind is involved in the Kantian vision of ocean and heaven'. The vision must not be submitted to a concept of any particular purpose, otherwise it could provoke only a teleological judgement, never a judgement of taste (which is what Kant, despite all the tensions which de Man notes between the sublime and the 'values and characteristics associated with aesthetic experience' insists on calling judgements about sublimity). But if the claim is pressed a little harder it becomes untenable. For Kant no determinate appearance to the eye is even possible without the intervention of the categories. Until the categories intervene there is only the indeterminate sensuous manifold of intuition. Without the categories we do not receive this sensuous manifold in any way which would allow us to see an ocean 'as a clear mirror of water only bounded by the heavens' or 'as an abyss threatening to overwhelm everything', or indeed *as* anything at all. It is not just that without 'mind' there is no determinate perception, but that without mind there is no 'presentation' of any kind.

No less significantly, the claim that 'no mind is involved', in order to work, would need to exclude 'reason' from 'mind'. Kant is working here with an architectonic parallel and distinction between the feeling associated with judgements of the beautiful and that associated with judgements of the sublime. The former are associated with a presentation which provokes the harmonious play of the faculties – imagination and understanding – necessary for cognition. The latter, on the other hand, are associated with the attempt and failure of imagination to provide an intuition adequate to *reason* (in the case of the 'mathematical' sublime, pure reason in its theoretical application, in the case of the 'dynamic' sublime, pure reason in its practical application). Our attempt and failure to imagine God is an instance of the imagination's sublime failure to provide an intuition adequate to reason. Sheer *Augenschein*, what appears to the eye, as invoked by de Man, can never for Kant provoke the feeling which is associated with the judgement of the sublime unless it provoke this sublime failure, whose value is that it is a failure which *reinforces* our sense, precisely of 'mind': '*Sublime is that which even to be able to think testifies to a capacity of the mind which surpasses any measure of sense.*'[45] So that while mind in the sense of understanding may not be present when we look at the ocean as the poet does in order to be sublime, reason certainly is.[46]

What matters about this is not primarily the accuracy or otherwise of de Man's reading of Kant – for my part, I continue to think that Kant is a transcendental idealist – but what is here imagined to be characteristic of 'materialism'. Materialism is here imagined to be what we get when what is invoked is a pure appearance to the eye in whose appearance 'no mind is involved'. In order to arrive at materialism, we are to delete any mediation of sheer *Augenschein* by our consciousness or by affectivity. On these criteria, Wordsworth's passage could not qualify because it thinks of 'the round ocean' as a 'dwelling'. Materialism depends above all for de Man upon the dispelling of anthropomorphic illusions, pathetic fallacies, about what we see. Materialism, in other words, is perfected disenchantment.

In many ways this is a curious terminus for a thinking so alert to the difficulties of separating the figurative from the literal as de Man's is to have arrived at. For the demand that the materialist may not think of the earth, for example, as a dwelling but must think of it, instead, as data, has as one of its implications the purging of figures from the materialist's literal language. As soon as Wordsworth thinks of ocean, air and sky as a 'dwelling' for anything, the literal *Augenschein* receives an idealizing figurative addition. The difficulties of such an approach can be seen if we return to the Kantian passage which de Man sets against Wordsworth. Is it really only the 'eye' and nothing else which 'reveals' the ocean 'as a clear *mirror* of water'? As 'an abyss *threatening* to overwhelm everything'? Are these not themselves already ways of *understanding* the ocean, through a language whose figures and concepts cannot but be contaminated with human experience?

RETHINKING MATERIALISM

Behind all this, I want to suggest, lies a deeper problem, which is the ruling idea itself – the idea that materialism is perfected disenchantment. It is no accident that de Man invokes such a notion of materialism in the book in which he devotes most attention to 'ideology'. In this essay Kant's supposed moment of 'materialism' is placed at the opposite pole to ideology. These materialist moments would be those elements of critical thought at the furthest distance from the ideologies, the speculations, which it is the unending task of critical thought to limit. Recall now that

Marx, by contrast, understands *ideology* as a form of disenchantment. May there not be a difficulty in understanding materialism and ideology as opposed polarities? Ideology was inaugurated as a science with a materialist programme; it was to be a branch of zoology. Yet these zoological demonstrations hoped to induce the end of social illusion. Social change, idealistically, is predicated by the ideologists upon a change in consciousness.[47]

What all this may be beginning to suggest is that it is very difficult indeed to be a materialist: much harder, for example, than declaring oneself a materialist or wishing to be such. Yet the central difficulty lies in the very idea that materialism is perfected disenchantment. It is often just where materialism is most zealously and literally pursued that its involuntary kinship with idealism is most in evidence. Two features of this view are especially striking. Firstly, the rise of what might be called materialism without nature. Boyle's assault on the vulgarly received conception of nature as idolatrous has cast a long shadow over subsequent materialisms. Any idea of nature as signifying more than the sum total of entities is thought of as a form of anthropomorphic projection, and hence as idolatrous, superstitious, or, more recently, 'ideological'. The development of oxymoronic programmes such as a cultural materialism in the humanities is an extension of this logic. It pursues the deletion of nature so far that materiality itself is deleted, in the sense that any notion of the real unmediated by culture is prohibited as, of course, 'ideological'. In its place are offered exemplary chunks of quoted socio-historical material specificity. Cultural materialism is one of Marx's sheep in wolves' clothing. If all is culture, then nothing is. Or one might say: if culture is everything, culture is – nature. 'No nature, no culture.'[48]

Secondly, we are offered the dismantling of subjectivity. Only when we can arrive at an invocation of a materiality free from contamination by subjective 'consciousness', affectivity or interpretation can we speak of materialism. But this scepticism about the subject is in fact an important feature of the development of idealism. It is not quite correct to think that idealism consists primarily in the absorption of everything by the subject. It is central to idealist conceptions of experience that the subject is *nothing at all* without its mediation by the object. This is clear enough in Kant's insistence that the pure concepts of the understanding produce no knowledge at all unless they are combined with intuition. We must be able to think the subject, but may not know whether it *is*. The subjectivity through which all is mediated in Hegel's thought is faithful to this Kantian conception in so far as it *is* nothing at all by itself, without the self-relinquishment in the realm of objects to which it alone owes the reality of its experience. The notion that what is characteristic of idealism is the monopoly of the subject over everything else is almost the opposite of the true situation. Rather, it is precisely because of idealism's allergic sensitivity to charges that it is relapsing into metaphysical soul-talk that it takes such pains to expel all ontological reality from the category of the subject. It is by just this means that the subject becomes pure consciousness; pure, that is, nothing at all until it gives itself away to objectivity.[49]

This may be illustrated by an example. What is pain, for Kant? Until it is operated upon by concepts, it is merely a sensuous manifold of intuition like any other. We do not *know* that we are in pain until this indeterminate manifold is made determinate by the application of the categories. But the problem does not arise, because pain has been conceived of on the model of an object. Because no sniff of soul-talk must be allowed in, all affectivity whatever has to be conceived of as a data set, sheer givenness. It is meaningless, qualityless data until it is processed by consciousness. Yet at the same time, this consciousness which is to grant meaning, qualities and determinacy is nothing at all by itself. Nothing plus nothing is made to equal something.[50]

Now this presents a real danger for materialism. The danger is that materialism will misdiagnose the problem. Materialism has wanted to dismantle the idealist subject or spirit. But it has used the idealist conception of the body – the body as sheer meaningless qualityless data set – in order to do so. Anything less disenchanted than such a data set would be 'idealist'. Yet it is idealism which has insisted on just this disenchantment! It is through this means that materialism becomes a self-misrecognizing idealism; an idealism, that is, in which my real experiences of hungering, suffering, desiring and thinking, are even more thoroughly disowned than they already are in Kant. These experiences remain characterized as givens, but it is even less clear than it is in Kant *to what* they are given. The deletion of both nature and subjectivity from materialism alike reflect the latter's recurrent practical idealism. Materialism becomes the unwitting shadow of idealism. It puts out its own eyes in order to see more clearly.

I want now to turn, then, to consider some alternative ways of understanding materialist thinking. What will be important here will not be the label itself, so much as the attempt to articulate a kind of thinking which could at once fulfil two desiderata. Firstly, it would need to reconsider its relation to the category of 'subjectivity'. In order to do this it would need to be able to do justice to the somatic element in thinking, the sense in which all thinking is entangled with affectivity and is itself a kind of affectivity. Such an account would not regard the claim of thinking to *be* thinking as dependent on, say, stripping thinking of its entanglement with somatic affectivity, for example by representing it as 'pure' consciousness. Accordingly it would demand a revised phenomenology of the body, one which could understand the body not as an originally insignificant and qualityless data set – materialism as the unwitting shadow of idealism – but rather as always already cognitive. The body is not merely a set of givens like any other processed by consciousness; it is itself also what must *know* any such phenomena. Secondly, such a materialism would need to reconsider its relation to the very category of 'nature'. The disenchantment of nature, followed by attempts to delete the very idea of nature altogether, must leave the concept of 'culture' no less indigent. But because this disenchantment is itself a real process, worked into the skin of our lives rather than merely held as a set of possessed opinions, it cannot be overcome simply by fiat. It is this that makes nature an aporetic category, a category subject, that is, to a set of contradictions which are not arbitrary but which are, instead, not eliminable by an act of will. Nature is a category which materialism deletes at its peril. If it does delete it, it cannot avoid becoming a degraded idealism. Yet nature is also a category which it cannot currently define. So materialism must understand itself as caught up in, rather than exempt from, a dialectic of disenchantment. Historically changing ways of conceiving nature could not legitimately be thought of as outworn superstitions unless we were confident of having a fully undeluded category available with which to replace them.

It is not at all my claim, therefore, that I already have such a materialism at my disposal, or that it can be taken off the peg from some master theorist of materialism, or that such a materialism could somehow be stitched up from selected body parts of existing authorships. Of course in arriving at my notions of materialism I have been particularly struck by the work of certain thinkers, my debts to whom are noted as appropriate; but these thinkers themselves speak of their work as preliminary, or as provisional, or as aporetic. It is just because materialism is currently entangled in a dialectic of disenchantment, rather than standing at some wholly undeluded vantage point, that its most valuable insights take a fragmentary and aporetic form. They cannot take the form of a 'materialist method'. The phrase is an oxymoron, because any method which remains the same whatever its object must be idealist, even if it calls itself materialist. They have not yet been able to take the form of a body of doctrine, because none has yet succeeded in stripping language utterly of its non-literal aspects. Nor is it certain that, were this possible, it would be desirable, or would be in any sense 'materialist'. 'Materialism', unlike, say, undeluded happiness, cannot properly count as an end. What we may learn from the historiography of idolatry, ideology and 'ideology-critique' is the impossibility of a painless exit from the logic of disenchantment. This means that the logic of social illusion cannot be delegated to a special science which has simply decided to say farewell to metaphysics, the science of ideology-critique, but will remain tied up with the persisting difficulties presented by the problem of cognitive illusion in general. It means that the logic of aesthetic illusion cannot be delegated to a sub-branch of that special science, a critique of aesthetic ideology, but will remain tied up with the persisting difficulties presented by the tasks of an aesthetic theory. What decides whether these problems can be solved, above all, does not depend only upon the discovery of the right method, doctrine or lexicon – the idea that this is the deciding factor is just what ideology means – but also upon the nature of the problems themselves, which are not yet exhaustively known.

For all these reasons 'poetic thinking' may be more important to any eventual 'materialist thinking' than has usually been thought. Marx and Engels's *Critique of Critical Criticism* already captured the ambivalence of a materialism caught in a logic of disenchantment:

In *Bacon*, its first creator, materialism still holds back within itself in a naive way the germs of a many-sided development. On the one hand, matter, surrounded by a sensuous, poetic glamour, seems to attract man's whole entity by winning smiles. On the other, the aphoristically formulated doctrine pullulates with inconsistencies imported from theology.

In its further evolution, materialism becomes one-sided. *Hobbes* is the man who *systematizes* Baconian materialism ... Materialism takes to *misanthropy*. If it is to overcome its opponent, *misanthropic, fleshless* spiritualism, and that upon the latter's own ground, materialism has to chastise its own flesh and turn *ascetic*. Thus it passes into an *intellectual entity*; but thus, too, it evolves all the consistency, regardless of consequences, characteristic of the intellect.[51]

In this view, Hobbes is more consistent, and less poetical, than Bacon. But he is not more materialist – only more miserable. What if our own era's critical criticism, its certainty about 'aesthetic ideology', were, in truth, *more idealist*, in its culturalisms, historicisms and pan-representationalisms, than

a poetic thinking like Wordsworth's (that staunch admirer of Bacon)[52] which has so often been found to fall short by its standards? In the following chapter I pursue this question by exploring the possibility of understanding Wordsworth's poetic thinking as a materialism of the beautiful.

CHAPTER 3

Materialism of the beautiful

'Do people still worry about higher things unless their bellies are full?'[1] Thus might any political economist working in an interdisciplinary institute face the prospect of yet another of those supersubtle seminar topics – that participants should discuss the nature of 'longing', for example, and consider its political and historical significances. The political significance of longing: the starving have no food, so they long for paradise.

Why do food riots happen? Because people get hungry, idiot! Then a distinction between needs and wants is the condition of the possibility of this kind of economics. Granted, it may be difficult to draw a precise border between these two. But when we get as far as *the beauty of nature*; when we are asked to consider what place *the beauty of nature* might have when we are distinguishing between needs and wants; should we be asked whether *beauty* need have any place in the calculation of that *strict nécessaire* without which the labour force must go under; then it will be clear what must be answered: that need comes first and beauty afterwards; that beauty is the extra, the more, the surplus that depends on the prior satisfaction of need and can be attended to only upon that condition; then it will be time to remind whatever fantasist has raised this question that only those with time on their hands have leisure for aesthetics, and that those who face real need are completely unsentimental. The question plays for time whilst more shall starve.

Yes, yes and yes. Meanwhile, might one of these ideas, that those who face real need are utterly unsentimental, not have its own sentimentality? What is it, in fact, to be *completely* unsentimental, and at what junction of necessity may this completed undeludedness be found? Is it not at this moment?

What is perhaps an occasion for surprise is the schizoid intellectual climate, which permits this quantitative historiography to co-exist (in the same places and

84

sometimes in the same minds) with a social anthropology which derives from Durkheim, Weber, or Malinowski. We know all about the delicate tissue of social norms and reciprocities which regulates the life of the Trobriand islanders, and the psychic energies involved in the cargo cults of Melanesia; but at some point this infinitely-complex social creature, Melanesian man, becomes (in our histories) the eighteenth-century English collier who claps his hands spasmodically upon his stomach, and responds to elementary economic stimuli.[2]

Thompson has done more than most historians to make clear that there is no such thing as purely economic behaviour. A genuine empiricism, one actually interested in getting the facts about historical *experience* of need, labour, exchange, is going to need to think quite carefully about what we might call the phenomenology of 'economics': about what working, exchanging, suffering feel like and about the extent to which those feelings are, not merely contingent or irrelevant or superstructural to 'need', but rather need itself. Not because economic history ought to *add* a phenomenology of exchange, as an 'interpretation', to the more fundamental facts of economic history, but rather because economic history is always in any case operating with some such account, usually one in which there is no time to waste on such extras.

'So *Wordsworth* saw all this? He was not, as we have been led to believe, a poet of the early nineteenth century, but instead an unusually subtle social scientist working in disguise against the moment when literary criticism should become well-informed enough to understand him?' The very reverse. It is just because Wordsworth wanted to be a poet, and not an ideologist, sociologist or political arithmetician, that he attempted to look steadily at singular cases – acts of attention which in practice begin to dismantle the misrecognitions of (what he would not have called) economistic thought.[3] If we do need to call it that, it is not with the foolish idea of securing praise for Wordsworth by showing how up-to-date he is, but rather with the idea that, if we are to recover a truth to experience in these poems, then more, rather than less, awareness of the obstacles which our own theoretical apparatuses provide is required.

THE BARE MINIMUM

Difficulty may be experienced in looking steadily at a subject, above all, when it *is* a subject. It is hard, for example, to look 'steadily' in the public road at someone who is weeping.

> Ten children, Sir! had I to feed,
> Hard labour in a time of need!
> My pride was tamed, and in our grief,
> I of the parish ask'd relief.
> They said I was a wealthy man;
> My sheep upon the mountain fed,
> And it was fit that thence I took
> Whereof to buy us bread:'
> 'Do this; how can we give to you,'
> They cried, 'what to the poor is due?'[4]

This is a logic of destitution in the straightforward sense that a man must be brought to destitution in order to qualify for relief from it. The destitute are those with no surplus, for, whilst a surplus remains, need cannot be understood to have been arrived at. When one can say, 'I have none', then may one properly become the object of mercy. The organism must be brought to a perfect minimum, so that it may be securely known that in supporting it, bare life alone is being sustained.

A sense of the barely perceptible, yet humanly decisive, transitions by which need and want pass over into each other, is part of Wordsworth's descriptive steadiness. This is evident in the critical passage from the appendix on poetic diction to the 'Preface' to *Lyrical Ballads* in which Wordsworth comes to see central obstacles to the founding of any poetic project on a philosophical anthropology: 'the true and the false became so inseparably interwoven that the taste of men was gradually perverted; and this language was received as a natural language; and, at length, by the influence of books upon men, did to a certain degree really become so'.[5] With that last phrase, the mutual interpenetration of wants and needs, and the difficulty of imagining a natural man of needs alone, is conceded.

This is an interpenetration which is still more subtly understood in the verse. Needs, the poetry is always showing, cannot but spill over into wants. As the farmer watches the destitution of his surplus, he 'wished they all were gone'. Nowhere could economic man ever wish so, or rather, the most that might be said from an economistic perspective is that the man's distress has induced insanity. The poem sees, instead, how the farmer's love for his sheep and his material interest in their life have become entangled in a way which cannot simply be undone when the base starts going down. This is the logic of the despairing self-destructiveness which economism can think of only as an aberration. For economism only the monk or madman would not wish to stay alive, and its instruction to the farmer is to exemplify this religion of bare life, something which, despite all this, he cannot be brought to do. 'Now I care not if we die.'

In that last expression – 'I care not if *we* die' – is harboured the peculiar quality of what we might think of as this poem's materialism – on condition that we do not build our materialism as a logic of destitution:

> Sir! 'twas a precious flock to me,
> As dear as my own children be;
> For daily with my growing store
> I loved my children more and more.
> Alas! it was an evil time;
> God cursed me in my sore distress,
> I prayed, yet every day I thought
> I loved my children less;
> And every week, and every day,
> My flock, it seemed to melt away.[6]

These lines insist that there is no spiritual property, even amongst those which are most often thought of as 'only human' – in the sense that it is 'only human' to love your children – which may not be taken away from us by material distress. In that insistence these lines are precisely materialist. Their bluntness far distances these lines from the usual tenor of poems about the virtuous poor: that, however far material distress should be pushed, the human and moral core shall remain unbroken. In that sense sentimental verse and economistic thinking properly complement each other as dejected humanisms, because both revolve around the exhibition of bare life as the irreducibly human. Wordsworth's poem is not humanist in that dejected sense, because it presents us with the disintegration of the human in the face, not even of absolute or 'natural' need, but of the economistic simulacrum of absolute need, the theoretical purification of need from want. Still more startling is that this is an entanglement, and a consequent collapse, whose recognition is not claimed by the poet for himself, but attributed, with real, rather than theoretical, generosity, to the farmer himself. It is the farmer who admits that he has made the scandalous equation 'love of my property : : love of my children'. I care not if *we* die, he says. So he makes it quite clear that he did not only *think* that he loved his children less.

A materialism of this kind is no fleeting appearance in Wordsworth's verse. When Robert, in 'The Ruined Cottage', loses his job, he too begins to love his children less. Instead of confirming a narrative in which a core of essential humanness remains unshakeable by all misfortune, he begins to speak 'lightly of his babes / And with a cruel tongue'.[7] This pressure runs right the way through to those poetic pleasures which Wordsworth is sometimes misconstrued as having taken to arise from a pre-established harmony fitting the 'mind' to 'nature':

> There is a law severe of penury
> Which bends the cottage boy to early thought,
> To thought whose premature necessity
> Blocks out the forms of nature, preconsumes
> The reason, famishes the heart, shuts up
> The infant being in itself, and makes
> Its very spring a season of decay.[8]

The forms of nature may very well be blocked out by penury. In one kind of account penury would do this by depriving the poor of the luxury for thought. Bent beneath immediate necessities, their views would become pitiably narrowed. This passage is not unrelated to that kind of account, but it also carries unusual emphases. The luxury of which the poor boy is here deprived is the opposite: the luxury of thoughtlessness. The lines contain within them, of course, an earlier sense of 'thought' as signifying preoccupation, unhappiness. They also carry, however, an acute sense of how the mind's fitting to the external world may be just the reverse of exquisite: of how it can be precisely an excess of thought which '[b]locks out the forms of nature'.

'FOOD FIRST, THEN BEAUTY!'

One way of thinking about the relationship between real need and ideal hopes is that represented by the following quotation:

The essence of Marxism (at least according to a certain and *restrictive* under-standing) is to give man mastery over nature, over what is nature in himself, by means of the thing: any other means of liberation that has recourse to ideal hopes would only prolong his enslavement and, furthermore, deceives him, lets him remain in an illusory state where he soon loses his footing and forgets what is. From this perspective, the liberator would thus be the man who is already at this moment the most purely thing, the man-tool who is already reduced, without travesty, to his material condition, who is 'nothing' except useful, the man of necessity, the necessitous, the man of need. Power must be given over to him, to this man: the man of labor, the productive man, that is, not immediately man (for he is 'nothing', he is only lack, negation, need) but labor itself, anonymous and impersonal, and the things produced by labor, the works in their becoming in which man, subjected to violence and responding with violence, would come to himself, to his real freedom. But it goes without saying that any man, if he wants to 'see' what he is (that is, nothing) through the unreality of values, is also this man of need.[9]

The passage is worth thinking about in some detail because it puts so forcefully a particular, and particularly influential, way of distinguishing the conditions of real emancipation from a merely ideal image of it. It is at a far remove from any straightforwardly humanist socialism. The condition of real emancipation would not be for some less inhuman world to be imagined, but precisely for things to get as bad as they could possibly do. Things are to get so bad, indeed, that the fundamental distinction itself which forms the condition of the possibility of understanding how surplus value is created – the distinction between living and non-living labour – should itself, apparently, go under. Marx, it will be remembered, continually reminds the reader throughout his account of surplus value that living labour and the action of tools are not the same.[10] It is just because humans are not tools that there can be surplus value. The human being's labour is bought and sold like any other commodity. Unlike any other commodity, though, it can produce further commodities, and it can thus, Marx thinks, be argued that the person who buys it is getting something extra, a surplus which has not been paid for. The difference between the living and the non-living, and the polemic against its effacement, echoes throughout Marx's books in a way which a marx*ism* schooled in the long after-effects of western metaphysics will find philosophically untenable and perhaps also embarrassingly melodramatic (or at least 'pre-deconstructive'[11]). 'Capital is dead labour which, vampire-like, lives only by sucking living labour, and lives the more, the more labour it sucks.'[12]

In the longer passage quoted earlier, however, it is not merely of no use, for example, for a given worker or group of workers to understand this difference between life and death; indeed, the case is rather the reverse. If the situation is to be changed, what must happen is not that workers should know the difference between living and non-living labour, but that they should be brought to a point at which it is quite impossible to know this difference, because the difference has ceased to apply: the point at which the worker is 'the man-tool'. What has happened in this reading? One genuinely pivotal motif in Marx's thought has been allowed to turn the rest of it. The pivotal motif is that emancipation is not a matter of changing ideas. Justly, the reading points out that for Marx emancipation can never depend upon providing to those who are suffering the ideal of a less dehumanized life. But the reading then springs from this defeat of false hopes into a theodicy of despair. Emancipation is to depend, it now appears, upon making the suffering embody the ideal of a *perfectly* dehumanized life. Only when the worker shall become 'the man of labor, the productive man, that is, not immediately man (for he is 'nothing', he is only lack, negation, need) but labor itself, anonymous and impersonal' may 'he' be 'the liberator'. As this quotation itself emphasizes, there is no such individual as 'the man of labour'; the man who is only lack, negation, need. Any such individual would be 'nothing'. There is such a personification, however: a personification which arises only in connection with the twinned personification of the capitalist as the hero of the narrative of capital. And here it is thought that emancipation requires that the worker perfectly inhabit this personification, that he perfectly embody this – ideal. For Marx, however, the living individual can *never* perfectly embody the personifications (whether of the absolute worker or of the absolute capitalist) through which capital is shaped. No individual can be 'labour itself'. Just this indicates the fact that 'labour itself' has no existence other than as a structuring chimera of capital. In these circumstances the idea that what is required in order for emancipation to take place is for the worker perfectly to inhabit this admitted chimera is powerfully superstitious. It is not less superstitious, but only more miserable, than the idea that what is required is for the worker to become, e.g., ethically responsible, or a believer in the possibility of a better world.

What has happened here? The desire to disentangle Marx from a sentimental humanism has produced an equally sentimental anti-humanism. (Indeed, the alliance between the two is well traced by the trajectory in this very passage from man's mastery over himself and over nature, understood as 'the essence of Marxism', to the recommendation of a personification deliberately emptied of life as the exemplary liberator.) The truth that Marx wished capitalist society to come to a condition of crisis, rather than to be ameliorated and helped to survive by useful reforms, has been allowed to efface the fundamental difference of his ontology between the living and the non-living; has been allowed to organize the critical moments in his thought around a kind of 'way of despair'[13] – things must get as bad as they could do before they will get better – which is in fact not its basis but only one aspect of a way in which he sometimes talks about one feature of a historical social process. And from this we can go on to affirm that it is indeed only in 'a *restricted* reading' that the essence of Marxism consists in giving man mastery of nature, whether the nature in him or the nature outside him. In the

Critique of the Gotha Programme, a text which is critical for the differentiation of Marx from the varieties of optimistic or pessimistic idealism which have been constructed from him, Marx insisted quite straightforwardly that labour was not the source of all wealth, but that nature was also a source of wealth and, with this, hinted that emancipation might have more to do with reconciliation with, than mastery over, nature.[14]

The liberator imagined by Blanchot is at the bare minimum. He is dead-and-alive; he has absolutely no surplus; he has *exactly* what is needed to survive and no more. One reason why Marx was so sceptical about the idea that we could know exactly what a human being needs to survive was that the fiction of the *strict nécessaire* was twinned in economistic apologetics with the concept of surplus value:

The agricultural labourer, depending on the minimum of wages, the *strict nécessaire*, reproduces more than this *strict nécessaire*, and this more is rent, *surplus-value*, which is appropriated by the owners of the fundamental condition of labour – nature. So what they [the Physiocrats] say is not: the labourer works more than the labour-time required for the reproduction of his labour-power; the value which he creates is therefore greater than the value of his labour-power; or the labour which he gives in return is greater than the quantity of labour which he receives in the form of wages. But what they say is: the amount of use-values which he consumes during the period of production is smaller than the amount of use-values which he creates, and so a surplus of use-values is left over. – Were he to work only for the time required to reproduce his own labour-power, there would be nothing over. But the Physiocrats only stuck to the point that the productivity of the earth enables the labourer, in his day's labour, which is assumed to be a fixed quantity, to produce more than he needs to consume in order to continue to exist. The surplus-value therefore appears as a *gift of nature*, through whose co-operation a definite quantity of organic matter – plant-seeds, a number of animals, enables labour to transform more inorganic matter into organic.[15]

The *strict nécessaire* is a crucial component in allowing profits and other forms of surplus-value to be represented as a species of unaccountable luck, a 'gift of nature', rather than as an unsurprising consequence of the fact that some people have all the luck; have, for example, a monopoly over what is needed to sustain life. The agricultural labourer depends on the minimum of wages. The gifts of nature start just where the labourer's minimum stops. How is the minimum settled? By a theory of what is absolutely needed, of what is 'strictly' necessary, and by the deletion of whatever falls above that – as luxury or surplus. How do you know what the bare minimum is? By waiting to see at just what point people start dying: an experiment whose course Marx charted in the section of *Capital* entitled 'The Working Day'.

If we keep this aspect of Marx's thought in mind we can see how mistaken it is to think of his thought as primarily determined by the moral critique of luxury. (It would be no less mistaken, of course, to think of it as a moral apologia for luxury.) That would be to take up a strict concept of need against the misappropriation of surplus. But the strict concept of need is twinned with the apologia for surplus. It is because of the strict theory of the nature of need that surplus comes to look like a gift of nature. And it is for this reason that Marx does not base his theory of surplus value in an anthropology of natural need, but rather in an account of the difference between the living and non-living components of production and in an account of monopolies over conditions of production.

From this perspective it can be seen that a programme which bases itself upon a theory of the strictly necessary and the otherwise surplus will not necessarily be socially critical. 'Food first, then beauty!' further reproduces as a moral demand the logic of need and surplus which is daily recorded in the existing business accounts. As a moral demand, its purpose is to strip the rich of their misappropriated surplus. Yet as soon as it builds upon the model of the *strict nécessaire*, it reinforces the logic of destitution which says that the farmer shall receive not one help until *all* his sheep are gone. It is possible that upon some individual occasion a poetic thinking, pleading specially for its own worth, for the need for this luxury, the luxury of poetry, may, none the less, and in part because of this partiality, come to look more steadily at particular cases of distress than will theories grounded in apriorized decisions about human nature. It is equally possible that its gaze may falter and drop back to some consoling sentiment of its own. These are possibilities whose result is shown only by the event.

FAITH IN CAPITAL

It is out of the consideration of points such as these that some of the most testing work on Wordsworth's understanding of social experience over the last two decades has emerged. Testing, because instead of setting itself at an imaginary ideo-logical vantage over the poetry, it has understood social scientific and historical enquiry themselves to be no less implicated in their objects of study than is Wordsworth's poetry in the world of his subjects. David Simpson's book, still in many respects unsurpassed on these aspects of Wordsworth's writing, has done a great deal to lay bare the deep affinities between the poetry's own rethinking of the experiences of working, needing, exchanging, and those present in the social-critical and philosophical traditions which have sometimes been brought to bear on it as though from another location entirely.[16] Another powerful, but more suspicious, reading is Jon Klancher's interpretation of Wordsworth's relation to his public in *The Making of English Reading Audiences*. Part of the power comes from a mode of interpretation deeply influenced by the thought of Pierre Bourdieu, yet which understands well how little susceptible is that body of thought to mechanical application. Bourdieu's own strengths, and in particular his ability to get beyond the bad choice between credulous reverence for, and equally credulous debunking of, the belief-system of literature – an ability to go beyond this choice not merely as an assertion but in the very texture of his practice, – are also Klancher's, and lead him to an account which travels at the poet's side as well as occasionally running ahead of him.[17]

Considering the applicability of such ideas to Wordsworth is impossible without taking a hard look at some central issues in the philosophy, history and anthropology of exchange and donation. Bourdieu himself has long understood, as Marx-ist social thinkers have sometimes not, that a rapid or insufficiently reflective application of a concept of 'ideology' to literary and other forms of cultural production can speciously relieve the ideology-critic of the need properly to interpret the mechanisms of mystification which are in play. This distance towards the concept of 'ideology', always present in Bourdieu's work, has recently been made explicit.[18] It is a distance which arises not from any desire to protect the literary field from disenchantment, but from a desire that the disenchantment shall actually work; from an understanding that abrupt idoloclasm is still enchanted by what it would take apart. Bourdieu is able to proceed otherwise primarily because he has himself undertaken a far-reaching reformulation of the anthropology of exchange. A passage such as the following offers a useful introduction to this reformulation:

Economism is a form of ethnocentrism. Treating pre-capitalist economies, in Marx's phrase, 'as the Fathers of the Church treated the religions which preceded Christianity', it applies to them categories, methods, (economic accountancy, for example) or concepts (such as the notions of interest, investment, or capital) which are the historical product of capitalism and which induce a radical transformation of their object, similar to the historical transformation from which they arose. Economism recognizes no other form of interest than that which capitalism has produced ...[19]

It is this failure of historical understanding, the particular failure of historical understanding characteristic of economism, which has dominated the abbreviated social science put to work in the service of literary historicism. It is an ethnocentrism which protects itself by rejecting as 'nostalgia' or as 'utopian fantasy' not merely an implicit or explicit *preference* for pre-capitalist social arrangements, but also the very idea of the existence of forms of work and exchange other than that which capitalism has produced.

Such thinking is protecting itself against the possibility of happiness. However it understands itself, the result is *Kapitalismusgläubigkeit*, a superstitious faith in capital. It is not at all Bourdieu's object, as such a passage makes clear, to contrast the providential harmony of self-interest in political economy's understanding of the market, for example with some more generous or disinterested culture of gift exchange, before or elsewhere. It is to show how the forms of interest at stake in pre- and non-capitalist societies, instead of operating according to our modern separation between the interested exchange, and the disinterested gift, work through a temporal delay present in a process which is at once gift and exchange. The gift comes back, but the fact that it does not come back *at once* is what allows what is in fact mutually necessitated or interested exchange to appear as freely chosen reciprocity. This is why, for Bourdieu, an interpretation such as Claude Lévi-Strauss's, which pays relatively little attention to the temporal dimension in gift-exchange, risks missing the extent to which such exchange conceals, as well as reveals, social necessity. What is thus opened up is a new way of interpreting extra-capitalist features of economic and social life – not only in pre- or non-capitalist societies, but within the never perfectible system which is capitalism itself.[20]

In this new space what begins to move and breathe again are the fundamental concepts of economic thought – not only of exchange and donation but, equally strikingly, of work and leisure. These concepts can now be seen to be, not technical counters with a fixed and unitary meaning, but fluid and mutually interdependent. One result of Bourdieu's enquiry, for example, is to question the dogmatic distinction between production and exchange which is so often used to truncate reflection upon exchange or to identify reflection upon exchange *as such* with 'liberal' political thought.[21] Work is itself a kind of gift or exchange with what is worked on; no disenchantment powerful enough completely to delete this aspect of work has yet been found. Exchange does not happen by itself. It always involves human labour.

No one would have thought of assessing the technical efficiency or economic usefulness of these indissolubly technical *and* ritual acts, the peasant's version, as it were, of art for art's sake, such as fencing the fields, pruning the trees, protecting the new shoots from the animals ... In short, the reality of production is no less repressed than the reality of circulation, and the peasant's 'pains' are to labour what the gift is to commerce ... The discovery of labour presupposes the constitution of the common ground of production, i.e. the disenchantment of a natural world henceforth reduced to its economic dimension alone ... measured by the yardstick of monetary profit, the most sacred activities find themselves constituted negatively, as *symbolic*, i.e., in a sense the word sometimes receives, as lacking concrete or material effect, in short, *gratuitous*, i.e. disinterested but also useless.[22]

This profound passage brings into a view a whole series of affinities and connections which economism destroys and conceals. Bourdieu points out that it is only within one particular historical kind of reason – the economistic reason which has become second nature to us – that it makes sense to wish exhaustively to divide production into the useful and the 'gratuitous', the technical and the ritual. What is the condition of this razor? 'The disenchantment of the natural world'. Our lived theory of value, which is not a matter of our opinions about economics, requires that value be created by us, by our labour or by scarcity with respect to us; that it not reside in the world, however much the poets in their elegies and songs may call upon the hills and groves to mourn. What we are finding, within one of the most tenaciously sceptical social-scientific accounts available to us, is the presence precisely of the link which is found nostalgic, or fantasized, or illusory in the poet: the link between the alienation of labour, the separation of gift from exchange, and the disenchantment of the earth.

It is important to see just how many of the comforts of unexamined scepticism this way of thinking must deprive us of. On such a view it is quite mistaken, and, indeed, an oddly Whig view, to think that, for example, the history of modern exchange is that symbolic exchange is gradually or in some way quantitatively being replaced by commodity exchange, so that there is 'more and more' commodification, or that symbolic exchange becomes 'more and more' a nostalgic fantasy. Once we have understood that the critical underpinning is the lived theory of a separation between gifts, which must be free, and exchanges, which are permitted to be interested, we notice that 'more and more' insistence on the self-interested character of exchanges is accompanied by 'more and more' insistence on the non-exchangeable: the 'more and more' it is insisted that judicial decisions may not be bought, for example. The mistake is to think it enough to regard the former insistence as shrewd realism, the latter as 'ideology'. The notion of a free gift is no more adequately understood as 'ideology' than is the word *ought* itself. At the same time it becomes more and more evident that this lived theory of separation is not perfectible. As Cornelius Castoriadis once pointed out, a factory in which literally every exchange was commodified would shut down in fifteen minutes.[23]

The fertility of Bourdieu's thought is produced by its holding with impressive tenacity to a thinking '*pace* both the unbelievers and iconoclasts and also the believers' – the believers and unbelievers, for example, in altruism, or in religion, or in poetry, or – in social science.[24] In practice this body of interpretation has much more often been put to use against the believers. This has sometimes been done so abruptly as to lose entirely the double force of Bourdieu's social thought.

But it is not only the result of abstract application. It also testifies to the fundamental structure which is in place beneath Bourdieu's double way, the way against the idolators and the iconoclasts. Economism is opposed because it is not economistic *enough*:

The only way to escape from the ethnocentric naiveties of economism, without falling into populist exaltation of the generous naivety of earlier forms of society, is to carry out in full what economism does only partially, and to extend economic calculation to *all* the goods, material and symbolic, without distinction, that present themselves as 'rare' and worthy of being sought after in a particular social formation – which may be 'fair words' or smiles, handshakes or shrugs, compliments or attention, challenges or insults, honour or honours, powers or pleasures, gossip or scientific information, distinction or distinctions, etc.[25]

This too is part of the exhilarating doubleness of Bourdieu's programme. When he was beginning work as an anthropologist, Bourdieu noticed something very simple which changed his work forever. He noticed that his colleagues, fine adepts and hermeneuts of the subtle exchanges of smiles, frowns and yawns in the seminar room, somehow lost all their eye for such nuance when in the field, and would come back instead with large systematizations of social structure. His theory of practice develops from the simple but revolutionary decision to apply to the apparently contingent minutiae of French life the systematic thought usually reserved for 'primitive societies'; and to observe the latter, conversely, in the manner of, as it were, an imaginary Flaubert of Kabylia.

Yet something also slips in this move. Bourdieu himself has noticed that the separation between 'interest' and 'disinterestedness' is a crucial, perhaps the crucial, historical achievement or misprision of modernity. In the programme to extend economism to all exchanges, that economistic separation tacitly becomes, not merely a working means of interpretation, but an anthropology in the philosophical sense: a theory of human nature. Interested exchanges are what are real. The means of disguise may vary, in the sense that the censorship of the direct expression of interest is stronger, and differently organized, in pre- and non-capitalist societies; beneath both situations lies a universal anthropology.

It is here that we must emphatically dissent from Bourdieu. At the last a particular historical separation, that between interest and disinterest, has after all been converted into the basis for a metahistorical anthropology. The consequences of this run right through Bourdieu's thought. They are especially evident in a passage such as this:

> The break necessary to establish a rigorous science of cultural works is something more and something other than a simple methodological reversal. It implies a true *conversion* of the ordinary way of thinking and living the intellectual enterprise. It is a matter of breaking the narcissistic relationship inscribed in the representation of intellectual work as a 'creation' and which excludes as the expression *par excellence* of 'reductionist sociology' the effort to subject the artist and the work of art to a way of thinking that is doubly objectionable since it is both genetic and generic.[26]

Once again Bourdieu's exemplary self-awareness is to the fore. The break implies a *conversion*, because, so Bourdieu is candid enough to imply, it is not a question of exchanging a mystified for a properly disinterested standpoint, but a question of changing one belief-system for another. When we move from aestheticism to social science, we renounce the cult of art, and are baptized into the church of social science. Yet, for Bourdieu, we may none the less speak here, not of a conflict between rival faiths, but of a 'rigorous science': the science of art.

THE GIFT OF NATURE

[The advance and return of capitals is] *what ought to be called the circulation of money*; that useful and productive circulation which enlivens all the work of society, which maintains movement and life in the body politic, and which is with good reason compared to the circulation of blood in the animal body.[27]

This is a passage from Turgot's 'Reflections on the Formation and Distribution of Wealth', written in 1766. When Wordsworth was proposing to his friend William Mathews that they should start a journal called *The Philanthropist* in 1794, he suggested that they should include biographical essays on 'eminent men, particularly those distinguished for their exertions in the cause of liberty'.[28] Turgot's name was at the head of Wordsworth's list; it seems possible that Wordsworth knew this work. Turgot's point here needs careful interpretation. The body politic needs circulation to keep it alive. Without circulation, it might die. Yet it is not just any circulation that keeps the body politic alive, but the advance and return of capitals: circulation, that is, which yields a surplus. For exchange to be a living exchange, one which animates and enlivens the body politic, 'more' capital must come back than was advanced. But how is it possible that the sums can come out like this? How can fair exchange yield a surplus? Turgot represents surplus value as originating in a 'pure gift' by nature to the proprietor of land. The first surplus, and the origin of surplus value, is the surplus above his needs which the proprietor's labour on his land yields, and which can be used to purchase the labour of those who are not proprietors. Surplus value is the 'pure gift' of nature.[29]

   I want briefly to link this account of the surplus value as a 'pure gift' from nature to Turgot's defence of usury. Turgot suggests that opponents of usury have been misled by the gospel principle, which he quotes from the vulgate text of Luke: *Mutuum date nihil inde sperantes*.[30] He goes on to argue that this text has been misread by scholastic critics of usury. Medieval scholasticism, following Ambrose and Jerome, reads this text and others like it to prohibit the free lunch, the usurer's unearned increment: 'one calls anything whatsoever usury and surplus if one has collected more than one has given'.[31] Turgot reads it instead to separate out disinterested giving from interested exchange. If you really are 'giving' – *date* – insists Turgot, expect nothing back, otherwise it is not really a gift; but if you are entering into a contract all that matters is that the contract should be voluntary on both sides. Fair exchange is guaranteed by the consent of the contracting parties. That fair exchange yields a surplus is not an ethical problem, but the secret of (social) life.

   Turgot's defence of usury establishes a distinction between gifts outright and giving in exchange. Exchange is opposed to donation; donation must not be a kind of exchange, nor is exchange conceivable as a kind of donation. This accompanies a crucial distinction between ethical discourse and economic discourse. The distinction is by no means peculiar to the Physiocrats. A developing insistence on the importance of separating ethical from economic discourse is what makes possible the idea of political economy. The importance of the process whereby the sphere of gifts could be depicted as not part of the possible subject matter of political economy, the process of privatizing the gift, can be seen in considering the response of Edmund Burke to demands that bread should be made available to feed the hungry in 1795.

Whenever it happens that a man can claim nothing according to the rules of commerce, and the principles of justice, he passes out of that department, and comes within the jurisdiction of mercy. In that province the magistrate has nothing at all to do: his interference is a violation of the property which it is his office to protect.[32]

Burke counters demands for *ex gratia* distributions of wheat, demands prompted by notions of moral economy, by representing the department of gifts as absolutely separated from that of exchange. All Christians do indeed have a direct duty of charity to the poor, but this is 'next in order after the payment of debts'.[33] Only when the books are legally balanced in the sphere of exchange may the surplus be ethically deployed in the sphere of gifts. To break 'the laws of commerce' by suspending them to give relief to distress is to break 'the laws of nature'.[34] As Adam Smith put it, 'It is not from the benevolence of the butcher, the brewer, or the baker, that we expect our dinner, but from their regard to their own interest.' This is not at all to say that the author of the *Theory of Moral Sentiments* thought that butchers, brewers and bakers need not be benevolent, but to insist upon a separation of powers between their actions as benevolent donors and as interested exchangers.[35]

It is easy to see how we might have here the basis for a study in 'spiritual economics'. The life of Wordsworth's imagination and the life of Turgot's body politic alike, it appears, need a surplus which is a 'gift of Nature'. They require a circulation which will yield 'more' than they began with. Without this 'more', this 'gift of Nature', they will be faced with standstill, breakdown and death. The continual references to Nature's gifts, to the poet's gifts, and to the hope of establishing a living relation between poet and readers, references which run through Wordsworth's poetry and poetics like a red thread, could easily look like a form of elaborate self-deception. Wordsworth thinks that the exchange between poet and reader might be one in which the naturally gifted poet can give more than the reader has bargained for; but suspicion naturally asks why this view should be any less conveniently naïve than Turgot's idea that the gift of nature is justly given to the owners of the means of production. Marx argued that surplus value arose not from unconstrained circulation but from forcible expropriation.[36] Does Wordsworth's idea of an overbalance mystify the physical labour off which it lives?

For Wordsworth reciprocity in the individual's experience of the world, and reciprocity in the individual's relations with others, are inextricably interconnected, which means that neither can be regarded as foundational, as coming 'first'. This is made clear even in the poem in which Wordsworth might most be thought to veer towards a kind of possessive individualism of the imagination, 'Home at Grasmere'. Wordsworth announces his intention to secure for himself and his family 'A portion of the blessedness which love / And knowledge will, we trust, hereafter give / To all the Vales of earth and all mankind.'[37] Such an announcement naturally raises suspicions. The poet will enjoy this blessedness now in the trust that others will enjoy it later, but if for some reason these others are unfortunately prevented from enjoying it later, at least this portion will have been put to good use by the poet himself. It may be seen that this is more than a reflex nod to sociality, though, if we look at a passage in which Wordsworth is trying to set out what this blessedness consists in:

> We shall not scatter through the plains and rocks
> Of this fair Vale and o'er its spacious heights
> Unprofitable kindliness, bestowed
> On Objects unaccustomed to the gifts
> Of feeling, that were cheerless and forlorn
> But few weeks past, and would be so again
> If we were not. We do not tend a lamp
> Whose lustre we alone participate,
> Which is dependent upon us alone,
> Mortal though bright, a dying, dying flame.
> Look where we will, some human heart has been
> Before us with its offering; not a tree
> Sprinkles these little pastures, but the same
> Hath furnished matter for a thought, perchance
> To some one is as a familiar Friend.[38]

It is possible for labour, including aesthetic labour, to be wasted. It might easily be that the adult Wordsworth in Grasmere might be 'wasting his kindliness on stocks and stones', no less than his younger self in 'Nutting'.[39] But Wordsworth insists that he is not wasting the gifts of feeling on objects which would be cheerless and forlorn were they not cheered by human meaning. One of the reasons for this, I have earlier tried to suggest, is because for Wordsworth there are *no* objects in themselves absolutely cheerless and forlorn – in the sense at least that they would utterly lack all significance – because the notion of sheer brute facticity is a chimera of dejected ontology, the ontology in which we despairingly think that we can only ever get back the life we have first given. But the reason given here is that these objects are not tended only by Wordsworth and his domestic circle. Two points are central here. First, if these objects were tended only by the Wordsworths this would be a shadow of reciprocity, as mortal as the human individual – 'a dying, dying flame'. The exchange between individual and world is structurally dependent upon an exchange between individuals. Second, Wordsworth's spiritual labour is saved from being wasted because others are also labouring – even though he may not know of their labour, before which objects they have placed their offerings, nor by whom those offerings have been placed.

At this point an increasingly urgent series of questions must make itself felt. What about need and suffering? We have heard much so far of a 'reciprocity' which depends on a continual overplus, but why should the account always be in credit? Wordsworth, however, does not think that a happy outcome must ensue, because no feeling is absolutely self-sufficing; feelings imply a dependence on objects. By themselves, Wordsworth's exchanges with the natural world could not yield an immortal spiritual possession, but are as mortal as the poet. That the farmer in 'The Last of the Flock' loves his children more and more the richer he becomes; that Robert in 'The Ruined Cottage' stops loving his children so much when he loses his job: these are not judgements on the accidental badness of these characters but acknowledgements that there is no human virtue or pleasure which we can never be deprived of by material distress. Wordsworth made sure that readers of *The Prelude* knew what Raisley Calvert's money had done for the growth of a poet's mind;[40] his sonnet acknowledging this debt affords one of the most impressive examples of Wordsworth's severe refusal of empty gesture in its failure to say almost anything about Calvert other than that he was sick and gave Wordsworth material help.[41] It is from this perspective that the following passage, also from 'Home at Grasmere', might be read:

> Nor deem
> These feelings – though subservient more than ours
> To every day's demand for daily bread,
> And borrowing more their spirit and their shape
> From self-respecting interests – deem them not
> Unworthy therefore and unhallowed. No,
> They lift the animal being, do themselves
> By nature's kind and ever present aid
> Refine the selfishness from which they spring,
> Redeem by love the individual sense
> Of anxiousness with which they are combined.
> Many are pure, the best of them are pure;
> The best, and these, remember, most abound,
> Are fit associates of the [ ] joy,
> Joy of the highest and the purest minds;
> They blend with it congenially; meanwhile,
> Calmly they breathe their own undying life,
> Lowly and unassuming as it is,
> Through this, their mountain sanctuary (long,
> Oh long may it remain inviolate!),
> Diffusing health and sober chearfulness,
> And giving to the moments as they pass
> Their little boons of animating thought,
> That sweeten labour, make it seem and feel
> To be no arbitrary weight imposed,
> But a glad function natural to Man.[42]

Few passages of verse so strikingly support the claim of one critic that 'ideology and truth in art are not like sheep and goats. Art cannot have the one without the other'.[43] It is not at once clear that the feelings of the workers by hand borrow '*more* their spirit and their shape / From self-respecting interests' than those of the workers of spirit. The words 'pure' and 'purity' are placed under stress; their repetition appears finally apologetic – '[m]any are pure, the best of them are pure' – without doing anything to clarify quite what they are pure from. Yet this passage also reflects subtly on the relation between labour towards self-respecting interests and that labour which is apparently given away for free, the 'little boons of animating thought, / That sweeten labour'. From one point of view it is clear that these boons could be an offer of spiritual gain in compensation for material hardship. The lines indicate the poet's awareness of this: these feelings spring from 'selfishness'. So how can they '[r]efine the selfishness from which they spring'? Once their real origin is understood as self-interested, the notion that these feelings are gifts, 'little boons of animated thought', can surely be nothing but an illusion, and one all too liable to be recruited into Paley's list of reasons for the poor to be cheerful?[44] We are reminded of what Bourdieu calls, in the very different context of Algeria in the 1950s, 'the peasant's version, as it were, of art for art's sake', pains which are at once technical and ritual, bestowed upon the earth, 'boons' whose material benefit cannot be determined, but which allow the peasant to bestow with largesse the one commodity of which he has plenty – time. For Bourdieu this indicates that just as apparent gratuities disguise interested exchanges, so these little boons of activity disguise the reality of sheer need.[45]

The notion, developed in the rise of political arithmetic, that gifts must be or constitutively are separated from exchange, involves an opposition between disinterestedness and interestedness. The two concepts appear to exclude any middle term: actions must either be interested or disinterested. Yet the concepts are inextricably twinned. As Jonathan Parry has suggested in an important reinterpretation of Marcel Mauss's work on exchange, the concept of an absolutely self-interested exchange emerges only together with the concept of the disinterested gift.[46] This means that, whilst there need be no difficulty in interpreting *particular* claims to disinterestedness as ideological covers for self-interestedness, there is a difficulty involved in regarding the concept of disinterestedness as *in principle* ideological. The concept of interestedness relies on the concept of disinterestedness for its very intelligibility. It may be, then, that the idea of *disguise* is inappropriate here, because the idea of absolute interestedness is no less 'ideological' than that of absolute disinterestedness. Wordsworth does not say either that these 'gifts of feeling' conceal the rural workers' self-interestedness, or that they replace it, but that they make a difference to it; that is, that they present us with a shape of feeling and action in which interestedness and disinterestedness can no longer be separated out from each other like goats from sheep. Similarly, it may be too quick to assume that the little boons of animated thought disguise the reality of labour when they sweeten it. The idea that labour is 'an *arbitrary* weight imposed' is no less and no more 'ideological', in its appeal to the chimera of sheer contingency, than the idea that it is 'a glad function natural to man'.

For Bourdieu it is clear what is reality and what is illusion. The real elements of his social ontology are forcible and interested exchanges. They are transformed into the illusion of elective and disinterested reciprocity by the mechanism of form for form's sake. No matter how socially necessary the illusion of elective reciprocity, therefore, it can never be more than an illusion, since interested exchanges are what is and must be real. But in practice Bourdieu cannot avoid presenting the work of the 'scientist' and in this case in particular that of the social scientist as a category escaping this mechanism of illusion. The professional social scientist presents us with an undeluded map of delusion. Bourdieu's work thus depends upon a form of the opposition between 'science' and 'ideology'.[47] The idea that the 'Realities of Life' ever have been and ever must be this dejected economy of tit-for-tat – '[s]o stinted in the measure of their grace' – turns out to depend on the very delusion which it would dispel.[48] This loop is repeated wherever the sociology of culture offers undeludedly to map the illusions of the aesthetic.

STRAY PLEASURES

Among Wordsworth's *Poems, in Two Volumes* can be found a remarkable account of a miller and two women dancing on a watermill floating on the Thames.

> ' – *Pleasure is spread through the earth*
> *In stray gifts to be claimed by whoever shall find.*'
>   By their floating Mill,
>   Which lies dead and still,
> Behold yon Prisoners three!
> The Miller with two Dames, on the breast of the Thames;
> The Platform is small, but there's room for them all;
> And they're dancing merrily.
>   From the shore come the notes
>   To their Mill where it floats,
> To their House and their Mill tether'd fast;
> To their small wooden Isle where their work to beguile
> They from morning to even take whatever is given;
> And many a blithe day they have past.
>   In sight of the Spires
>   All alive with the fires
> Of the Sun going down with his rest,
> In the broad open eye of the solitary sky,
> They dance, – there are three, as jocund as free,
> While they dance on the calm river's breast.
>   Man and Maidens wheel,
>   They themselves make the Reel,
> And their Music's a prey which they seize;
> It plays not for them,– what matter! 'tis theirs;
> And if they had care it has scattered their cares,

While they dance, crying, 'Long as ye please!'
>They dance not for me,
>Yet mine is their glee!
Thus pleasure is spread through the earth
In stray gifts to be claimed by whoever shall find;
Thus a rich loving-kindness, redundantly kind,
Moves all nature to gladness and mirth.
>The Showers of the Spring
>Rouze the Birds and they sing;
If the Wind do but stir for his proper delight,
Each Leaf, that and this, his neighbour will kiss,
Each Wave, one and t'other, speeds after his Brother;
They are happy, for that is their right![49]

This poem is one of the most original and unusual in the two great volumes which appeared in 1807. It at least complicates the idea that, for instance, what worries Wordsworth about St Bartholomew's fair is its 'carnivalesque logic'.[50] It confirms, rather, the sense that what is wrong with the fair is that it is not really carnivalesque at all. The poem begins (I can't think of a precedent for this) with an epigraph which is a quotation from itself. The self-quotation indicates the focus of its interest. What is described is the standing defeat of the fondest superstition of economic reason, that there is no such thing as a free lunch. The music which the three are dancing to is something they seize: played and paid for to some other purpose, they get it for free; they are dancing only for themselves, but Wordsworth gets the pleasure of it anyway, in a stanza which brings all these thefts and gifts to elation. It is important that these 'stray gifts' are spread about without any particular altruism, merely the excesses of the 'stray pleasures' which give rise to them. They can be claimed by whoever finds them, who will owe no recompense or even gratitude to the disseminators. The stanza goes beyond this. This is not merely the way with the occasional moment of pleasure. It is what pleasure is like. Pleasures which are really pleasures must be 'stray', the stanza implies. What is more, this is the logic, or the absence of logic, of nature itself: 'a rich loving-kindness, redundantly kind, / Moves all nature to gladness and mirth.' The final stanza develops this, again with the emphasis on the dissemination of pleasure through its excess: the wind is not imagined as engaging in a mutually beneficial exchange with the leaves, as it might be in some horrible physico-theological extension of the logic of providential economism to winds, leaves and birds, but as pursuing his own pleasure alone: 'his proper delight'. The gift can only really be sent if it is not thought of as a gift, rather as, in a surprisingly couched passage of the 'Preface' to the *Lyrical Ballads*, Wordsworth suggests that the poet can best fulfil any ethical or instructive potential open to poetry by obeying 'blindly and mechanically' his or her habits of mind.[51] The poem does not wholly escape the whimsicality which is its calculated risk, but in its articulation of its thematic centre, 'a rich loving-kindness, redundantly kind', it seizes something critical to Wordsworth's poetry. For the kindness to be real it must be 'redundant', more than was needed. Yet this 'more' is not adventitiously or calculatingly added, but comes from the thoughtless enjoyment of the pleasure itself. The poem thus opens a wish which animates the whole authorship: for an unconscious reciprocity of excess. (It is perhaps not accidental to this poem to mention that Wordsworth had seen many such mills when travelling in France in 1793.[52]) The redundance which expresses this wish appears in the verse itself at moments of imaginative power; that is, at moments when something significant is actually experienced.

One of the things which theories of surplus value in classical political economy have in common, despite their many differences, is that they increasingly rely upon a strict separation of the disinterested gift from interested exchange. Disinterested donations, should they be found to exist, are part of the subject matter of ethics; political economy undertakes to show how even if benefactions are bracketed out, social harmony may still be understood to emerge from interested exchange. Surplus value is the crucial expression of this harmony, because it embodies that overplus – whether understood as a gift of nature or a gift of labour – which comes simply through following the logic of interested but voluntary exchange. For Wordsworth, however, the idea of a total separation between disinterested gifts and interested exchanges is just the condition he wishes to diagnose – both in the sphere of social reciprocity and in that of our reciprocal relations with the material world. Crudely put, it is only half the problem for Wordsworth that 'everyone is becoming so selfish'; it is just as much the case that 'everyone is demanding selflessness', and the two developments are inextricably connected. The fact that 'we are selfish men' is the mirror image of our total unselfishness in theory.

Wordsworth's deep dissatisfaction with Godwin's empty 'ought', his 'bald and naked reasonings', is the necessary complement to his loathing of enlightened self-interest. Of course Wordsworth is well aware that this separation is nothing like a simple intellectual or moral mistake – to imagine that it were such would be to set up another system of bald and naked reasonings – but is closely connected with a transformation in the fabric of social life itself. It could not be averted just by using a different set of words, and accordingly Wordsworth often refers to selfishness and to unselfishness alike – but more often with an interest in understanding the connections between these two, than in protecting a theoretical disinterestedness from a real selfishness. Turgot's gift of nature is the surplus which comes to one class of us provided we keep gifts and exchange strictly separated, but Wordsworth's gift of nature and gift to nature is the 'more' which would prevent this separation between gifts and exchange – between 'ought' and 'is' – from becoming totalized. We give largely, we give more than enough, not so as to distinguish our disinterested gift from an interested exchange, not so as to return to purely symbolic exchange, but so as to allow the gift to animate exchange. That we do not only receive exactly what we have already given, give only what we need do in order to receive, is not an 'aesthetic ideology', but an illusion or an intimation of 'blessedness', 'the pleasure which there is in life itself', an illusion or an intimation which it is impossible even for the most determined and dogmatic dejection wholly to extirpate.

It is to the poetic thinking of this blessedness that the second part of this book must now turn.

PART II

Common day

Whoever desires the infinite does not know what he desires. But one can't turn this sentence around.

CHAPTER 4

Happiness

J. G. A. Pocock begins his study of Edward Gibbon's relation to the various currents of enlightenment to which he was exposed by quoting the self-description which gives Pocock his own title: 'I have described the triumph of barbarism and religion', remarks Gibbon, towards the close of his philosophic history. Pocock's study does much to show that barbarism and the Christian religion were for Gibbon not so nearly synonymous as has sometimes been thought; and, in particular, that Gibbon's peculiar variety of philosophical history owes much to varieties of enlightenment unlike those which we are most used to hearing about: an 'Arminian' enlightenment with English, Dutch and Swiss origins, as well as a tradition of deep historical erudition which D'Alembert praised faintly in his preliminary discourse to the *Encyclopédie*. If there was one aspect of early Christianity of which it can be said with some confidence, however, that Gibbon regarded it as barbarous, the early asceticism of the desert fathers is a strong candidate.

The prince or magistrate, the soldier or merchant, reconciled their fervent zeal, and implicit faith, with the exercise of their profession, the pursuit of their interest, and the indulgence of their passions: but the Ascetics who obeyed and abused the rigid precepts of the gospel, were inspired by the savage enthusiasm, which represents man as a criminal, and god as a tyrant. They seriously renounced the business, and the pleasures, of the age; chastised their body, mortified their affections, and embraced a life of misery, as the price of eternal happiness.[1]

Although Gibbon sometimes takes the line that early Christian ascetics were more self-interested than they pretended to be – genuinely pious impulses towards retreat, he remarks, 'were strengthened by secret remorse, or accidental misfortune; and they might derive some aid from the temporal considerations of vanity or interest' – he more often insists on their alarming fanaticism, remembering sympathetically that '[t]he philosophic eye of Pliny had surveyed with astonishment, a solitary people, who dwelt among the palm-trees near the Dead Sea; who subsisted without money, who were propagated without women; and who derived from the disgust and repentance of mankind, a perpetual supply of voluntary associates.'² Christian princes, magistrates, soldiers, and merchants reconcile faith and the world; monks, though, are 'recluse from profession'. For Gibbon it was the particular characteristic of the desert fathers that they were 'obscure and abject plebeians' and hence ignorant. 'Recluse fanatics have few ideas or sentiments to communicate.'³ Gibbon's mild distaste for the desert fathers arises, less from a suspicion that their own motives are more worldly than they pretend, than from a conviction that their motives are indeed, unfortunately, every bit as insanely ascetic as they appear.

Gibbon's double view of religious asceticism is typical of a good deal of comment on the subject in his century. The early monks are generally viewed either as hypocrites or as fanatics. At the end of the century, of course, discussion of asceticism and monasticism was strongly coloured by the Revolutionary assault on French monasteries. Supporters of this assault were able to recruit in their aid a long tradition of Protestant and other enlightenment anti-ascetic commentary. Its opponents found themselves drawn to defend religious retirement even where this had not previously been a concern of theirs. Edmund Burke's *Reflections* offers one of the most important instances:

The monks are lazy. Be it so. Suppose them no otherwise employed than by singing in the choir. They are as usefully employed as those who neither sing nor say. As usefully even as those who sing upon the stage. They are as usefully employed as if they worked from dawn to dark in the innumerable servile, degrading, unseemly, unmanly, and often most unwholesome and pestilentious occupations, to which by the social oeconomy so many wretches are inevitably doomed. If it were not generally pernicious to disturb the natural course of things, and to impede, in any great degree, the great wheel of circulation which is turned by the strangely directed labour of these unhappy people, I should be infinitely more inclined forcibly to rescue them from their miserable industry, than violently to disturb the tranquil repose of monastic quietude.⁴

Passages like these have usually given a series of cues for interpreters of the politics of religion in the decades following the French Revolution. Sympathy for religious asceticism and retirement, for monks and for monasteries, can easily be taken as evidence either of outright Romanism or of a conservative strain of Romanticism. The question is particularly important when we come to consider a much-discussed case like that of William Wordsworth, in whose work ruined abbeys so often appear at critical moments. Wordsworth's developing interest in monasticism and its monuments, his increasing reluctance to think their destruction representative simply of Protestant or rational progress, appears to offer useful evidence for a straightforward narrative of apostasy from the revolutionary cause.

Discussion of this issue has naturally enough focussed on Wordsworth's writing about the majesty of the Grande Chartreuse. In this chapter, however, I want to focus less on Wordsworth's responses to contemporary Romanist monasticism than on a less often discussed fragment of Wordsworth's planned and unfinished philosophical poem 'The Recluse'. This fragment, 'The Tuft of Primroses', written in 1808, has in my view crucial importance for the way we think about Wordsworth's life work. In it, Wordsworth is undertaking something which is both very ambitious and, I believe, central to the way in which he came to think of the 'Recluse' project. He offers a sustained implicit analogy between the significance of poetic retirement, in particular his own poetic retirement to Grasmere, and the devotional retirement of early monasticism. After an account of his retirement at Grasmere in which features of the landscape are recurrently imagined through metaphors drawn from ecclesiastical architecture, Wordsworth develops in detail a verse exchange of letters between the two most celebrated Cappadocian fathers, St Basil and St Gregory Nazianzen, on the value and pleasures of religious retirement.

I want to argue in this chapter that Wordsworth knew exactly what he was doing when he compared his retreat in Grasmere to St Basil's in Pontus. Poets, like monks, are felt to fall within that class of persons who 'ought to get a proper job'. Poets and monks alike are to be compelled to useful labour. For Wordsworth, the assumption that this kind of *ressentiment* is politically progressive is deeply misleading. His work of the early 1800s does not retreat from egalitarianism and universalism, but only from the idea that egalitarianism and universalism are best served by aprioristic moral philosophy and by a political arithmetic of universalized economic reason. It is this universalization of economic reason which the poem contests, both by contesting the adequacy of received understandings of the origins of monasticism, and by attempting to imagine a model of the individual not reducible to *homo economicus*.

This chapter takes the following form. First I explore some of the reasons for Wordsworth's choice of the Cappadocian fathers, and develop a contrast between his treatment of them and the sceptical approach followed by much eighteenth- and early nineteenth-century ecclesiastical history and other commentary. I shall argue, in particular, that Wordsworth's poem implies a subtle critique of Protestant and enlightenment history-writing's hostility to religious and ascetic retirement. Wordsworth's poetic reimagining of patristic asceticism suggests that the categories of enlightened economic reason – and in particular its opposition between 'useful labour' and 'idleness', an opposition common to iconoclasts and political arithmeticians alike – are inadequate to its interpretation. The poem is central to the way in which we imagine the politics of the unfinished project of 'The Recluse', because in it Wordsworth tries to imagine an individualism not founded on an idea of *homo economicus*, and to imagine a community of such individuals – a community which would really be such, rather than a 'vacant commerce' of pre-socialized ciphers.

'SACRED SLOTH'

When Joshua Lucock Wilkinson visited the Chartreuse in the early 1790s, he was not impressed:

I was there a witness to the most absurd ceremonies, the most abject devotion and debasement, to genuflections, holy wild and mysterious signs of the cross, submissive bows of the head, ringing of a bell, and many applications of [the coadjutor's] forehead to the pavement – advancing to, and suddenly retreating from, the altar. I concluded, that nothing of this world belonged to these pious fathers ... But in the kitchen, I observed a very different appearance of the good things of this world; and from the numerous cooks and attendants on the thirty-seven monks, who were then in the house, I presumed, that they enjoyed every delicate variety, which art could give to their numerous dishes of fish, vegetables, and luxurious deserts.[5]

Wilkinson's experiences led him to look unfavourably on all monasticism, as a passage later in the same volume indicates:

The hermitages of Lucerne, the Rhine, the Moeuse, or the Mozelle, are filled by men, who are recluse from profession, and who support an idle life upon the benefactions and labour of the poor believer; but upon the mountains and lakes, or in the narrow vallies of the Alps, where innocence still holds its slippery reign, and as much above the failings of humanity as above the common level of mankind, the friend of solitude and nature might find the most delicious retreats. At the chapel of Wilhelm Tell, he might hear infant children sing, in full chorus, songs in praise of their warlike ancestors.[6]

Wilkinson wishes to distinguish between monasticism and the solitary's retreat. Monks are 'recluse from profession', and must live off the labours of others, whereas the friend of solitude and nature is implied to possess a capital which is the fruit of his own labours. The pretended unworldliness of monks is a ruse to deprive poor believers of their cash; the delights enjoyed by the friend of solitude and nature are more legitimately his own.

Wilkinson's view was hardly novel. Bayle's *Dictionary* had already expressed scepticism about monastic renunciation towards the end of the seventeenth century. Although abbeys were not at first very rich, 'in a little time they discovered a safe, secure, and inexhaustible fund, by which they gained immense riches, I mean the foolish and superfluous credulity of the laity'.[7] Nor, despite their belated accession to such riches, were even the first monks genuine renouncers. Where monastic asceticism was not motivated by covert greed, it could only be the product of fear: '[t]he monastic life began in Egypt about the year 300, where a great many Christians being persecuted for religion, were obliged to fly their native country'.[8] For Bayle the desert fathers were in essence exiles, whose retreat resulted less from genuine zeal than from political circumstance. Even chroniclers more devout than Bayle often shared this pragmatic view of the origins of ascetic retreat. In his *Christian Antiquities*, an often reprinted account of the institutions of the early church, Joseph Bingham regarded persecution as the most important initial motive for the establishment of monasticism:

The Rise of it was thus: In the *Decian* Persecution, which was about the middle of the third Century, many Persons in *Egypt*, to avoid the Fury of the Storm, fled to the neighbouring Deserts and Mountains, where they not only found a safe Retreat, but also more Time and Liberty to exercise themselves in Acts of Piety and Divine Contemplations; which sort of Life, though at first forced upon them by Necessity, became so agreeable to some of them, that when the Persecution was over they would not return to their Ancient Habitations again, but chose rather to continue in those Cottages or Cells, which they had made themselves in the Wilderness.[9]

Although the motives for remaining in the wilderness surpass mere self-preservation, the initial impulse to exile is represented as pragmatic.

Such a view of the origins of ascetic monasticism remained influential throughout the eighteenth century. When in his 1808 sketch towards 'The Recluse', 'The Tuft of Primroses', William Wordsworth asked what had prompted the first Christian renouncers, he came up with a rather different series of answers:

> What impulse drove the Hermit to his Cell
> And what detain'd him there his whole life long
> Fast anchor'd in the desert? Not alone,
> Dread of the persecuting sword, remorse,
> Love with despair, or grief in agony; . . .
> Not always from intolerable pangs
> He fled; but in the height of pleasure sigh'd
> For independent happiness, craving peace,
> The central feeling of all happiness,
> Not as a refuge from distress or pain,
> A breathing time, vacation, or a truce,
> But for its absolute self, a life of peace,
> Stability without regret or fear,
> That hath been, is, and shall be ever more.[10]

This answer reads almost as a direct rebuttal not only of Bayle's view, but of the more complex account given by Gibbon. Several items in the catalogue of worldly motives which Wordsworth regards as an insufficient explanation of patristic asceticism might have been drawn from Bayle and Gibbon (who cites Bingham as a source): '[d]read of the persecuting sword' from Bayle, and 'remorse' from Gibbon, who suggests that although the initial motives of the ascetics were unworldly, 'they were strengthened by secret remorse, or accidental misfortune; and they might derive some aid from the temporal considerations of vanity or interest'.[11] As indicated, however, Gibbon more often insists on the unworldly fanaticism of the early ascetics. He is not primarily worried that the desert fathers might be concealing more worldly or more self-interested motives beneath their asceticism; on the contrary, what worries him most is the thought that they might really mean it. His sentiments find an echo in those of some eighteenth-century travellers to Egypt, one of whom wondered at the monks' lack of business sense:

The books and manuscripts in their libraries are eaten by the dust, and yet the good friars, rather than sell them for a very high price, chuse to let them be spoiled, and make no kind of use of them. The patriarch who lives at *Cairo* represented to them, that they could rebuild their churches and cells with the money which these books would fetch, but they answered him, they would rather be buried in the ruins, than agree to that.[12]

Such views were often shared even by more devout writers. Words-worth's friend Francis Wrangham, in his 1798 sermon *Rome is Fallen!*, regarded the spirit of early Christian asceticism as so alien to that of the gospel that it could only be understood as an essentially Jewish survival:

we are at a loss to find the origin of those enormous errors – which removed millions from their allotted stations in society; and begot the superstitions that darkened the cloister, and the fanaticism that added savageness to the desert. The greater of these extravagancies seem indeed to have been of foreign growth: The Jewish Essenes may in some sense be pronounced the founders of the Christian Hermitage, and the authors of that wild scheme of austerity – which has excited the admiration of ignorant, and the compassion of enlightened ages. The seat of this phrensy, however, was not wide. A DISEASE OF CLIMATE (as it may be called) scarcely known in the Western world, it was confined principally to EGYPT and to SYRIA; There, plunged in the depths of unexplored solitudes, the saints of the Pillar and the Cavern long ago had their day – a day, never to return. But the less inhuman seclusion of the Monastery prevailed for many centuries throughout the extent of CHRISTENDOM: ... it is not perhaps at present too bold to affirm, that henceforward the *European* community will assert with effect its claim upon the services of every individual member.[13]

Asceticism is of foreign, which here means oriental, growth. Essene-derived asceticism matches 'Superstition's ghastly brood', later imagined by Wrangham on the banks of the Ganges.[14] In this view he is joined by, for example, the 'dissertation' prefixed to Thomas Dudley Fosbrooke's *The Economy of Monastic Life*, a recreation of medieval monastic life written in Spenserian stanzas: Fosbrooke, then a curate in Gloucester-shire, refers to 'monachism' as 'a system, whose archetype existed in the Jewish sect of Essenes', and finds its primary motivation in Diocletian's persecutions.[15] Wrangham distinguishes between Oriental asceticism and Western monasticism, which is 'less inhuman'. Yet the latter still shares the fundamental culpability of the former – the wish to take a free ride, life without self-preservation. The end of monasticism, happily presaged by the capture of Rome and the humiliation of the pontiff (Wrangham exults 'to behold Him, who once trod upon the neck of Monarchs, crouching himself beneath the insolent foot of a ferocious and implacable Republic'[16]) promises the end of such parasitism. None shall live idle when the 'community will assert with effect its claim upon the services of every individual member'. In this Wrangham's Protestant attack on monasticism joins the more systematic attacks of the French radicals. For Volney, self-preservation was 'the law of Nature', a law which, once overturned by asceticism, 'a sacred sloth established itself in the world'.[17]

More sympathetic views of early asceticism could occasionally be found. Joseph Milner's *History of the Church of Christ* insisted on the purity of the motives of the first recluses: 'the flower of the flock of Christ, in these days, is to be looked for amongst them'.[18] Milner also argued that contemporary derision of monasticism was founded in an excessive veneration for the value of labour alone:

How many, whose reading has scarce reached further than a monthly review or a magazine, are apt to felicitate themselves on their exemption from superstition, and to deride all monks as perfect fools? If we conceive a man in Basil's days, possessed of the same contracted spirit, and capable of foreseeing the exclusively mercantile task of the present race of men; would he not be disposed to censure their covetousness; and would not the vice appear as ridiculous to such an one, as superstition does to the moderns?[19]

Yet even for Milner, the undoubted qualities of a man such as St Basil could not be understood as essentially connected with his monasticism, but, rather, as surviving despite it: 'It is much to be lamented that a man so strangely pious, so profoundly learned, and of so elegant and accomplished a genius, should have suffered so much, both in mind and body, from the monastic spirit.'[20]

Every aspect of Wordsworth's answer to the question of the motives for asceticism differs from these varieties of enlightened contempt. Bayle's theory of covert worldliness fails to explain why those who lived 'in the height of pleasure' should become renouncers. Gibbon's theory of superstitious delusion presents renunciation as an instrumental trade-off, pain now for celestial jam tomorrow; he can only share Pliny's astonishment. Both answers, as I shall argue shortly, speak the language of economism, in which disinterestedness and interestedness operate a law of the excluded middle. For Wordsworth, by contrast, the desert fathers are neither taking a brief holiday from the world, nor buying salvation with a life of misery, but making this life in the image of those attributes which have been regarded as reserved to the next. The life of peace which they seek here and now '[f]or its absolute self' is also a transcendent peace, '[t]hat hath been, is, and shall be ever more'. Immanence and transcendence, pleasure and altruism, are not traded off against each other but, utopianly, reconciled.

But why should Wordsworth have been asking this question? Joseph F. Kishel has made the significant discovery that the life of St Basil in William Cave's collection of lives of the church fathers, *Apostolici*, was an

important source for 'The Tuft of Primroses'.[21] He points out the reso-
nance of the story of the friendship between SS. Basil and Gregory
Nazianzen for the relationship between Wordsworth himself and
Coleridge. As I hope to show, there are also reasons for thinking both that
Wordsworth's research went beyond Cave, and that his interest in the
earliest Christian recluses was central to the very idea of his projected
philosophical poem. Throughout 'The Tuft of Primroses' one can see
Wordsworth considering through an ambitious analogy with early
Christian retirement those questions which perplex him when he thinks
of the costs, pleasures and virtues of his own, poetic, retirement.

THE CAPPADOCIAN MOMENT

When Wordsworth's excursus on the Cappadocian fathers arrives, it is
perhaps not what readers of 'The Tuft of Primroses' have most immediately been expecting. The long passage concerns the relationship
between St Basil, the author of the monastic rule of the Eastern church,
and his friend Gregory Nazianzen. Wordsworth offers a verse appeal from
Basil to Nazianzen to come to join him in his ascetic retreat at Pontus. As
Kishel notes, the relationship between Basil and Nazianzen has suggestive
parallels with that between Wordsworth and Coleridge, with which
Wordsworth was certainly preoccupied at this date. But the more
important purpose of this excursus, I want to suggest, is that it offers an
extended, if fragmentary, consideration of the prehistory of poetical
retreat. Far from regarding the pleasures of his retirement as unprecedented, Wordsworth understands that they are entangled, together with
the conceptions of the individual which sponsor them, in a lengthy
genealogy. This genealogy is at least in part religious. The poem develops
an extended implicit parallel between the poetic life and certain aspects of
the history of monasticism.

   Wordsworth's choice of St Basil and St Gregory Nazianzen as the
central figures of this meditation has so far been given little consideration.
Kishel's discovery of a proximate source can have the effect of making
Wordsworth's selection look contingent, as though the primary motive
for the choice were convenience or the coincidental parallel with his own
closest friendship. Certainly that parallel is important, and it is given the
more weight, perhaps, by the fact that Gibbon, in a striking footnote,
goes out of his way to emphasize the extraordinary depth of Nazianzen's
feeling.

Gregory's poem on his own life contains some beautiful lines (tom. ii. p. 8.).
which burst from the heart, and speak the pangs of injured and lost friendship:

... ['our shared commitment to our studies, / our life together sharing hearth
and home:/ one mind, not two, in both of us ... ./ all this has been scattered,
dashed to the ground, / and the winds carry off our former hopes.']

In the Midsummer Night's Dream, Helena addresses the same pathetic complaint to her friend Hermia:
    Is all the counsel that we two have shared,
    The sister's vows, &c.

Shakespeare had never read the poems of Gregory Nazianzen: he was ignorant of
the Greek language; but his mother-tongue, the language of nature, is the same
in Cappadocia and in Britain.

Gibbon's account emphasizes the breach between Basil and Nazianzen.
When Basil was elevated to the Archbishopric of Caesarea, he offered his
friend only an unalluring minor bishopric in 'the wretched village of
Sasima'.[23]

Yet there may have been less simply personal reasons for Wordsworth's
interest in Basil and Nazianzen. Although Gibbon is doubtless right to say
that Shakespeare had never read Nazianzen's poems, a copy of the works of
Nazianzen was in Wordsworth's Rydal Mount library at his death.[24] He is
also known to have owned or read a number of works in which the councils
of the early Church were discussed at length, amongst them Meredith
Hanmer's expanded Elizabethan Eusebius.[25] Wordsworth always took seriously the notion that writing 'The Recluse' would demand broad research as
well as deep self-scrutiny.[26] And Coleridge, whose notes for 'The Recluse'
Wordsworth kept hoping to receive, later compared the work of Nazianzen
favourably with that of the ante-Nicene fathers.[27] I want to explore, then, the
possibility that Wordsworth's choice may have been connected with the
particular significance of the lives and works of the Cappadocian fathers.
Such an idea is certainly suggested by Wordsworth's own description of Basil
as 'An intellectual Champion of the faith, / Accomplish'd above all who then
appeared, / Or, haply, since victoriously have stood / In opposition to the
desperate course / Of Pagan rites or impious heresies' (453–7). Basil is here
emphasized to be both the scourge of idolatry, 'Pagan rites', and of Arianism,
the most notable of the 'impious heresies' with which he struggled. Basil and
Nazianzen matter particularly to Wordsworth not only because of Basil's
unique impact upon the idea of monasticism, but also because of the role of
both in the formation of the Christian doctrine of the Trinity, an aspect of

their work which Meredith Hanmer also emphasizes.[28] That doctrine should matter to us, not out of any misplaced concern for Wordsworth's orthodoxy, but as the central expression of two critical mediations: that between immanence and transcendence, but also, as Louis Dumont has persuasively argued, that between the world and the otherworldly or 'out-worldly', a mediation which was one of the most urgent problems confronting the early Church.[29] These ideas are important to Wordsworth, I want to suggest, not for any merely historiographical reason, but because he wishes speculatively to recruit from them a model of the poetic individual, a model which might escape the misrecognition of the life of the individual under the mutually exclusive options of economic reason.

SS. Basil and Gregory Nazianzen are remarkable for a number of reasons. Their role in the formulation of Church doctrine was pivotal. The decisive features of Trinitarian orthodoxy emerged only in the course of the struggle against Arianism, the denial of the divinity of Christ. In this campaign Basil and Nazianzen played a central part. It was not accidental that Basil and Nazianzen were also prominent in redefining the meaning of Christian asceticism. For Joseph Milner, 'these two friends formed the rules of monastic discipline, which were the basis of those superstitious institutions which afterwards overran the church'.[30] Two features of this redefinition are especially important here. Firstly, although the monastic regimen imagined by Basil is hardly easy, it is sharply distinguished from the ostentatious mortifications practised by several of the desert fathers. In the letter from Basil to Nazianzen which Wordsworth paraphrases in 'The Tuft of Primroses' we have an early example of contemplative retreat not as self-inflicted agony, but as what Augustine was later to call *Christianae vitae otium* – loosely paraphrased, Christian indolence.[31] Secondly, Nazianzen offers a striking account of the union of the active and the contemplative life. His model for this is Athanasius, the scourge of Arianism – a fact which indicates the connection between the Cappadocians' redefinition of Christian contemplation and their Trinitarianism.[32] Monks had been divided into solitaries inhabiting an isolated cell at some distance from other human beings, and coenobites living communally. Nazianzen represents Athanasius as having unified the varieties of monasticism:

he thus reconciled hermitism and coenobitism by showing that there is both a philosophical ministry and a mystical philosophy ... He harmonized in this way the two kinds of life and associated them under the form of activities compatible with retirement, and retirement compatible with an active life, in such a way as to convince all that what is essential in the monastic profession consists in the constant fidelity to a way of life rather than in the material fact of being retired from the world, following the principle which made of David the great at once the most active and the most solitary of men.[33]

The resonances of such lines for Wordsworth are many. The problem of the reconciliation of the active and the contemplative life pervades everything ever written towards 'The Recluse'. Of course it is given particular point by revolutionary upheaval. Much enlightenment anti-clericalism was united in regarding religious asceticism as a simple *truc des prêtres*. For Condorcet and for Volney, religion was the Ur-form of social non-transparency, closely bound up as they thought it with the division between intellectual and manual labour.[34] Ascetic retirement constituted a more cunning variant upon clerical freeloading.[35] Nor was this view confined to the French materialists. Adam Smith understood religious asceticism as a political gambit:

> In every civilized society, in every society where the distinction of ranks has once been completely established, there have always been two different schemes or systems of morality current at the same time; of which, the one may be called strict or austere, the other, the liberal, or, if you will, the loose system. The former is generally admired and revered by the common people, the latter is commonly more esteemed and adopted by what are called people of fash- ion ... Almost all religious sects have begun among the common people, from whom they have generally drawn their earliest, as well as their most numerous proselytes ... Many of them, perhaps the greater part of them, have even endeavoured to gain credit, by refining upon this austere system, and by carrying it to some degree of folly and extravagance ... [36]

Devout austerity accumulates symbolic capital which will help its adherents to positions of power. Hence the potential political significance of Wordsworth's *parallel* between ascetic and aesthetic retirement, between Pontus and Grasmere. Must the ascetic's, must the poet's retirement be understood as either parasitism, on the one hand, or ideology, on the other? Or might this *otium* – Volney's 'sacred sloth' – turn out to be strangely indispensable to the possibility of any *action* not simply identical with production?

INDIVIDUALS

In 'The Tuft of Primroses' Wordsworth attempts to rethink the idea of the individual. The difficulty he faces may be put like this. As we saw in the previous chapter, for economic reason, as well as for the various derivatives of it which have governed some of our most influential genealogies of the individual (often equated with the 'possessive' individual, or with the 'Cartesian subject', or both), the fundamental units of social ontology are interested individuals. The complement to this real interestedness is an 'ideology' of disinterestedness. Such a classification is not simply a mistake of economic reason but is bound up with the real separation in modern economic life between exchange, which is acknowledged as necessarily interested, and donation, which it is thought ought to be undertaken without any view to a return. From such a perspective ascetic and aesthetic experience are alike forms of mystification or self-mystification. In both, a real interestedness is masked by an illusion – not necessarily a pretence – of varying forms of disinterestedness, whether renunciatory or aesthetic. Within such rationality, interestedness and disinterestedness operate an excluded middle, whereby to contest the absolute reality of interestedness is to be thought to endorse an ideology of *dis*interestedness. In the realm of the individual the choice apparently faced is that between the outworldly renouncer, the ascetic, or the possessive individual.

It is just this bad choice and its false absoluteness that 'The Tuft of Primroses' begins to contest. The choice of the Cappadocians rather than the Palestinian or Egyptian anchorets as the central figures is itself significant. Wordsworth himself draws attention to the contrast between the two kinds of recluse when he has Basil remark that 'a solitude this deep / Thebais or the Syrian Wilderness / Contains not in its dry and barren round' (398–400). Thebais and Syria point up the contrast between two varieties of retirement. Pontus is more solitary, but also more pleasurable than Egypt and Palestine. The latter contain a life not merely of aridity and infertility but also of mechanical repetitiveness, a 'round'. Pontus, by contrast, is a place of superabundant excess where one may live upon what nature freely gives: 'the fruits that hang / In the primaeval woods ... / Ungrudgingly supply that never fails, / Bestowed as freely as their water' (423–8). The language here implicitly contrasts the freely bestowed excess of the Pontic solitude with exchange in the service of self-preservation: a supply dispensed 'ungrudgingly', not with the 'stinted grace' of calculation. Pontus is an 'enduring paradise'. Central to Basil's pleasure is the entirely non-instrumental way in which it has been discovered. He set out in search of a 'strict life of virtuous privacy', yet when he arrived 'found the same beyond all promise rich' (326–38).

Yet this is not the utopia of sheer indolence – paradise as a never-expiring meal ticket – but rather a frame of life in which the opposition between consumption and production has not yet been absolutized as economic reason tends to absolutize it. 'Labour itself / Is pastime here.' St Jerome on Bethlehem, as paraphrased by Bingham, comes to mind: 'there was nothing to be heard but psalms: one could not go into the field, but he should hear the ploughman singing in his hallelujahs, the sweating mower solacing himself with hymns, and the vine-dresser tuning David's Psalms. Thus the ancient monks joined their bodily and spiritual exercise together, and made their common labour become acts of devotion to God.'[37] Another of the poem's formulations of the difference between Cappadocian and Egyptian reclusiveness underlines this point. Basil is 'neither first nor singular' in his retirement, but his 'common life' with Nazianzen was 'More beautiful than any of like frame / That hitherto had been conceived' (464–6). In treating Basil and Nazianzen, Wordsworth does not claim to fix the chronological origins of monastic retirement, but rather a critical stage in its development. Basil allows the ascetic to become beautiful. The beauty of this life has an exemplary value. Its happiness refuses the bad choice between the pleasure of sheer consumption and the ascesis of pure renunciation. Hence the importance of contesting modern interpretations of the motives to exile. The hermit did not always flee from 'intolerable pangs', but 'in the height of pleasure sigh'd / For independent happiness ... ' (285–7). The hermit leaves neither to renounce all pleasure, nor simply to obtain a greater quantity of it, but rather to seek a different kind of pleasure, a 'happiness' which escapes that antithesis. Basil is the poet of this beautiful life '[t]o which by written institutes and rules / He gave a solid being': this is no mere isolated incident but rather the invention of a life which 'did not thence / Depart with him, nor ceas'd when he, and they / Whom he had gathered to his peaceful vale / In that retirement, were withdrawn from earth' but rather 'hung through many an age, / In bright remembrance, like a shining cloud, / O'er the vast regions of the western Church' (467–74).

In some important ways this pleasure recalls 'the pleasure which there is in life itself' for Michael: a pleasure which appears not to be some particular pleasure, but rather to attach to the very element in which experience occurs, a pleasure without which life becomes unthinkable and unliveable. In Michael's case this pleasure is indissoluble from his attachment to the land which he owns. As recluses, we might expect Basil and Nazianzen to represent individualism without ownership, yet Wordsworth's account does not quite represent them thus. Of the early

Christian hermit in general it is said that 'Therefore on few external things his heart / Was set, and those his own, or if not his, / Subsisting under Nature's stedfast law' (294–6). The point which Wordsworth emphasizes here is not simply that the hermit had his heart set on few external things, but that those things were either his own or part of his environment. The torpid heart must ever rely upon the next extra item for continual resuscitation; the heart of the recluse, by contrast, is not set on the commodity which he does not have. Such an interpretation of early Christian asceticism qualifies both the self-understanding of many of the anchorets themselves and the view of a figure like Gibbon. For both, the essence of such hermitism was in its other-worldliness, its detachment from the world: 'The candidate who aspired to the virtue of evangelical poverty, abjured, at his first entrance into a regular community, the idea, and even the name of all separate, or exclusive, possession.'[38] The important point was not that ascetics would simply refrain from acquisitive behaviour, but that they would renounce all attachment to the world, including the world of lakes and mountains. Once again the significance of Wordsworth's choice of Basil rather than, for example, St Antony, is foregrounded. Basil's adaptation of the classical *locus amoenus* to Christian retirement marks a difference of emphasis, a difference which is hardly accidental to his central role in the establishment of the orthodox doctrine of the Trinity, and thus in the establishment of a particular kind of mediation between the outworldly and inworldly aspects of Christianity.

Slowly we are approaching an appreciation of the reasons for Wordsworth's excursus on early monasticism. His reconstruction recovers particular senses of terms such as 'happiness', 'pleasure' and 'beauty', senses of those terms which have become impossible to articulate within the framework of economic reason, and within its pair of mutually opposed derivatives, philosophical aesthetics and the sociology of culture, but which are essential to the way in which Wordsworth thinks of poetry and the poetic life. The point can be made by a contrast. For Kant, 'the understanding can intuit nothing, the senses can think nothing'.[39] Pleasures must accordingly be seen from one of these two standpoints, which operate an excluded middle. Pleasures are either empirical gratification or they are disinterested delight. This is neither merely Kant's opinion, nor merely a mistake. It is the most consistent statement of modern epistemology. Yet the excluded middle between these two terms is the place where we must think Wordsworth's notion of happiness. Wordsworth must think differently of happiness because for him human pleasure, unlike the pleasure of empiricism, rationalism, or transcendentalism, is itself *cognitive*. It is not simply an instrument for, a consequence of or a stimulus for, cognition happening somewhere else. So pleasures may be true or false. The pleasure which we feel in nature is not an extra element *accompanying* true or false propositions or perceptions.

The idea of happiness which Wordsworth recovers through his imaginative reconstruction of early Trinitarian thought is not to be confused with an attempt to *bridge* the gulf in modern valuation which Kant lays bare. Kant, indeed, already understood his own *Critique of Judgement* as an attempt to do this. When we attempt to bridge this gulf we arrive at solutions such as Schiller's 'aesthetic state', a harmony of duty and inclination. In this respect the choice of early Trinitarianism, rather than Schiller's classical Athens, is telling. Wordsworth's notions of pleasure and happiness cannot be understood if they are thought under the rubric of 'the aesthetic' as it is usually understood – that is, the aesthetic as an impossible mediation between the exclusive options of economic reason – regardless of whether aesthetic value, in such a rubric, is treated as an ideology or as genuinely disinterested. One of the greatest obstacles to addressing the question of 'the aesthetic' in Wordsworth, and its ideological status or otherwise, is that the notion of pleasure which is at stake in such readings is constructed according to a quite inadequate phenomenology of pleasure, a phenomenology which Wordsworth's poetry in various ways contests. The separation of pleasures into sensual pleasures, on the one hand, and disinterested (or, alternatively, 'ideological') pleasures on the other, is governed by the progressive perfection of the distinction between production and consumption in modern economic reason. The image of this perfected separation can be found in the stand-off between the pure activity of concepts and the given passiveness of intuition in Kant's criticism. Wordsworth is less interested in forcing these two mutilated opponents into a dubious harmony than in recovering a different language for happiness, pleasure and the beautiful.

THE WORKING DAY

Of course this cannot really be thought of simply as an act of 'recovery'. Wordsworth's account of Basil's Pontic solitude adds much which is hardly present in any of the possible sources. Because Wordsworth has continually in mind the parallel with poetic retirement, we are offered something which is much more like a speculative reconstruction of the life of the Cappadocian recluses than it is like a historiographical exercise.

This becomes clear if we consider one of the possible sources beyond Cave's volume. We need to look not only at Basil's fourteenth epistle, which Wordsworth is ostensibly paraphrasing, but at his second (also to Gregory) in which he is attempting to formulate a monastic rule. The latter may well also have been a source for Wordsworth. Wordsworth's Basil promises Nazianzen that he will be 'often lifted to the calm / Of that entire beatitude in which / The Angels serve'. Basil's letter asks, 'What then is more blessed than to imitate on earth the anthems of angels' choirs; to hasten to prayer at very break of day … to season our labours with sacred song as food with salt?'[40] When not at this exquisite pitch, Wordsworth's Basil suggests 'Searching in patience and humility / Among the written mysteries of faith', just as Basil's letter insists that 'a most important path to the discovery of duty is also the study of the divinely-inspired scriptures'.[41] Wordsworth's Basil emphasizes the delights of his retreat by a list of privatives:

> No loss lamenting, no privation felt,
> Disturb'd by no vicissitudes, unscarred
> By civil faction, by religious broils
> Unplagu'd, forgetting, and forgotten, here
> Mayst thou possess thy own invisible nest,
> Like one of those small birds that round us chaunt
> In multitudes, their warbling will be thine,
> And freedom to unite thy voice with theirs,
> When they at morn or dewy evening praise
> High heaven in sweet and solemn services.
>
> (373–83)

The repeated privatives are formally reminiscent of a striking passage from Basil's second letter: 'withdrawal from the world does not mean bodily removal from it, but the severance of the soul from sympathy with the body, and the giving up city, home, personal possessions, love of friends, property, means of subsistence, business, social relations, and knowledge derived from human teaching'.[42] The effect of the catalogue is made much starker in the Greek by the repeated privative form.[43] Although Wordsworth's list of privatives is formally reminiscent of Basil's second letter, its content is very different. Basil emphasizes what one gives up of the world when one leaves it, Wordsworth what one is freed from in leaving the world. What they have in common is the renunciation of the absolute rule of self-preservation. Wordsworth takes the ideal of Christian retirement to mean that we give up only the 'world' which 'is

too much with us, late and soon', the economized world of infinitely
protracted getting and spending. We do not renounce the world 'in
which / We find our happiness or not at all.'

The point is further emphasized in an another important instance of
Wordsworth's adaptation of his sources, the incorporation of elements
from the charter of Furness Abbey into Basil's letter. The incorporation is
important partly because it indicates the extent to which Wordsworth is
reflecting on the character and fate of religious asceticism itself in this poem:

> What if the Roses and the flowers of Kings,
> Princes and Emperors, and the crowns and palms
> Of all the great are blasted, or decay –
> What if the meanest of their subjects, each
> Within the narrow region of his cares,
> Tremble beneath a sad uncertainty?
> There is a priviledge to plead, there is,
> Renounce, and thou shall find that priviledge, here.

Wordsworth himself drew attention to the use of lines from the charter
of Furness Abbey – 'Considering every day the uncertainty of life, that the
roses and flowers of Kings, Emperors, and Dukes, and the crowns and
palms of all the great, wither and decay' – when he printed a revised
version of these lines in book 7 of *The Excursion*. He may have found the
charter in Thomas West's *The Antiquities of Furness*; the translation given
there is identical to that quoted in the note to *The Excursion*.[44] West's
work also gives a brief account of the origin of monasticism which
follows Bingham both in its insistence upon persecution as the initial
motive for ascetic retreat, and in its concession that '[t]his kind of
life ... was afterwards embraced by choice'.[45] That the future Eastern
Metropolitan, Basil, is made to speak a version of the charter of Furness
Abbey decisively refuses any absolute opposition between Eastern and
Western monasticism. Yet the charter's force is significantly altered by its
transposition to the Cappadocian context. The charter of Furness granted
to the monks some quite particular privileges – rights, for example, to
hunt and fish – by gift of the landowner who drew it up in 1127, Stephen,
Earl of Boulogne and Moreton.[46] The 'privilege' referred to in the
concluding lines of Wordsworth's adaptation, by contrast, is one conferred not by a landowner but by the indestructible possibility of
renouncing the world which is at the origin of all monasticism: the
privilege of contemplative retreat. Retreat is contrasted not only with the
transitory glory of the state and its commanders, but also with the world

of perpetual self-preservation of each subject 'within the narrow region of his cares', a 'narrow region' later implicitly contrasted with 'the vast regions of the western church' which later develop from the rule framed by Basil. Yet this is not so much self-mortification as its reverse: the renunciation only of those fixated and not very delightful delights in pursuit of which we lay waste our powers, getting and spending. Why amaze yourself with merely emblematic flowers – the roses and the flowers of kings (or the palm, the oak or bays) – when you can have 'fruits that hang / In the primaeval woods'?

The Cappadocian model, then, suggests an individual who differs radically from the instrumental agent of economic reason. Accordingly, it also suggests a different kind of community than the providential harmony of interests, and a different kind of lived time than capital's working day. Wordsworth is fascinated by the improvised character of this community, which is always a community of individuals. What he emphasizes is the non-instrumentality, the happenstance of its formation. To speak of this group as a 'flock' or 'congregation' has more than a merely conventional force. The monks are 'like a troop of fowl / That, single or in clusters, settle on the breast / Of some broad pool, green field, or shady tree . . . ' Elsewhere, Wordsworth emphasizes that they are '[o]ne after one collected from afar', which does not stop them being '[a]n undissolving fellowship'. Only because the recluse is an individual, rather than the hollow cipher of one, does community become possible. The monks are drawn not by the wish to belong, but by

> The longing for confirm'd tranquillity,
> Inward and outward, humble and sublime,
> The life where hope and memory are as one,
> Earth quiet and unchanged, the human soul
> Consistent in self rule, and heaven revealed
> To meditation in that quietness.
>
> (303–8)

'The life where hope and memory are as one' is the still, yet living centre of this earthly paradise. It is in this sense that 'peace' is described as 'the central feeling of all happiness' – a present tense which is not constantly destroyed by the possibility of its removal. Wordsworth's turn away from perfectibilitarian thought in the final years of the 1790s, a turn which is most emphatically seen in the prose fragment on systematic moral reasoning and in the essay on the character of Rivers, does not delete the utopian dimension of his work, nor suppress it in favour of what a lesser poet called 'the pleasures of memory'. Rather that dimension migrates into the very way in which he thinks of memory, which would not have the force it does did it not intimate a future which might hereafter come to all the vales of earth and all mankind. The model of happiness recovered from the Cappadocian fathers proposes a present continually animated by past and future, hope and memory. The world of getting and spending, by contrast, proposes a present which is like a series of points along a line, each one instantaneously passing from future to past, so that the point in which the present exists is in fact shrunk to dimensionlessness – a *nothing*, yet a nothing fetishized and generalized into the measure of life.

It is the possibility of a different life, a life where hope and memory are as one, which monastic and poetic retirement alike hold out, and which grounds both Wordsworth's analogy between them and his defence against the evident objections to which both kinds of retirement are open. This analogy is the central axle of the fragment. Grasmere's 'little avenue / Of lightly stirring Ash-trees' (108–9), which the Wordsworths found cut down on their return in 1807 is a 'consecrated visto' (120) which has its echo in the 'cloistral avenues' (483) of the ruined abbeys. Grasmere and the Chartreuse alike constitute exceptional cases, whose destruction risks not only the loss of these particular places, but of a particular kind of life, the life made beautiful by Basil, which might otherwise be lost from the world altogether. The *exceptional* character of Christian and poetic retreat is central to the analogy between them. 'Here, if here only', Wordsworth pleads for Grasmere, let one small place be protected '[i]nviolate for nobler purposes' (269, 267). For the Chartreuse, '[l]et this one Temple last – be this one spot / Of earth devoted to Eternity' (542–3). It is useful to consider the episode of the Chartreuse in its original context in Wordsworth's account of the Cappadocian model of monasticism: it helps us to understand the subtlety of the sense which we are to give to 'Eternity' here. The Chartreuse does not merely turn away from the world towards transcendence. It *embodies* – rather than simply theorizing or describing – the 'blissful pleasures' of a life where hope and memory are as one.

It is easy to see how this could be understood as a retreat from political universalism. Yet it is no part of these pleasures to relish one's distinctiveness. The monks are driven by '[t]he *universal* instinct for repose' (302, my emphasis), just as the happiness of Grasmere is one day to come to *all* the vales of earth. What would really be utopian is not that *no* individual should ever be allowed to hold on to anything, but rather that *all* should share in the security and the happiness which are currently protected for *some* by property. Wordsworth's meditation on the ruined abbeys points out how rapidly rage against injustice becomes a rage against happiness itself. Some indulge their instinct for repose whilst others can barely scratch a living: so there is of course a desire to make lazy monks, or poets, do a proper job. Yet the fury at repose thus expressed is, when elevated to a measure and a system of life, to an Economy, just what makes it impossible to tell what a 'proper job' – one which would be transparently related to real human need – really is. This fury against repose, in its conversion of production into an absolute good and primary source of value, becomes the economy of production for its own sake, an economy in which *need* is in fact no longer a consideration.

Gregory Nazianzen is Christendom's first ever genuinely auto-biographical poet.[47] Whereas Joshua Lucock Wilkinson draws a firm distinction between 'the friend of solitude and nature' and the idle monk, 'recluse from profession', Wordsworth explores an analogy between the religious and the poetic recluse. His position is by some distance the less self-exculpatory. In a shining page of the *Phenomenology of Spirit*, Hegel once pointed out the limits to the good faith of any enlightened contempt for religious asceticism. Enlightenment's allergic reaction to 'super-stitious' asceticism is in part prompted by its own guilty conscience, since its own ascetic rhetoric – of *inner* or *moral* sacrifice – has become purely theoretical. What frightens the sceptic is that the ascetic actually puts his rhetoric into practice. Hence the temptation to think renouncers not merely foolish, but morally dangerous:

Insight also finds it *wrong* to deny oneself a meal and to give away butter and eggs, not for money, nor money for butter and eggs, but simply to give them away without receiving anything in return; ... it also affirms as a pure intention the necessity of rising above natural existence, above acquisitiveness about the means of existence; only it finds it foolish and wrong that this elevation should be demonstrated *by deeds*; in other words, this pure insight is in truth a deception, which feigns and demands an *inner* elevation, but declares that it is superfluous, foolish and even wrong to be *in earnest* about it, to put this elevation into *actual practice* and demonstrate its truth.[48]

All Wordsworth's poetry resists economistic reason, yet not in the name of a merely inner elevation, but rather because that reason rests on a concept which, where it is not unclarified and unintelligible, is abstract to the point of contentlessness: the concept of happiness itself. To begin to find the language in which the concept of happiness could have a meaningful and undiminished content is to begin to understand how Wordsworth imagined the individuality of the recluse, and of 'The Recluse'.

In the next chapter I turn to confront this individuality with what might at first sight seem for Wordsworth to be its antitype: London.

CHAPTER 5

Infinity

In one of Walter Benjamin's notes to himself, abutting the long arcades of quotation in his *Passagenwerk*, can be found the following:

The student 'never stops learning'; the gambler 'never has enough'; for the flâneur, 'there is always something more to see'. Idleness has in view an unlimited duration, which fundamentally distinguishes it from simple sensuous pleasure, of whatever variety. (Is it correct to say that the 'bad infinity' that prevails in idleness appears in Hegel as the signature of bourgeois society?)[1]

Wordsworth is sometimes thought of as a poet for whom there is no such thing as a bad infinity. Yet the 'endless way' of 'Stepping Westward', radiant with promise, *does* have its miserable counterpart, in the 'illimitable walk' which the poet encountered in London: 'Still among streets with clouds and sky above . . .' In the first, the illimitability of travel is a blessing; in the second it can appear almost to be a curse. Where do we stand with respect to the infinities, the endlessnesses, the illimitabilities with which Wordsworth is so often concerned? Are they, for us, merely so much devalued currency? Or is it possible that, by trying to distinguish among the precise tenors and weights of their various occurrences – in the city as well as at the summit – we might arrive at a sense of their real value?

'BAD INFINITY'

Benjamin asks a good question. *Is* it correct to say that the 'bad infinity' that prevails in idleness appears in Hegel as the signature of bourgeois society? Answering it needs care. We could start with Hegel's most serious attempt at explaining the idea of 'bad infinity'.

It is this reciprocal determination, negating both itself and its negation, which appears as that *progress to infinity* which is in so many forms and under so many applications taken for an *ultimate* beyond which it is impossible to go; at which instead thought, once having arrived at this '*and so on* to infinity', has usually come to an end. – This progress comes forward wherever *relative* determinations are driven to the point of coming to oppose each other, so that they are in an inseparable unity, and yet each is attributed a self-sufficient existence in opposition to the other. This progress is therefore the *contradiction* which is not resolved, but which is only ever expressed as *present*.

What is present is an abstract going-beyond, which remains incomplete because this *going-beyond* is never *gone beyond*. What is present is the infinite; however we go beyond the infinite, since a new limit is posited, but with just this positing we only return, rather, to the finite. This bad infinity is in itself the same as the perennial *Ought*; it is indeed the negation of the finite, but it is in truth unable to free itself from the finite; the finite emerges *within* this negation itself as its other, because this infinite is, only as it *relates* to the finite which is other to it. The progress to infinity is thus nothing other than the self-recapitulating monotonousness, one and the same boring *alternation* of this finite and infinite.[2]

This looks rather a long way from Benjamin's suggestion, since it seems to have nothing at all to say about social experience. An example may help. In the third antinomy of the *Critique of Pure Reason*, Kant asks whether 'causality in accordance with the laws of nature is the only one from which all the appearances of the world can be derived', or whether 'it is also necessary to assume another causality through freedom' (for examples: a free will, a God) 'in order to explain them'.[3] What makes this an antinomy is that Kant gives two contradictory answers which he declares equally true, and therefore equally false. These two answers can be made to refute each other to infinity. Hegel's broader target is the limitation of reason undertaken in Kant's critiques and their successors. Wherever we arrive before what is declared to be an absolute limit to reason, there we have an instance of what Hegel calls 'bad infinity'. Something which is only finite or relative has been falsely promoted to be an infinite absolute. The critical instance of this in Kant's thought is the *ought*, the moral law. It is an absolute which we must obey, without being able fully to know.

Characteristically of him, Hegel's *Science of Logic* turns out not to be a logic in the conventional sense, but also to be concerned with ontological, ethical and aesthetic ideas. 'This bad infinity is in itself the same as the perennial *Ought*...' Bad infinity is the perennial ought. The large scope of the figure of bad infinity in Hegel's thought thus appears. Universalizing morality, floating free an *ought* from the historical, political and institutional life which has made it possible; ascetic religiosity, insisting that transcendence *ought* to become manifest within an immanence it has

already decreed radically forsaken; sceptical or fideistic or critical epistemology, insisting that we *ought* not to try to say what ought is; ersatz
sublimity, congratulating itself on the awe which it feels at the notional
contrast between the finite and the infinite which it has itself confected:
all these share the structure of bad infinity, its promotion of limitation
into an absolute. To which, of course, Hegel's response cannot be that we
'ought' to have nothing to do with it, but rather that, as we live out these
bad infinities, we find them less than infinite: if fascinating to ourselves,
then as boring to others as any fixation of student, gambler or *flâneur*. 'It
is usually declared that thinking must come to a standstill when it sets out
to consider such an infinity. It certainly is true at any rate that in the end
we let it alone, but this is not because the business is so sublime, but
because it is so boring.'[4]

If this is the false, bad or boring infinity, what is the true, good or
sublime one? Not, as we might expect, the opposite of the former, but
rather the bad infinity which has come to comprehend itself. 'The
solution of the contradiction is not the recognition of the equal correctness and equal incorrectness of both assertions' (this is where Kant's
antinomies come to rest), 'this is only another form of the persisting
contradiction –, but the *ideality* of both, an ideality in which both
assertions, as reciprocal negations, are only *moments*; this monotonous
alternation is, factically, just as much the negation of the *unity* as it is of
the *separation* of these moments.'[5] Instead the true infinity is the com-
prehension that there is no such 'thing' as finitude, but that 'the finite' is
no less an ideality than 'the infinite'.

The proposition that the *finite is ideal* constitutes idealism. The idealism of
philosophy consists in nothing other than in not recognizing the finite as anything really existent. All philosophies are essentially idealisms or at least have
idealism as their principle, and the question then is only to what extent this
idealism is actually carried through.... The opposition of idealist and realist
philosophy is thus without meaning.[6]

Bad infinity, in fact, is, for Hegel, the structure of *Verstand* (understanding) itself. *Vernunft* (reason) is not something simply higher than or
apart from *Verstand*, as though these were two different regions of spirit.
It is a *Verstand* which has come also to understand itself as a whole – to
see the interrelation of its own elements as something essential to
understanding itself, rather than accidental to it. So that the 'good' and
the 'bad' infinity turn out after all to be connected to each other. The
good infinity comprehends, yet also emerges from, the bad one.[7]

That Hegel despite all this still calls bad infinity *bad* is one of the undialectical blows which give his speculative logic its purchase upon experience. The motif of bad infinity connects a series of such crises in Hegel's work: the distinction of morality from ethical life; of ersatz sublimity from real grandeur; of speculative thinking from romantic irony: all these distinctions share the structure of the reproof to bad infinity. It is thus a motif whose significance is hard to pin down. From one point of view the discussion of bad infinity is an attack upon a self-deceiving yearning to transcend all restriction and limitation. Hegel can use its structure, for example, to talk about growing up:

> That the individual at first resists the idea of settling on a particular social position, and regards this as a restriction of his universal character and as a merely *external* necessity, results from the abstract thinking which remains with what is universal and, thus, with what is not actual, and which does not recognize that, in order to exist at all, the concept entered into the distinction between the concept and its reality and thus into determinacy and particularity, and that it is only in this way that it can obtain actuality and ethical objectivity.[8]

Yet this example itself shows how multiple is this structure. It might look as though Hegel is issuing familiar instructions: get used to it. But it is because the individual thinks that particularity is just something he or she has to get used to, rather than part of what he or she is, that it is experienced as external limitation. The path from spurious to real infinity is not the acceptance of limitation but, in a direction which is hard to follow, to move 'beyond the universal': to move, that is, beyond the abstract beyond. Although this can be turned to the service of an abrupt realism – 'Philosophy does not waste time with such empty and other-worldly stuff. What philosophy has to do with is always something concrete and directly present'[9] – it also leads into the (for modern common sense) distinctly utopian realm of the speculative proposition, a realm in which a 'science of logic' can include near its close a long chapter on 'Life'. This equivocality can be seen in the afterlife of the motif. From it runs a line not only to conservative attacks on utopianism but also to Marx's comic treatment of ideo-logy.[10]

Not only might it be correct, then, 'to say that the "bad infinity" that prevails in idleness appears in Hegel as the signature of bourgeois society' – for so long as it is realized that this bad infinity is the signature also and first of all of that society's noblest and most moral self-understandings or self-misprisions; and once it is recalled that for Hegel 'bourgeois' or what he more often calls modern society is defined by a *longue durée* which stretches back to Roman law and Christianity – not only might this be correct, but Benjamin's deployment of it shows how his theological materialism has been educated in absolute idealism. Benjamin's use of the motif of 'bad infinity' is much more than a chance appropriation. These urban pleasures are also punishments. Their immediacy is ideal; their inner logic, an internalized asceticism. The more we help ourselves to the authentic taste of the nineteenth-century city from this table, the hungrier we become. It presents not a series of facts, but unfinished work towards a composition wishing to get us to where we could first see the facts: wishing to release us from our own bad infinity; – our 'long Etcetera'.[11]

ILLIMITABLE WALK

The elevation of the finite to infinite significance has often been thought of as a governing trope of Wordsworth's work. It has then been easy to think that his problem with London – an environment in which he sometimes felt uncomfortable[12]– was that it failed to achieve this elevation; that urban life fixated on the merely finite, contingent or accidental at the expense of loftier or more permanent objects better suited to successful spiritual lift-off. The work on London thus comes to look satirical. From the pure and permanent vantage of Helvellyn or philosophy, a pettier life is to be mocked or denounced. This was certainly what Coleridge wanted, when he was giving an account of Wordsworth's poem in 1832: Wordsworth, recall, was to assume 'a satiric or Juvenalian spirit as he approached the high civilization of cities and towns'.[13] The difficulty, though, is that many precisely of the most striking lines in Wordsworth's account of his experience in London do not fit this, and indeed that broader features of its articulation and placement do not support it.

It is clear from the start of Wordsworth's account of his London experience that the difficulty of register which has so often confronted modern poets attempting to write about cities – which is at bottom a difficulty of register consequent upon attempting to write poetry about modern experience itself – persists for him too. Wordsworth gives a history of his own advances and setbacks in writing the poem to Coleridge. He announces that he is now ready to continue in terms which make it clear that special difficulties pertain to rendering urban experience in verse: 'we will now resume with chearful hope, / Nor check'd by aught of tamer argument / Which lies before us, needful to be told' (vii. 54–6).

He starts again; but he has to start again twice. London has fallen below his fancies of it twice. In childhood a friend of his had gone to London and had, to Wordsworth's astonishment, returned looking and sounding much the same as when he left. Although as a man he no longer expected to find a golden citadel, other fond imaginations had taken its place.

> These fond imaginations, of themselves,
> Had long before given way, in season due,
> Leaving a throng of others in their stead;
> And now I look'd upon the real scene,
> Familiarly perused it day by day
> With keen and lively pleasure, even there
> Where disappointment was the strongest, pleased
> Through courteous self-submission, as a tax
> Paid to the object by prescriptive right,
> A thing that ought to be. Shall I give way,
> Copying the impression of the memory,
> (Though things remember'd idly do half seem
> The work of Fancy) shall I as the mood
> Inclines me, here describe, for pastime's sake,
> Some portion of that motley imagery,
> A vivid pleasure of my youth, and now,
> Among the lonely places that I love,
> A frequent day-dream for my riper mind.
> – And first ...
>
> (vii. 145–54)

The difficulties which Wordsworth had in getting the poem to start in the first place afflict him again. Just as he has initially sidled into the poem by asking himself whether all his youthful intimations of grandeur were really only building up to this failure to write, and then by failing to answer the question and instead starting to talk about what those youthful intimations of grandeur were, so here another logical slippage allows him to start writing about London. 'Shall I ...' proposes a question mark which never arrives. After this he simply does get under way, tellingly, with a connective: '– And first, ...' The leap appears decisionistic rather than decisive, in the sense that it is made for the very purpose of obviating the anxiety of blockage. The difficulty of thinking the apparently idiotically contingent minutenesses of one's own experience fit to write a poem about, a difficulty which, after Wordsworth, it has become hard even to think of as a difficulty, was, fatefully, broken through at the start of the poem; but here it apparently has to be broken through, and in a similar way, all over again. It is as though going to the city makes us feel with renewed defeat that our own silly singularity can carry no general weight. That Wordsworth does feel anxious about this emerges from the apologetic nature of this passage: from the quite unconvincing suggestion that this part of the poem should be thought of as a bit of hobbyism ('for pastime's sake'); from the connection made between idle remembering and fancy, a connection which implies the opposite connection between involuntary remembering and imagination; and, most of all, from the account of the mingled disappointment and pleasure which Wordsworth says he felt when he arrived. It is hard to enter into this account of 'keen and lively pleasure', because pleasure is not usually thought of as a 'tax', nor felt 'by prescriptive right'. Wordsworth seems to be saying that although he was in fact disappointed he made himself be pleased. We could remove this difficulty by thinking that saying that these pleasures were 'keen and lively' is just a way of being polite. Yet Wordsworth generally has little trouble admitting that youthful pleasures were forced ('The tragic super-tragic, else left short' (viii. 532)). The difficulty therefore needs to be preserved, rather than erased. It gains force in the subtle parataxis which closes the sentence: what is the 'thing that ought to be'? Thematically and primarily, it is the pleasure which Wordsworth feels because he ought to feel it. Yet syntactically and secondarily it may also be the 'object', London itself. London is *a thing that ought to be*, this under sense insinuates. The city perhaps remains in itself an ideality, retains also the shape of a norm rather than becoming a bare fact, even after successive fantasies of it have been chastened. It cannot be seen at once; it never ends. 'There is always something more to see.'

It is, in fact, this 'always more' which hangs over the attempt to 'describe' into which Wordsworth now plunges.

> And first, the look and aspect of the place,
> The broad high-way appearance, as it strikes
> On Strangers of all ages; the quick dance
> Of colours, lights and forms; the Babel din;
> The endless stream of men, and moving things;
> From hour to hour the illimitable walk
> Still among Streets with clouds and sky above; . . .
>
> (vii. 154–60)

It is not hard to see here at least one reason why poets immediately preceding Wordsworth should have found mock a comfortable medium in which to versify the city. Johnson's remark about Thomson's difficulty in organizing *The Seasons*, that '[o]f many appearances subsisting all at once, no rule can be given why one should be mentioned before another'[14] can be felt to apply equally acutely to descriptions of cities, and it reminds us of what is unusual in this passage within the whole poem's frame, that although he is continuing, as throughout, to describe his own memories, yet none the less, to describe one's own memories of the city is to begin to describe the multiplicity of the city itself; so that whereas Wordsworth's accounts of his Lakeland memories are distinguished from picturesque precisely by their lack of interest in any attempt at exhaustive description of what is merely given, he here at once pitches himself or finds himself pitched into a catalogue which, in trying to do more than merely give a list of notable items, he begins at a level of extreme generality. This generality attempts to offer something of the universal phenomenology of the city, its look and aspect in so far as that look and aspect is the same for all. It is just this which exposes the writing to the guffaw at apparent vacuity which most critics and many readers of Wordsworth's time still had in their repertoire. ('Mr Wordsworth first undertakes to tell his readers 'what *look*' the city bore, and also with what '*aspect*' it appeared; and his conclusion is, that it had a 'broad high-way *appearance*'.') These first two lines do indeed appear emptied of purchase by the willed arbitrariness of getting started: something must be written, at any rate. The thought drops into a list which continues for the whole passage and recurs often throughout the book. Yet that there really was something Wordsworth wanted to say about the highways appears a few lines later: 'From hour to hour the illimitable walk / Still among Streets with clouds and sky above.' But of course there is nothing about the 'many appearances subsisting at once' of the city which makes them in themselves more or less difficult to describe simultaneously than the appearances of a mountainous region; nor is the city in itself more multiple than such a region. So the illimitability which is referred to here cannot be simply the fact that one could walk forever without coming to an end. That goes for everywhere else too. The implication, rather, as the remainder of the passage suggests, is that the walk is illimitable because one can never in truth *arrive* anywhere, and thus that one can never in fact *go* anywhere either. 'Still among Streets' grasps this in one move: the primary sense, that however far we walk we are still walking among streets, also contains a secondary possibility, that however far we walk we are still, that is, motionless.

> Here, there, and everywhere, a weary Throng!
> The Comers and the Goers face to face,

Face after face; the string of dazzling Wares,
Shop after Shop, with Symbols, blazon'd Names,
And all the Tradesman's honours overhead;
Here, fronts of houses, like a title-page,
With letters huge inscribed from top to toe;
Stationed above the door like guardian Saints,
There, allegoric shapes, female or male;
Or physiognomies of real men,
Land Warriors, Kings, or Admirals of the Sea,
Boyle, Shakespear, Newton; or the attractive head
Of some Scotch Doctor, famous in his day.

(vii. 171–83)

One of the habitual ways of organizing appearances subsisting all at once in the century preceding Wordsworth was the conveniently arbitrary 'Here ... there'. These markers gave the pointedness and apparent meaningfulness of spatial apposition to an otherwise too evidently contingent ordering. Wordsworth resorts to this device too, but only after he has already destroyed it with the opening line of this passage. Once 'Here, there, and everywhere' have been forced into a list they no longer bear any organizing power. 'Here' and 'there' are instances of 'everywhere'. The tacit resonance of 'Still among streets', that we walk without being able to arrive anywhere, is developed in these lines. The possible destinations are pointers to something else.

The illimitability of the city raises a problem of knowledge. The scarcely precedented speculation in Wordsworth's writing – that universality, if at all, is to be attained precisely by attention to what seems entirely personal or idiosyncratic – is brought up against difficulties there. In so far as the city is in any way one city, its unity consists not in a place or a series of places but in an ideality which sublates or abolishes any particular place, in *a thing that ought to be*. How is such an ideality to be known? Wordsworth's solution to this problem is abrupt. It repeats the decision which allowed him to begin to write about the city in the first place.

From those sights
Take one, an annual Festival, the Fair
Holden where Martyrs suffer'd in past time,
And nam'd of Saint Bartholomew; there see
A work that's finish'd to our hands, that lays,
If any spectacle on earth can do,
The whole creative powers of man asleep!
For once the Muse's aid will we implore,

And she shall lodge us, wafted on her wings,
Above the press and danger of the Crowd
Upon some Show-man's Platform: . . .
                                             (vii. 649–59)

'– And first, . . .'; 'From these sights / Take one . . . ' The appeal to the Muse
which follows reinforces this decisionism with a poetic *metabasis eis allo
genos*, a resolution of a difficulty by a leap into a different order of being.[15]
Wordsworth notes the emergency character of this leap: 'For once . . .'[16]
'The Muse' is by this date flightless. But '[f]or once' she is needed, since she
allows us to imagine a vantage which we cannot really have. The sudden
ascent is all the more conspicuous because Wordsworth's writing is usually
so cautious about the kind of knowledge which elevation is supposed to
confer over what, either figuratively or literally, is looked down upon. It is
from this willed aerial perspective that we can see the production of consumption: 'as if the whole were one vast Mill' (vii. 692). The solution comes
at a critical point in the book, because Wordsworth is going on to treat the
fair as a model for understanding the whole city:

O blank confusion! and a type not false
Of what the mighty City is itself
To all except a Straggler here and there,
To the whole swarm of its inhabitants;
An undistinguishable world to men,
The slaves unrespited of low pursuits,
Living amid the same perpetual flow
Of objects, melted and reduced
To one identity by differences
That have no law, no meaning, and no end;
Oppression under which even highest minds
Must labour, whence the strongest are not free!
                                             (vii. 696–707)

What constitutes the City as 'itself' is not, as so much poetry of city life
would have it, an ungraspable or even infinite plurality, but a single
ideality. It is a lived ideality of unchanging self-sameness: the same perpetual flow, one identity. The *rich variety* of city life is usually thought of
as lying in its many differences. But here these 'differences' are not
opposed to that blank identity. They establish it. This seems not to make
sense. How can it be the case that *differences* make this '[a]n undistinguishable world to men'? The writing implies that there might
be differences which do have a law, a meaning and an end. For these

differences to be distinguishable, we must find a way to stand outside the perpetual flow of illusory plurality – a plurality, for example, of many 'moveables of wonder' (vii. 680). That perpetual flow is the element in which we live and breathe, however 'high' our minds may be. There is no spiritual aristocracy which may stand above it. If there were, the appeal to the Muse would not be needed. Yet it is only from this no-place that the whole view has been delivered. It is this difficulty that the passage immediately comes back to:

> But though the picture weary out the eye,
> By nature an unmanageable sight,
> It is not wholly so to him who looks
> In steadiness, who hath among least things
> An under sense of greatest; sees the parts
> As parts, but with a feeling of the whole.
>   (vii. 708–13)

The city is '[b]y nature an unmanageable sight' or 'picture' because it is not really a sight or picture at all. It has only been possible to represent it as such with the Muse's help. We can have no knowledge of the whole, but only 'a feeling of the whole'. More strangely, this feeling of the whole is the opposite of the 'one identity' mentioned before. *This* feeling of the whole requires that we wrest our attention from that abstract unity. It requires that we see the parts as parts; that we feel those differences which really do have a law, a meaning and an end. It is an *under*, not an *over* 'sense of greatest'. What may be hoped for from this under sense is kept carefully limited. It cannot untie anyone from the string of dazzling wares. It forms a rub or botch in that surface seamlessness. The gaze is 'not wholly' blinded by the false whole. It may see something if it look in steadiness.

'NOT WHOLLY SO'

The exceptional difficulty of London as an object or illusory-object for verse is confirmed by the recursion to it in the following book. This book is given the indicative title 'Retrospect', but the subtitle, 'Love of Nature leading to love of Mankind', hardly lets us know that we are to return to London. Wordsworth begins the book on a physical vantage-point, Helvellyn, which is implicitly contrasted with the fantasized vantage afforded by the 'Muse' in book 7, as though to recruit from 'fields and their rural works' that steadiness which he has just invoked. Whereas in the earlier book Wordsworth became continually anxious that his subject

matter was too tame, asking himself whether he needed to fear men-
tioning a place name as humble as Sadler's Wells in verse, and thus
indicating that he did fear to do it (as one might even today fear to
mention Cricklewood or Finchley Road); whereas he concedes there that
his matter is likely to 'seem / To many neither dignified enough nor
arduous'; here, by contrast, the difficulty is to attempt again first to give
an adequate sense of the grandeur which he experienced in entering
London and then to give an adequate sense of the blankness he felt when
that grandeur had almost at once passed away:

> On the Roof
> Of an itinerant Vehicle I sate
> With vulgar men about me, vulgar forms
> Of houses, pavement, streets, of men and things,
> Mean shapes on every side; but at the time
> When to myself it fairly might be said,
> The very moment that I seem'd to know,
> The threshold now is overpass'd – Great God!
> That aught external to the living mind
> Should have such mighty sway! yet so it was –
> A weight of Ages did at once descend
> Upon my heart, no thought embodied, no
> Distinct remembrances; but weight and power,
> Power, growing with the weight: alas! I feel
> That I am trifling: 'twas a moment's pause,
> All that took place within me, came and went
> As in a moment, and I only now
> Remember that it was a thing divine.
>   (viii. 693–710)

The experience of entering the city was so powerful that he remembers
almost nothing about it. Now he feels that he is trifling, not because the
matter is too light for his grander verse, but because his verse is too
mundane or too restricted to seize the grandeur of his experience of the city;
– and yet not, in truth, of his experience of the city, but his experience of
the ideality of the city. For this weight of ages descends not at the sight of
a picture, but at the point when he seemed to know, when to himself it
fairly might be said, that he was now in the city. We might expect to be
given some idea of the sensory cues which allowed him to say this to
himself, but he draws attention to the fact that he has no distinct
remembrances to offer at all. The experience of weight and power arises
from an encounter with an ideality of the city: 'a thing that ought to be'.

Wordsworth's own chiasmic play on 'weight' and 'power' strikes him as empty, and so he embarks on an extended simile which is intended to make clearer in what way this was 'a thing divine':

> As when a traveller hath from open day
> With torches pass'd into some Vault of Earth,
> The Grotto of Antiparos, or the Den
> Of Yordas among Craven's mountain tracts;
> He looks and sees the Cavern spread and grow,
> Widening itself on all sides, sees, or thinks
> He sees, erelong, the roof above his head,
> Which instantly unsettles and recedes
> Substances and shadow, light and darkness, all
> Commingled, making up a Canopy
> Of Shapes and Forms, and Tendencies to Shape,
> That shift and vanish, change and interchange
> Like Spectres, ferment quiet, and sublime;
> Which, after a short space, works less and less
> Till every effort, every motion gone,
> The scene before him lies in perfect view,
> Exposed and lifeless as a written book.
> But let him pause awhile, and look again
> And a new quickening shall succeed, at first
> Beginning timidly, then creeping fast
> Through all which he beholds: the senseless mass
> In its projections, wrinkles, cavities,
> Through all its surface, with all colours streaming,
> Like a magician's airy pageant, parts,
> Unites, embodying everywhere some pressure
> Or image, recognis'd or new, some type
> Or picture of the world; forests and lakes,
> Ships, rivers, towers, the Warrior clad in Mail,
> The prancing Steed, the Pilgrim with his Staff,
> The mitred Bishop and the throned King,
> A Spectacle to which there is no end.
>   No otherwise had I at first been mov'd
> With such a swell of feeling follow'd soon
> By a blank sense of greatness pass'd away
> And afterwards continued to be mov'd
> In presence of that vast Metropolis,
> The Fountain of my Country's destiny
> And of the destiny of Earth itself,
> That great Emporium, Chronicle at once

>   And Burial-place of passions and their home
>   Imperial, and chief living residence.
>
>   (viii. 711–51)

This simile is the unmasking of an unmasking. Its shape is important. By the time readers reach 'Exposed and lifeless as a written book' they may be ready for 'So' to reply to 'As', for the relevance of this vehicle to the tenor, the entry into London, to be delivered. What follows instead is a second look at the vehicle: 'But let him pause a while . . . ' The cave at first provides an unusual kind of sublimity, one which follows not from the grandeur or fearfulness of the object, nor from any attempt, and failure, to provide an intuition to reason, but simply from the attempt and failure to see what is there, a 'ferment *quiet*, and sublime'. This recedes as the traveller does see what is there, and arrives at a kind of dead letter of perception.[17] The second cathexis which follows appears at first to be a rebirth of the power just lost. Yet its shape is quite different. The roof now offers a world of representations. It is a surface in which the traveller can if he wants see infinitely many representations. It is 'A Spectacle to which there is no end.' This second attempt repeats the illimitable character of the city. 'There is always something more to see.'

Its strangeness hinges on the imagined dead letter. The book is lifeless, like any book, yet it can be read. But what we do when we read a book is not really to bring it back to life. The scene is a train of spirits which appear animated but are not alive. This strangeness persists into the tenor, which after this delay now arrives. Wordsworth's initial sense of sublimity (not, however, as in the cave, a sense of sublimity prompted by an appearance, but rather a sense prompted by his own act of understanding) is replaced by a 'blank' disappointment, the city as a dead letter; and this in turn is replaced by a long or endless period in which he 'continued to be mov'd': moved, that is, not by what he may now solidly perceive as a reality, but by the illimitable train of spirits of urban life. The simile is the unmasking of an unmasking in the sense that it does not take us from illusion to reality, but from appearance to appearance: to the recognition that the city, as city, is infinite appearance, 'A Spectacle to which there is no end.'

Although this passage is legitimately read as a compensation for the critical treatment in book 7 (a reading which is most trenchantly put by Mary Jacobus when she argues that 'The Cave of Yordas saves the city from satire and gives it back to romance'[18]) – and although, indeed, Wordsworth himself thinks of it (viii. 678–85) as a more serious attempt to return to a subject which was only played with or puzzled at there – its

fundamental thoughts and feelings are of a piece with the earlier treatment's equivocality. As Thomas Pfau remarks, the simile 'gradually
reattaches itself to that ambivalent heart of civilization, London, whose
semiotic and perceptual entropy it was meant to counterbalance'.[19] The
concluding lines of the passage, with their breathless conjunctive linking
of opposites, indicate this equivocality: 'Chronicle at once / And Burial-
place of passions and their home / Imperial, and chief living residence.'
Burial-place *and* living residence. This gathering of the *personae* of distinction or vocation ('the' warrior, 'the' pilgrim, 'the' bishop) was not
accidentally a meeting of spirits, of the living dead. The city's living-dead
character is awesome. It is for the poet to feel that awe, but also to look
steadily through and beyond it. He is to feel the power of those spirits
without worshipping them: 'not wholly so'.

Nothing could be more alien to Hegel than Wordsworth's 'not wholly
so'. This is still more true of a reservation which depends, as Wordsworth's does, on what, he goes on to explain, are the steady habits of
thinking and feeling which his mountain childhood and youth have given
him. Hegel described his own thinking as a highway of despair. By this he
meant not that it ended in despair but that it had to pass through it. His
thinking was a 'self-completing scepticism'.[20] It would defeat scepticism,
not by clinging to illusions, but by pushing sceptical claims as far as they
would go. This fearlessness has its own mythical aspects. It is at once an
internalization and an outbidding of the logic of sacrifice. To sacrifice is
to give something up in order to secure something else. But in Hegel,
only to a relinquishment of everything, including any guarantee of a
return, will all be given back.[21] This is what differentiates self-perficient
scepticism from the 'unhappy consciousness'.[22] Something like this way
of thinking and feeling, the feeling of having gone in so far that going
back would be impossible and in any case worse than going further, is
present in Rivers, the anti-hero of Wordsworth's play *The Borderers*:
'Uneasiness must be driven away by fresh uneasiness.'

ENDLESS WAY

We are used to being told that oneness, wholeness, unity, or an overcoming or bridging of dualisms was Wordsworth's governing *ought*.
When he tries to think about his experience in London, though, what
makes that thinking possible is rather to keep open or to prise open a
difference, – a difference, that is, which could have a law, or a meaning or
an end. What kind of difference might this be? One ready place to start

would be to try to specify just how the questionable infinities presented
by the ideality of the city – the illimitable walk, the same perpetual flow
or the spectacle to which there is no end – differ from another kind of
infinity, a valuable or good infinity which is, if reading follow the letter,
so close to the bad one as to be right up against it. 'Still among Streets the
illimitable walk' easily recalls an earlier passage of the poem in which the
complexity of the word 'still' is mobilized in an analogous way. The clear
meaning in both cases is 'always', and yet it is hard not to hear, as an
under sense, 'motionless':

> the soul,
> Remembering how she felt, but what she felt
> Remembering not, retains an obscure sense
> Of possible sublimity, to which,
> With growing faculties she doth aspire,
> With faculties still growing, feeling still
> That, whatsoever point they gain they still
> Have something to pursue.
>
> (ii. 334–41)

Here too 'there is always something more to see'. The more 'still' as
'continually' or 'yet' is repeated, the more the motionlessness of all this
infinite striving is glimpsed beneath it. The fourth and fifth lines here,
moreover, take the form of just that chiasmic redundance which in book
8 leads Wordsworth to think that he is 'trifling'.

   In what respect does this kind of infinity differ from the city-idea's
illimitability? How, for instance, does an 'illimitable walk' differ from an
'endless way'?

> I liked the greeting; 'twas a sound
> Of something without place or bound;
> And seem'd to give me spiritual right
> To travel through that region bright.
> It's power was felt; and while my eye
> Was fixed upon the glowing sky,
> The echo of the voice enwrought
> A human sweetness with the thought
> Of travelling through the world that lay
> Before me in my endless way.[23]

   One ready answer comes forward, of course: the difference lies in the
'greeting' which gives the poem its title: 'What you are stepping

westward?' When Wordsworth corrects himself in the course of describing the streets of London – where people are not so much 'face to face' as 'Face *after* face' – the qualification matters, because it presents a central feature of the city's unintelligibility, the 'mystery' of each single passer-by, the next-door neighbours who don't know each other's names. Here we have the counterpart to the indifferent neighbour: the hospitable stranger. The way is not in fact endless because, as a note prefixed to the poem has already let us know, Wordsworth and his companion are walking to a hut which they have already visited earlier in their tour, and where they had been 'hospitably entertained'. So it may be suspected that the 'human sweetness' is enwrought with the taste of endlessness not only by the friendly greeting but also, as the note has implicitly conceded, by the anticipation of a good supper. Part of the greeting's power is that the kindness of these strangers recalls the hospitality which has already been experienced, and which is expected again at the end of the endless way. The thought which the first stanza has raised, of how frightening it would be to be walking without knowing where you were going to in this isolated country, and of how nevertheless you might dare to do just that with just this sky to lead you on, is thus qualified in advance by the knowledge that in fact Wordsworth knows quite well where his next meal is coming from.

The 'endless way' is thus bracketed, both in the facts of the narrative and in readers' minds, as a seeming endlessness. Yet in the shape of the poem it is not bracketed. It forms the last words of the poem, and comes as the final elation of a gathering syntactical propulsion and stanzaic excess; an elation which may (it is unscientific to imagine) lead a reader to close the book and walk out into the street as though in that movement the same illusory elation might be experienced. This gap between what the poem says and what its shape seems to say does not issue in irony, because the appearance-character of this endlessness is explicitly noticed: 'stepping westward seem'd to be / A kind of heavenly destiny.' Might this not be one hiding-place of the poem's power – a hiding-place which, if it seems to close every time we approach it, then this is perhaps for the reason that the poem presents us with an illusion which may be truer than what, from any illusory vantage of perfected disenchantment, dissolves it? That the illimitable walk and the endless way, what Wordsworth for just this reason would never have called the *bad* infinity and the *good*, are almost indistinguishably intertangled with each other, is just the extent to which the wish for bliss has never yet appeared without illusion.

Hospitable stranger, indifferent neighbour. It is the firmest belief and dearest wish of indifferent neighbours that there are not and should not be any hospitable strangers. Fortunately the words *nostalgia, ideology, pastoral, utopianism* are ready, all the more serviceable for having been worn featureless, to block off that possibility. In this case it is worth pausing before sorting Wordsworth's near-indiscernible opposition between the illimitable walk and the endless way into one of those boxes. The account of his experiences in London and that of his memories of France are connected.

> Even files of Strangers merely, seen but once,
> And for a moment, men from far with sound
> Of music, martial tunes, and banners spread
> Entering the City, here and there a face
> Or person singled out among the rest,
> Yet still a stranger and beloved as such,
> Even by these passing spectacles my heart
> Was oftentimes uplifted, and they seem'd
> Like arguments from Heaven that 'twas a cause
> Good, and which no one could stand up against
> Who was not lost, abandon'd, selfish, proud,
> Mean, miserable, wilfully depraved,
> Hater perverse of equity and truth.
>
> (ix. 281–93)

Like the unmanageable sight of London, these too are 'spectacles', a word which has thus far appeared with a sense of suspicion surrounding it, because of the way in which the spectacle can lay the powers of the viewer asleep. The passage accelerates into a catalogue whose shape, the list, strongly recalls that of many passages in the account of Wordsworth's experience of London, except that this time the list of reproaches describes his then feelings about the opponents of the Revolution; describes, that is, those who cannot feel the power of this 'spectacle' rather than those who are unable to resist it. The relation between the two cities is peculiar. It is as true here as it is in London that the face of everyone who passes by Wordsworth is a mystery. Yet just the opposite conclusion is drawn. Not only did Wordsworth love the strangers who passed by, he says that he loved them *as strangers*. Just that which seemed to concentre the bad infiniteness of London, the face-after-face as against a face-to-face, is here what allows the intimation of that 'Bliss' which Wordsworth felt, and felt that everyone felt, simply by being alive in the Revolution.

It would be a mistake to delete this difficulty by forcing it too quickly into the broader rhetorical context of this book of the poem: by treating the passage, for example, as only another instance of the Quixotism which often attaches to revolutionary sentiment in the book. For that Quixotism in any case shares the equivocality which many readers have found in Cervantes. Michel Beaupuy

> thro' the events
> Of that great change wander'd in perfect faith,
> As through a Book, an old Romance or Tale
> Of Fairy, or some dream of actions wrought
> Behind the summer clouds. By birth he rank'd
> With the most noble, but unto the poor
> Among mankind he was in service bound
> As by some tie invisible, oaths profess'd
> To a religious Order. Man he lov'd
> As man; ...
>
> (ix. 305–14)

The 'illimitable walk' of the London streets now finds a further counterpart: the endless wanderings undertaken by poetic heroes in Ariosto's or Tasso's or Spenser's forests. Wordsworth later describes how he himself 'wander'd on' with Beaupuy through the forests in the Loire and allowed himself to imagine himself walking through the *Orlando Furioso* or the *Gerusalemme Liberata*. The implication is not that Beaupuy should, instead of 'wandering' through that time, have marched briskly through it from A to B. Instead the whole passage differentiates Beaupuy's 'perfect faith' from the principled apriorism which came to dominate revolutionary *raison d'état*. What marks the latter is continual self-legitimation, which Wordsworth came to think of as a sign that there was something going on that was difficult to justify.[24] The difference between Beaupuy's perfect faith and moral apriorism seems to be the difference between loving man as man and having a theory that one should do so.

The same modernity which brings us indifferent neighbours, then, appears to bring us, if not the beloved stranger, then the stranger beloved as such. Wordsworth sees how strange it is to love a stranger *as* a stranger. What appears in countless secular theodicies of the time not merely as something which is quite easily attainable, provided only that one have sufficient respect for the rational component of a rational animal, is for Wordsworth something so rarely found as to risk appearing Quixotic when it does. Despite the readiness with which Wordsworth has been understood as a humanist by admirers and critics alike, the word 'human' in his writing rarely signifies something whose meaning is altogether clear, and certainly not something which can readily be assimilated, for example, to the presence to itself of consciousness or any of the moral or social theories for which that metaphysic lays the ground. It is 'not a punctual Presence, but a Spirit / Living in time and space, and far diffused' (viii. 763–4). The human is not what we always in any case have as members of a set; yet nor is it empty abstract possibility floating free from our living bodies like the perennial ought. In the following chapter I turn to consider Wordsworth's sense of that 'life' which has so often been invoked in the course of this study.

CHAPTER 6

Life

'*Life* is a Term, none more familiar. Any one almost would take it for an Affront, to be asked what he meant by it. And yet if it comes in Question, whether a Plant, that lies ready formed in the Seed, have Life: whether the Embrio in an Egg before Incubation, or a Man in a Swound without Sense or Motion, be alive, or no, it is easy to perceive, that a clear distinct settled *Idea* does not always accompany the use of so known a Word, as that of *Life* is.'[1] It is irritating to have to think minutely about known words. It is especially irritating in connection with a poet who could write that a breeze in a spring wood could teach you more than anything in the library. Kierkegaard once mocked theologians who gave the impression that salvation depended upon keeping up with the literature. Wordsworth would have sympathized with that. Something of the same feeling can be heard in his remark to Crabb Robinson that 'he had never read a word of German metaphysics, thank Heaven!'[2] But today's super-subtlety can become tomorrow's common sense, and the question of 'Wordsworth and philosophy', which had perhaps been widely hoped finally exhausted, reopens continually. First of all because, as has already been suggested, the bad choice between Wordsworth as verse metaphysician and Wordsworth as anti-philosophical craftsman has been allowed to determine the terms of that question. But in the second place (and it is with this that this chapter will deal) because that determination has too often wanted to position Wordsworth on intellectual-historical maps which themselves become so abbreviated in the course of being invoked as means to interpreting his poetry – which so readily shrink to the labels, 'rationalism', 'empiricism', 'idealism' – as greatly to simplify and fore-shorten the ontological landscape in which Wordsworth's writing moves. This chapter will argue that quite a wide variety of interpretations of the philosophical background to Wordsworth's poetry have rested on broad narratives of seventeenth- and eighteenth-century philosophy which close down some of the most important possibilities which were in fact available; that there are good reasons for thinking that Wordsworth's own ways of thinking about that aspect of intellectual history, despite (or because of) his suspicion of technical philosophy and the limits on the time which he wished to give to reading it, was in significant ways shaped differently from the shared narrative of contemporary interpretation; and that whatever might be of real philosophical interest in his 'philosophic song' – whatever, that is, opens up possibilities for thinking which exceed what is available from technical philosophy – emerges from elective affinities between the syntax and lexicon of his verse and suppressed or marginalized features of philosophical writing itself. The result of the chapter is to increase, rather than reduce, the difficulty of providing a sketch map of Wordsworth's philosophical 'opinions'. It hopes to show that some important features of what Wordsworth thought about the kinds of issue which were increasingly being reserved to philosophy in this period have simply been overlooked because they do not fit in with what we already think we know about Wordsworth.

WORDSWORTH AND THE PHILOSOPHERS

Among the most resonant attempts to think about the relation between philosophy and poetry in Wordsworth's writing have been those of Paul de Man. De Man's critics have of course been able to foreground the violence of his reading.[3] But when the critic's alternative is brought forward, we at once remember what was valuable in de Man, and which has not been foregrounded: a determination to continue to think about the relation between philosophy and poetry and not to be bullied out of it by the bad choice between metaphysics-in-verse and sheer craft. De Man's revision of his own question about Wordsworth remains exemplary: 'is he a poet or a philosopher – or, somewhat less naïvely put, what is it in his work that forces upon us, for reasons that philosophy itself may not be able to master, this question of the compatibility between philosophy and poetry?'[4] De Man and others pursuing this question open up a special field of interest: a region between the understanding of Wordsworth's poetry as versified philosophy, and the insistence on its autonomously poetic, i.e. cognitively empty, character. In some of the adverse commentary on de Man since his death, the object has, perhaps, been not merely to contest de Man's singular way of writing this field, but actually to close down the space for it altogether: and thus to end for good the privileging of philosophizing interpretation of philosophical poetry; and thus to recover all the lived historical particularity which that privileging is understood to have suppressed.

Rodolphe Gasché has recently argued that a powerful impulse behind de Man's anti-systematic yet closely self-interwoven essays is a (paradoxical) 'systematic denunciation' of all 'figures of totalization'. This is a denunciation 'conducted in the name of what I [Gasché] shall call the "absolutely singular," that is, a singularity so singular as to defy all relationality – a singularity, hence, that would indeed be idiosyncratic in an absolute sense'. This is an 'absolutely singular that at the limit, and unlike Adorno's nonidentical, rebuffs all attempts at intelligibility'.[5] Although Gasché has little to say about the work on Wordsworth, the idea helps us to understand that part of the authorship. What de Man made it impossible for later reading not to consider in Wordsworth is the insufficiency of chiasmic or dialectical models for understanding the ontologies implied or invoked in passing or at length in his poetry. The idea of a simple shuttling back and forth between mind and nature of the same spiritual capital is one which in Wordsworth finds, not the grand secret, but the image of 'dejection'. There has to be something 'more' than this, otherwise the whole game is peculiarly dismal: we take out of nature, pointlessly, only the spiritual assets we have first banked. In this sense the charge of 'nihilism' sometimes sent the way of such interpretations is too abbreviated, because it fails to see that one important impulse which lies behind them is, rather, averse to the nihilisms which inhabit modern common senses: that you only get out what you put in, that nothing will come of nothing, and that there is no such thing as a free lunch. I think it is partly because they seize the aspect of Wordsworth's writing that does not fit in with this sort of zero-sum game that de Man's interpretations of Wordsworth continue to exert a pull even after their inaccuracies or 'violences' have been catalogued. The apparent melodrama of discovering this 'more' in irreducible arbitrariness, blindness and death would not exert the fascination it does, did it not, however hopelessly, shelter all those hopes which a cost-accountancy of meaning would delete. Why else must the dead, decaying, or mutilated human body be returned to ever and again? Not because that is really what is wished for but, on the contrary, because it seems better to promise what might really be alive than the nihilated theory of the living, healthy and whole one. Whenever the human is made to consist in the rational bit of a rational animal it at once feels not only not human but barely alive; it is as though the human is so frail that it is visible only where it is about to go over into the inhuman, into rocks or stones or trees. Yet

finally to sink hopes into the damage undergone by that damaged
countenance would be the most forlorn fixation, and its terminus the
need to prove that nothing can possibly have been lost, by proving that
none was given in the first place. 'He inscribes the eye / I in the face of the
mother. In the slippage of a pun or a pen (or a pen-knife?), the child
"slashes" the eye of the mother.' Translation: 'Rest in peace! The love you
fear was always already *positing!*'[6]

   In a note to the last chapter I suggested that it was a task still remaining
to philology to detach Wordsworth from Hegel in the right way, always
assuming that such a way be in fact available. One key moment in the
way Wordsworth and Hegel have been associated and disassociated can be
found in Paul de Man's reading of 'Time and History in Wordsworth'. In
the course of an account of the interest of Geoffrey Hartman's study of
Wordsworth, de Man also demurs:

We cannot follow him in speaking of an apocalyptic temptation in Wordsworth.
The passages that Hartman singles out as apocalyptic never suggest a movement
towards an unmediated contact with a divine principle. The imagination is said to
be 'like an unfather'd vapour' and is, as such, entirely cut off from ultimate origins;
it gives sight of 'the invisible world' [536], but the invisibility refers to the mental,
inward nature of this world as opposed to the world of the senses; it reveals to us
that our home is 'with infinity', but within the language of the passage this infinity
is clearly to be understood in a temporal sense as the futurity of 'something
evermore about to be'. The heightening of pitch is not the result of 'unmediated
vision', but of another mediation, in which the consciousness does not relate itself
any longer to nature but to a temporal entity. This entity could, with proper
qualifications, be called history, and it is indeed in connection with historical
events (the French Revolution) that the apostrophe to Imagination comes to be
written. But if we call this history, then we must be careful to understand that it is
the kind of history that appeared at the end of the Duddon sonnet, the retrospective recording of man's failure to overcome the power of time.[7]

   Attention to this sort of passage in de Man's thinking since this essay
was published has usually focussed on the way of putting the relation
between 'time' and 'history' which it arrives at. David Bromwich provides
a chiasmic vignette of a central aspect of Wordsworth-reception in the last
two decades: 'Much of the argument about his poetry in the latter half of
the twentieth century has involved those who want to translate History
into Time against those who want to trace Time into History' (although
it is doubtful whether what the words, in this particular case, say could be
read as performing the kind of 'translation' which Bromwich mentions).[8]
Here I should like to look at a different aspect of the passage. It is how far

the passage goes in denying the invocation of immediacy in Wordsworth's writing. It is not only that de Man does not believe there is any invocation of an immediate contact with the divine in Wordsworth's writing; but, more remarkably, that there is never any 'movement' towards such a moment, so that Hartman is wrong even to speak of an apocalyptic 'temptation' in Wordsworth's writing. Certainly, Hartman 'has noticed, more clearly than most other interpreters, that the imagination in Wordsworth is independent of nature and that it leads him to write a language, at his best moments, that is entirely unrelated to the exterior stimuli of the senses'.[9] This is what is to be praised in Hartman's reading. This absence of an invocation of 'immediate vision' thus accepts Hartman's qualifications to the notion that everything subjective is always found to be mediated by 'nature' in Wordsworth but uses them to move instead to a further mediation, the mediation of consciousness itself by a peculiar kind of time or history, and thus, implicitly, the impossibility of ever finding a point at which consciousness is present to itself. The absence of an immediate vision of divinity is thus linked to the absence of immediate self-presence of any kind. If a certain supposed Hegelianism of Hartman's is being rejected here, then, it is not being rejected because Hegel or Hartman give too little room to immediacy, but too much. For Hegel, whenever we appeal to immediacy, we always find that our appeal was itself a kind of mediation. Sheer immediacy is thus not susceptible of statement. Yet for de Man this is not enough. There is a 'further' mediation which is to remove the very 'movement' towards or 'temptation' towards immediate vision.

Whatever we think about the entire history of de Man's relation to Heidegger, it is clear that this sort of work could not have arisen without Heidegger's interpretation of the *cogito* and his dismantling of the metaphysics of presence to consciousness. (The 'kind of history' constituted by 'the retrospective recording of man's failure to overcome the power of time' would hardly have been imaginable without Heidegger's idea of histor*icity*.) But woven into that dismantling, as we shall now see, lies in fact an *acceptance*, not of Descartes's original insight, but of a *lapsed* Cartesianism in which the *cogito* is my act of representing *to* myself.

WHAT IS CALLED THINKING?

What do we mean when we say 'thinking'? Here is one kind of answer:

We have thus already before us a putative science, built on the single proposition I t h i n k; and we can, in accordance with the nature of a transcendental philosophy, quite appropriately investigate its ground or groundlessness. One should not be brought up short by the fact that I have an inner experience of this proposition, which expresses the perception of oneself, and hence that the rational doctrine of the soul that is built on it is never pure but is grounded in part on an empirical principle. For this inner perception is nothing beyond the mere apperception I t h i n k, which even makes all transcendental concepts possible, which say 'I think substance, cause, etc.' ... The least object of perception (e.g., pleasure or displeasure) which might be added to the general representation of self-consciousness, would at once transform rational psychology into an empirical psychology.[10]

In this interpretation, it is part of the essence of thinking that it not be contaminated by any object of perception. In giving this interpretation of thinking, an interpretation of affectivity has also been given at the same time. Affectivity – pleasure or displeasure, for example – is an *object* of perception. This decisively constitutes the 'inner experience' which is spoken of here. It is experience without affectivity. It must be so, because were this experience in any way to be affective, the least addition of pleasure or displeasure would mean that this would no longer be inner but outer experience. And the psychology based on it would no longer be something which thinking alone might undertake, that is, a 'rational psychology'. It would be an 'empirical psychology', a science to which experience of objects – here, of 'objects' such as pleasure or displeasure – is indispensable. To the very extent that experience experiences affectivity, it is no longer an experience of thinking. The extent to which this can be called 'experience' remains a significant problem for this way of thinking about thinking.

Here are other answers to the question of what we mean when we say 'thinking':

It is true that no one can be certain that he is thinking or that he exists unless he knows what thought is and what existence is. But this does not require reflective knowledge, or the kind of knowledge that is acquired by means of demonstrations; still less does it require knowledge of reflective knowledge, i.e. knowing that we know, and knowing that we know that we know, and so on *ad infinitum*. This kind of knowledge cannot possibly be obtained about anything. It is quite sufficient that we should know it by that internal awareness which always precedes reflective knowledge.[11]

9. What is meant by thought. By the term 'thought', I understand everything which we are aware of as happening within us, in so far as we have awareness of it. Hence, *thinking* is to be identified here not merely with understanding, willing and imagining, but also with sensory awareness. For if I say 'I am seeing, or I am walking, therefore I exist', and take this as applying to vision or walking as bodily activities, then the conclusion is not absolutely certain. This is because, as often happens during sleep, it is possible for me to think I am seeing or walking, though my eyes are closed and I am not moving about; such thoughts might even be possible if I had no body at all. But if I take 'seeing' or 'walking' to apply to the actual sense or awareness of seeing or walking, then the conclusion is quite certain, since it relates to the mind, which alone has the sensation or thought that it is seeing or walking.[12]

Among the things which it is sometimes thought that Descartes did to us all is to inaugurate a dualism between mind and body in which knowing, truth, and meaning are reserved exclusively to the former, and in which the latter counts as a kind of mechanical vehicle, devoid of significance until mind should bestow it. The view is conveniently abbreviated by Gilbert Ryle, who gives an account of '[t]he official doctrine, which hails mostly from Descartes' at the beginning of *The Concept of Mind*: an official doctrine of which he promises that he shall often speak 'with deliberate abusiveness, as "the dogma of the Ghost in the Machine"'. (Ryle's expression may be a variant upon Maritain's formally similar but semantically opposed expression: 'the angel in the machine'.)[13] From such a turn of phrase it appears to follow very naturally that we should go the whole way and have the ghost exorcised too. What if, however, what is in the machine is not a ghost at all? Perhaps a still more influential reading of the *cogito* than Ryle's (and certainly one which, through its various literary-theoretical tributaries, has borne more forcefully upon Wordsworth criticism) was that offered by Martin Heidegger in the section 'Das cogito Descartes als cogito me cogitare' from the second volume of his lectures on Nietzsche. Heidegger justly points out that we sometimes too hurriedly think we know what is meant by thinking:

We translate *cogitare* by 'thinking' and thus persuade ourselves that it is now already clear what Descartes means by *cogitare*. As though we knew at once what 'thinking' is, and as though, above all, with our notion of 'thinking' taken, perhaps, from some textbook of 'logic', we might be sure of hitting upon exactly that which Descartes wants to say with the word *cogitare*. In important passages Descartes employs for *cogitare* the word *percipere* (*per-capio*) – to take possession of something, to master a thing, and here indeed in the sense of a placing-to-oneself of the type of a placing-before-oneself, a re-presentation [*im Sinne des Sich-zu-stellens von der Art des Vor-sich-stellens*, des '*Vor-stellens*']. If we understand *cogitare* as re-presentation in this literal sense of placing-before, then we already come closer to the Cartesian concept of *cogitatio* and *perceptio*.[14]

For Heidegger the *ego cogito* is essentially a representation, a placing of what is represented before the self: 'Because in every representing there is a representing person *to whom* what is represented in representation is presented, the representing person is involved with and in every representing – not subsequently, but in advance, in that he, the one who is placing *before* [or re-presenting] brings what is represented before *himself*.'[15] Despite its reception history, Heidegger's attentive reading ought really to make it harder, rather than easier, to place Descartes in a simple narrative of the inauguration of modern rationalism and of the modern subject. Nevertheless, as a group of French phenomenologists and Descartes scholars, and above all the 'material phenomenologist' Michel Henry, have demonstrated, it rests upon a decisive prior interpretation: the interpretation 'that *cogito* means "I represent". Hence there is no conclusion leading from *cogito* to *sum*, but merely the recognition of an "I" who is necessarily deployed in the structure of representation and who, finally, is identical with it.'[16]

Henry argues that this is a significant misreading of Descartes's fundamental proposition, a misreading which is not simply Heidegger's mistake but which confirms Descartes's own later misreading of his own central insight, a misreading later continued in the Kantian paralogisms. Henry draws a distinction between what he calls 'beginning Cartesianism', the Cartesianism of the central insight, and a latter Cartesianism which loses this insight. Henry's re-reading of the Cartesian *cogito* depends upon an exact attention to the precise sense of the terms in which it is written. It depends upon the recovery of those terms from what they have been made to mean in the philosophical history determined by latter Cartesianism. Above all it depends upon a recovery of the sense of *thinking*, and of *res cogitans*, from the over-hasty identification of these terms with 'representation to consciousness'. It is precisely because he does not understand thinking as 'representation to consciousness', Henry argues, that he responds so vehemently to Bourdin:

He removes the true and most clearly intelligible feature which differentiates corporeal things from incorporeal ones, *viz.* that the latter think, but not the former; and in its place he substitutes a feature which cannot in any way be regarded as essential, namely that incorporeal things reflect on their thinking, but corporeal ones do not. Hence he does everything he can to hinder our understanding of the real distinction between the human mind and the body.[17]

(Heidegger repeats Bourdin's interpretation in the very title of this passage on Descartes: *Das cogito Descartes als cogito me cogitare*. Indeed as early as the *Introduction to Phenomenological Research* (1923–4) he can identify Descartes's *cogito als cogito me cogitare* with Husserl's *Reflexion*.[18]) 'Thinking', as Descartes understands it, thus has 'nothing to do with what we now call "thought," with thinking that . . . judging that . . . considering that . . ."[19] Instead it signifies the radical difference of original appearance from what appears, the ontological difference between Being and beings, the refusal to ground Being on beings.

If we compare Heidegger's passage with those from Descartes and Kant offered above we can see that something strange has happened to the way Descartes is understood. Descartes makes it extremely clear that the *cogito* is not first of all reflective knowledge. It is not thinking-about, thinking-that, judging-that, representing-that *x*. It is first of all *that I experience*. For this reason, then, what 'thinking' means here is something quite different from what it has come to mean in most post-Cartesian thought and the common sense determined by it. It does not mean – what I have left when I have erased all trace of affectivity, of desire, of the senses, so that, as it were, I should be left with pure reflection, the 'I think' which accompanies all my representations. What I bracket out is not affect but transcendence: the existence of exterior objects of which I cannot be certain. So far is affectivity from being an exterior object that Descartes can say, quite explicitly, that '*thinking* is to be identified here not merely with understanding, willing and imagining, but also with sensory awareness'.

This sense for the word 'thinking' changes the geography of every other fundamental question. '[T]he actual sense or awareness' is what is meant by *cogito*. What we do when we hunger, when we are in terror, when we desire, is part of thinking. What we are hungry for, what we desire, what we are terrified of, may or may not exist. Of that we cannot be certain. What we cannot not be certain of is that we are hungering, terrified, desiring. This means first of all that, although the dualism between mind and body is every bit as absolute as it has always been considered in Descartes's work, the two sides of the dualism do not mean the same as what we have come usually to mean by mind and body. There are thus as it were two bodies in Descartes. There is the objective body, my body which I may *have* and which I can myself see or touch, whose existence I may doubt in so far as it appears to me as an object; and there is the subjective body, that is to say, the body who I *am*, whose being I cannot doubt however hard I try. This body is part of what Descartes calls *res cogitans*, and its experiences are 'thinking'. This 'changes the geography' in the specific sense that the writing of the Cartesian 'world' with which we have become familiar through Heidegger's interpretation[20] and through the numerous post- and anti-humanist tributaries of that interpretation, that this story is only half the story. If 'to think' can no longer be understood as 'to represent to myself', what this means is that thinking is no longer primarily this arbitrary power by which man is the measure and lord of beings, able freely to order, combine, divide his ideas, sensations or impressions, but, first of all and not at all in my power, what I am. And it follows that this beginning Cartesianism is, in fact, not a humanism in the sense which Heidegger's famous letter on that topic wished (in the service of *humanitas*) to overcome.[21]

It is hard to keep hold of this thought, because the notion that what thinking means is something opposed to sensory awareness, the notion that thinking is reflection, has become so powerfully embedded as common sense. It was hard, indeed, for Descartes himself. As Henry has shown, in his brilliant and also minutely close re-reading, there are for this reason also two Descartes: the Descartes for whom suffering and desiring are also thinking; and the Descartes who, later, and against his own essential insight, instead of beginning always from an affective awareness which he cannot doubt, begins to interpret suffering and desiring instead as effects of beings whose very existence cannot certainly be known, effects *presented to* a consciousness which is now understood as defined by intentional clarity and distinctness. The contrast between the beginning Descartes and the later Descartes can be well grasped by the shift in the way the term 'idea' is understood. Descartes affirms that 'I did not doubt that I "had a clear idea of my mind," since I had a close inner awareness of it. Nor did I doubt that "this idea was quite different from the ideas of other things".'[22] This view is confirmed by the definition which Descartes gives of the term. '*Idea*. I understand this term to mean the form of any given thought, immediate perception of which makes me aware of the thought.'[23] The idea is not, for example, a proposition but, for example, the immediate perception which makes me aware of it. In this interpretation it is clear that the (phenomenological) 'clarity' of an idea and its *affectivity* are one and the same. But as Descartes's train of thinking proceeds to deal with 'the body' and with external sources of affectivity, affectivity increasingly gets represented as what clouds clarity, what makes it, that is, 'obscure'. It is then an easy step to begin to think (or rather to resume thinking, since it is this way of *opposing* mind to affectivity that has a heavy tradition behind it) that the pursuit of certain knowledge requires the decontamination of affectivity from thinking: that affectivity in which the very possibility of the *cogito*'s certainty has already been grounded!²⁴ It is *this* latter Descartes whose thought is most influentially transmitted through his disciples and his opponents alike; *this* conception of thinking as reflection or activity or representation; of affectivity as exterior objectivity represented to consciousness; and the other Descartes, the Descartes of the suffering-desiring-thinking subject, who goes under.

Or rather, who almost goes under. The conception of subjectivity as always and necessarily affective, rather than always presented with affectivity as a transcendent object of merely possible existence, nevertheless continues to surface. This has its ground in the nature of the case, in the impossibility of imagining reflection without affective immediacy. And this is what also means that so many of the route maps taken from intellectual history and applied to literature are faulty. As Jean-Luc Marion has pointed out:

It appears incoherent on the one hand to admit, with Hegel, Husserl and Heidegger, that all modern thought of subjectivity depends from top to bottom on the *ego cogito* instituted by Descartes, and on the other hand to claim to interpret this subjectivity with the help of concepts which, far from preceding it, one and all result from it, as, precisely, intentionality and representation. If only the *ego cogito* makes the deployment of representation possible, then, through representation, that of intentionality, it must in principle *exclude* the possibility that the model of representation or intentionality could suffice to make intelligible the *ego cogito*.²⁵

When Blake asserts that 'This Lifes dim Windows of the Soul / Distorts the Heavens from Pole to Pole / And lead you to Believe a Lie / When you see with not thro the Eye', the thought, for all the supposed 'subversion' of rationalism, etc. attributed to Blake, is a direct development of an idea of Descartes: 'it is the soul which sees, *and not* the eye'.²⁶ The long-standing difficulty of understanding Blake's double attitude to the body – an attitude in which bodily delight is prized and defended, yet in which worlds can be understood as 'clos'd by your senses five' – arises partly because we ourselves so readily think in terms determined by the second Cartesian dualism, even while we claim to be labouring to subvert, blur or overcome it. Blake's formulation of an opposition between the *spiritual body* – the body which I am, the body which imagines and suffers and desires – and the *natural body* – the body, and the senses, as they are conceived of by empiricism – is quite unintelligible from an empiricist, or a transcendental idealist, or a standard-rationalist viewpoint; the only philosophical option in terms of which it makes sense is this beginning Cartesianism, elements of which Blake probably found in Berkeley. This is an opposition to 'blur' which is not for Blake an imaginative or subversive emancipation, but *idolatry*. 'The hard and wiry line' between life and death must be graven ever more deeply. It is one of the lines of which it may be said: 'Leave out this line, and you leave out life itself.'[27]

It is by no means necessary to adhere to Henry's programme of 'material phenomenology', then, to see how his attention to Descartes illuminates in one of its important sources a fundamental tension subsisting in the ways that thinking, subjectivity and affectivity have been thought about since.[28] The possibility of a phenomenology of the subjective body is always potentially open. Sometimes it may open up inadvertently even where the primary aim is to close it. But this also means that, from one point of view, a question which has so often seemed central to literary historians of Romanticism – the question of 'dualism' and its overcoming or subversion or displacement or dismantling – is by itself not nearly precisely enough formulated. Because if the meaning which is given to each half of that dualism is understood in accordance with Kant's lapsed Cartesianism – the empty representing form marshalling intuition which is featureless until determined by the concept – it matters not in the least whether these empty halves should be added up together or left apart from each other. Indeed, one can go further: lapsed Cartesianism is not really a dualism at all, but a monism, because the sceptical bracketing of transcendence has then been read back into what makes that bracketing possible in the first place, with the result of a comprehensive nihilation of all the terms available: with the result, in the end, of the conception of the path of truth as a highway of negation.[29] '[A]s precondition of representation, of objectivity, the Cartesian cogito is already a Kantian cogito ... deprived of its radical interiority, reduced to a seeing, a precondition of objectivity and representation, taken instead as constitutive of and identical with that structure, the subject's subjectivity is nothing but the object's objectivity.'[30] This is the monism of 'All is meer outside'.[31] It is not a true sublation of the difference between the interior and the exterior, because the interior has been destroyed or evacuated before the sublation takes place.[32]

Perhaps we are in a position to think about the possible consequences of some of these considerations for reading the interpretations of 'life' that inevitably subsist in literary works even where those works understand themselves precisely in opposition to any philosophical discussion of this kind of question. One important motive behind Heidegger's interpretation of the *cogito* as representation, and his sense of its epochal decisiveness to a historical situation in which humans think of themselves as the 'masters of beings' rather than as 'shepherds of Being',[33] is to open up the possibility of another way of understanding what *life* is than that which he finds in Descartes. The contrast is especially evident if we compare the treatment of animals in *The Fundamental Concepts of Western Metaphysics*, for example, with Descartes's view of animals as not essentially different from machines. In the wake of this rethinking it has been an obvious step to understand writers as different as Wordsworth and Blake as fundamentally motivated by a desire to overturn Cartesian dualism. This is understandable, because when *cogito* is read as 'reflection' we have, precisely, a completed 'universe of death'. Bodies, as *res extensa*, cannot be understood as emphatically alive. Yet when interpreted as a pure act of *reflection*, the *cogito*, as empty of all affectivity, has also been emptied of everything which makes life life. As we have seen, Descartes himself came partly to read himself in this way. Yet the doubleness of Descartes's texts means that the same enterprise which grounds the project of a universal mathesis at the same time opens up precisely the area which refuses such mathesis: a life which can never be understood as an object, that life which I am. This is historiographically surprising only if we uncritically accept a scientistic reading of Descartes's authorship. We should remember that while from one point of view that body of work aims to ground the possibility of finally securable results in the sciences, from another, it is – not at all merely influenced by, but pre-cisely the most powerful of many *continuations* of – Augustine's description of the life of the soul.[34] Although lapsed Cartesianism is generally supposed to be suffering the agonies of unbridgeable dualism, its component parts in fact sort rather well together, because in it the *cogito* has retrospectively been reinterpreted on the model of *res extensa*. Life, except as an object, has been expelled from both. In beginning Cartesianism, on the other hand, a fundamental difference is torn open which it has been the vain labour of much philosophy ever since to close: the difference between the living and the non-living.

'[?LIF]'

'Wordsworth copied quotations from Descartes into DC MS 31, leaves 71–2, *c*. Feb. 1801. They appear to have been copied from C's own transcriptions and do not imply serious study of Descartes by W (though it should be noted that two books by Descartes were retained at Rydal

Mount; see Shaver 76). Significantly, C's first serious study of Descartes also dates from Feb. 1801 . . .'[35] This is reasonable, except that it may not be quite accurate to say that the copyings *do* not imply serious study. They *need* not imply serious study, certainly. But they also prove that Wordsworth (who so disliked the physical act of writing and who so often had others do it for him) was interested enough in these quotations to write them down himself. Duncan Wu is usefully sceptical, here as often in his indispensable work, about the extent of Wordsworth's interest in technical philosophy; and the fact that these quotations also appear in the letters which Coleridge was writing at this time to Josiah Wedgwood makes it almost certain that Coleridge was Wordsworth's source. The same provider is now usually named as the origin of Wordsworth's acquaintance with the dream-narrative by Descartes which is an important source for the dream of the 'Semi-Quixote' Bedouin in book 5 of the 1805–6 poem to Coleridge. These views together have made it easy for critics not to pursue a possible pattern of a Wordsworthian interest in Descartes. Few of the many readings of the relevant passage of book 5 since Jane Worthington Smyser discovered the source have wanted to say much about the striking fact that a dream of *Descartes's* should figure at this point in the poem.[36] It may not be accidental to this reluctance that many of the readings are proposing the passage as a sort of dismantling of what is often supposed to be a Cartesian set of presuppositions, or a set to which Descartes gave an especially fateful modern formulation.

Some of the quotations are in fact particularly interesting for the way in which they bring to light aspects of Descartes often overlooked by our maps of 'Cartesianism'. This is a passage from Coleridge's letter to Wedgwood of 18 February 1801. The italicized passage was all that Wordsworth copied from it into his notebook.

In the Objectiones Tertiae, which were undoubtedly written by Hobbes, the word Idea is obstinately taken for Image, and it is objected to the Passage '*nullam* Dei habem<u>us</u> imaginem sive ideam.' To which Des Cartes answers 'Hîc nomine ideae vult tantum intelligi imagines rerum materialium in phantasiâ corporeâ depictas, quo posito facile illi est probare, nullam Angeli nec Dei propriam ideam esse posse; atqui ego passim ubique, ac praecipue hoc ipso in loco ostendo me nomen ideae sumere *pro omni eo quod immediate a mente percipitur, adeo ut cum volo et timeo, quia simul percipio me velle et timere, ipsa Volitio et Timor inter Ideas a me numerentur, ususque sum hoc verbo, quia jam tritum erat a Philosophis &c; et nullum aptis habebam*[']. ['Here my critic wants the term "idea" to be taken to refer simply to the images of material things which are depicted in the corporeal imagination; and if this is granted, it is easy for him to prove that there can be no proper idea of an angel or of God. But I make it quite clear in several places throughout the book, and in this passage in particular, that I am taking the word "idea" *to refer to whatever is immediately perceived by the mind. For example, when I want something, or am afraid of something, I simultaneously perceive that I want, or am afraid; and this is why I count volition and fear among my ideas. I used the word "idea" because it was the standard philosophical term used. . . . And besides, there was not any more appropriate term at my disposal.'*] Locke in his second Letter to the B. of Worcester gives the same definition and assigns the same Reason; he would willingly change the Term 'Idea' for a Better, if any one could help him to it. But he finds none that stands so well *'for every immediate object of the mind in thinking, as Idea does'*. As Des Cartes & Locke perfectly coincide in the meaning of the *Term* Ideas, so likewise do they equally agree as to their Sorts and Sources. I have read Mr Locke's Book with Care, and I cannot suppress my feelings of unpleasant doubt & wonder, which his frequent claims to originality raised in me; . . .[37]

The passage confirms the inadequacy, outlined above, of understanding *cogito* as 'reflection' or 'self-consciousness' in Descartes. Volition and fear are counted among my ideas. But Coleridge's larger rhetorical purpose – the depreciation of Locke's originality – leads him to overstate the coincidence between Locke and Descartes. In fact the passage from Locke's letter which Coleridge quotes indicates this. 'Idea' does not stand in Descartes for 'every immediate *object* of the mind in thinking'. Volition and fear are not only *objects* of thinking. For the 'beginning' Descartes, they *are* thinking. There is no trace of *that* Descartes in Locke. So he goes missing from Coleridge's account too. The difficulty reappears when Coleridge describes a passage from Locke's *Essay* as 'almost a free translation' of another quotation from Descartes. Locke suggests that

[t]he mind receiving certain ideas from without, when it turns it's view inward upon itself and observes it's actions about those Ideas, it has, takes from thence other ideas, which are as capable to be the Objects of it's Contemplation as any of those, it derives from foreign Things. Likewise the Mind often exercises an active power in making several combinations: for it being furnished with simple Ideas, it can put them together in several compositions, and so make variety of complex ideas without examining whether they exist so in nature.[38]

The text and note from Descartes of which this is supposed to feel like a free translation run as follows.

Among my ideas, some appear to be innate, some to be adventitious, and others to have been invented by me. My understanding of what a thing is, what truth is, and what thought is, seems to derive simply from my own nature. But my hearing a noise, as I do now, or seeing the sun, or feeling the fire, comes from things which are located outside me, or so I have hitherto judged. Lastly, sirens, hippogriffs and the like are my own invention. But perhaps all my ideas may be thought of as adventitious, or they may all be innate, or all made up; for as yet I have not clearly perceived their true origin.[39]

(Again the italicized passage is that copied by Wordsworth.) Even if one sets aside the pertinent point that the passages are not comparable, because whilst Locke's makes a firm assertion, Descartes's clearly signals itself as a point in a narrative of a course of introspection not yet completed, it is still difficult to believe the passages so similar as Coleridge thinks them. Locke could hardly entertain in Descartes's sense the notion that 'my understanding of what a thing is, what truth is, and what thought is, seems to derive simply from my own nature'. For Locke each of these ideas is a complex idea built up inductively from simple ideas. The connection that Coleridge sees, of course, is in Locke's reference to the mind's observation of its own 'actions', and in the possibility that both therefore have a kindred account of innate ideas as referring not to propositions innately known, but to the operations and activities of the faculty of thinking itself. But the self-consciousness described by Locke – the ideas at which the mind arrives by reflection upon its own operations – is not what Descartes means by saying that my understanding of what a thing is may derive from my own nature. For Descartes I know what a thing is because I know what I am. *Res cogitans* derives its meaning from the fact that I am, thinking. First of all and as the condition of possibility of any other knowledge I know that I am. This difference becomes clear in the last of the quotations from Descartes which Wordsworth copied, this time in full, into his notebook:

In article *twelve* the author's disagreement with me seems to be merely verbal. When he says that the mind has no need of ideas, or notions, or axioms which are innate, while admitting that the mind has the power of thinking (presumably natural or innate), he is plainly saying the same thing as I, though verbally denying it. I have never written or taken the view that the mind requires innate ideas which are something distinct from its own faculty of thinking. I did, however, observe that there were certain thoughts within me which neither came to me from external objects nor were determined by my will, but which came solely from the power of thinking within me; so I applied the term 'innate' to the ideas or notions which are the forms of these thoughts in order to distinguish them from others, which I called 'adventitious' or 'made up'. This is the same sense as that in which we say that generosity is 'innate' in certain families, or that certain diseases such as gout or stones are innate in others: it is not so much that the babies of such families suffer fom these diseases in their mother's womb, but simply that they are born with a certain 'faculty' or tendency to contract them.[40]

It is not difficult to see why Coleridge seizes on this passage. Like the others, it appears to confirm that Descartes did not any more than Locke believe in 'innate ideas', in the sense in which Locke wished to attack them. But the contrast with the quotation Coleridge elsewhere gives from Locke, with the mind's sortings, combinings and other classificatory activities, is striking when Descartes writes of 'certain thoughts within me which neither came to me from external objects nor were determined by my will, but which came solely from the power of thinking within me'. The source which Descartes names, neither external objects nor determined by the will, is neither active nor passive. It is a 'power of thinking within me', and thus appears to be active; yet this 'power' is in fact not under my control, it is not 'determined by my will', and thus appears to be passive. It is thus strangely ambiguous because it *is* me: it is that in my experience which I cannot doubt however hard I try.

It is unlikely that Wordsworth took the trouble to copy passages from Descartes because he was interested, like Coleridge, in settling a question of intellectual priority, or even in Coleridge's broader aim of rewriting the historiography of modern philosophy. It is much more likely that he wrote down what he did because he was interested in what Descartes was saying. What Wordsworth leaves out in his transcription of the reply to Hobbes's objection is striking, because it leaves out what was the point of the reply: the demonstration that it was possible to have an idea of God. What Wordsworth finds interesting enough to write down, instead, is the explanation of why volition and fear are counted among my ideas. The passage thus loses, in being excerpted, any reminder of its place in an argument for the idea of God, and stands instead as an account of affective subjectivity as such. The idea that to desire and to fear is part of what it is to *think*, the idea that desire and fear are not 'stimuli' or results of stimuli which reflection then processes so as to make knowledge, but themselves knowledge: this idea is, as I have suggested, a possibility which repeatedly reopens in thinking of this epoch.

A self-vexing or desperate passage of drafting from Wordsworth's work towards book 13 of the poem to Coleridge illustrates this:

> { And
> { [?] chiefly must such [?men have] been trained up   [XIII, c 71–3]

To stand in awe of mighty presences
Tha~~t somethin in himself that is not though~~t
~~But more~~
Image or consciousness but more than these
And deeper that whereby [?thinks and] & makes
One
Himself & that whereby he thinks & is
That somethin in himself that is not though
              but the power
[?Image] ~~& consciousness~~ but Where whereby
          And [?Lif]
              in the [?soul] to Human life
And last the great feeling of the world   [182–4]
God & the immortaity of life
[?Beneath] being ever more to be[41]

The relationship between this and any passage of book 13 as it stands in any more extended manuscript is distant indeed. Reed's parenthetical nominations of the passages in the AB-stage text for which these might be considered drafts are reproduced where he places them. His AB-stage reading text for xiii, 71–3 reads:

> That is exalted by an underpresence,
> The sense of God, or whatsoe'er is dim
> Or vast in its own being; above all [...][42]

If 1ᵛ of DC MS 38 is indeed drafting for this, it is drafting at such an early stage that the relation between the two is now almost unrecognizable. Reed's footnote to his transcription remarks that 'entry is draft toward "Higher Mind" material developed further on 7ᵛ–8ʳ.'[43] 7ᵛ and 8ʳ themselves, however, are hardly closer to the material on 1ᵛ than is Reed's AB-stage reading text, so that they are 'developed' out of it, if at all, only in a loose thematic sense rather than in a closely textual one. The core of the material on 1ᵛ is a kind of relentless negation, whether in the words themselves or by the physical act of striking through, of the available language for describing 'somethin in himself':

> Tha~~t somethin in himself that is not though~~t
> ~~But more~~
> Image or consciousness but more than these
> And deeper that whereby [?thinks and] & makes
> One

> Himself & that whereby he thinks & is
> That somethin in himself that is not though
>   but the power
> [?Image] &~~consciousness~~ but Where whereby
> And [?Lif]

Not an image, not consciousness, and not 'thought / But more' (a thought which is itself crossed out and then returned to, but this time without the 'more'). What is it, then? The terms that are allowed to stand are 'that whereby he thinks', 'the power' (with the implication that Wordsworth will go on to say the power *of* something or other) and '[?Lif]': perhaps the beginning of the word 'Life'. Wordsworth seems to be trying to articulate something which is not thought, yet which is in the subject and which makes thought possible. It is not consciousness, the faculty of organizing or combining or reflecting upon my impressions; yet nor is it impression, an 'image'. Some of the key terms in the passages transcribed in Coleridge's letters are here in play. Even though 'thought' here appears clearly to be used in a non-Cartesian way, as equivalent to 'reflection', it implicitly shares with Descartes's account of what is native to the mind the negation of both sheer passivity and sheer activity: 'the power', whatever it is, which makes thinking (in the sense of reflection) possible, is perhaps something like 'Life' itself, a life upon which the language and concepts of reflection and representation are always dependent, and whose attempts to capture it are therefore not themselves foundational, but after the fact, and so must proceed through a series of negations. This possibility is further suggested by what immediately follows, with its apparent attempt to address a specifically 'Human' life.

> in the [?soul] to Human life
> And last the great feeling of the world   [182–4]
> God & the immortaity of life
> [?Beneath] being ever more to be[44]

The drafting seems to be attempting to open access to a region which clearly belongs to human subjectivity, and yet which is not adequately thought along the lines of the common-sense lapsed Cartesianism which Wordsworth often, elsewhere, like most other writers of the period, takes as exhaustively dividing the possible ontological options: 'sensuous or intellectual',[45] 'discursive or intuitive'.[46] Nothing can be said for certain about any potential thesis aimed at by a passage so fragmentary as this;

but what it does make fully evident is Wordsworth's sense that the languages usually available to him are not adequate here.

It is instructive to compare this blockage in face of the way an inherited lexicon maps out and misclassifies the contours of experience with a rather different early draft towards 'The Recluse', the beginning of which was briefly examined in chapter 3:

> There is a law severe of penury
> Which bends the cottage boy to early thought,
> To thought whose premature necessity
> Blocks out the forms of nature, preconsumes
> The reason, famishes the heart, shuts up
> The infant being in itself, and makes
> Its very spring a season of decay.
> The limbs increase; but liberty of mind
> Is gone for ever, and the avenues of sense
> Are clogg'd, and this organic frame,
> So joyful in its motions, soon becomes
> Dull, to the joy of its own motions dead;
> And even the touch, so exquisitely poured
> Through the whole body, with a languid will
> Performs its functions, in the basking hour
> [   ]
> Scarce carrying to the brain a torpid sense
> Of what there is delightful in the breeze,
> The sunshine, or the changeful elements.[47]

These verses are strikingly different in emphasis from the kind of account in which penury deprives the poor of the luxury for thought: the kind of account in which, bent beneath immediate necessities, their views would become pitiably narrowed. The luxury of which the poor boy is here deprived is the opposite. It is the luxury of thoughtlessness. The lines contain within them, of course, an earlier sense of 'thought' as signifying unhappy preoccupation. They also carry, however, an acute sense of how the mind's fitting to the external world may be just the reverse of exquisite. It can be precisely an excess of 'thought' which '[b]locks out the forms of nature'. In this sense 'thought' is *opposed* to reason, which it 'preconsumes'.

So that when this account of the damage is extended, it escapes the usual typologies. It is unsurprising to be told that 'liberty of mind / Is gone for ever'. With this, we perhaps begin to suspect that a familiar machinery is at work; that, for example, reflection in the service of self-preservation ('thought') is to be contrasted with a disinterested reflection in no service but its own ('liberty of mind'). Yet what that means looks more surprising in the light of what follows. It is not that liberty of mind is gone because too much weight has been placed upon the senses: rather, the passage implies, part of what it means for liberty of mind to disappear is for 'the avenues of sense' to be 'clogg'd'. These 'avenues of sense' are part of what distinguishes 'reason' from 'thought'. As the passage goes on, the idea that such avenues are there merely to collect data for reason to process and subsequently to confer meaning upon is put in doubt. What happens in this passage is that the ontology of the body operating in phenomenalism and the discourses determined by it – the ontology in which all species of bodily experience must first become data in order to be processed by the mind – that this ontology of the body becomes inoperable. *The touch* is undecidably both passive – exquisitely poured through the whole body – and active – possessed of a 'will' which may, as here, be languid, or may be energetic. Yet what we have here is unlike the monism brought out under the banner of a 'one life' which, as it is usually constructed, rather resembles 'one death'. Instead we find a cut between an inner and an outer body which the dejected ontologies available to Wordsworth habitually take to be one and the same. The limbs increase, yet this organic frame decays: how can this be? The lines suggest that 'this organic frame' is perhaps not quite the same as limbs, organs, and whatever else increases under the pressure of penury. A gap is implied between what might be meant by 'the organic frame' and that thriving musculature. If we are ever to experience what there is delightful in the breeze, we must first be alive to the joy of our own motions. A *pure organic pleasure*, a pleasure which is not received by a subject, processed by a subject, endowed with meaning by a subject, but which is a subject itself already both cognitive and embodied, is the necessary precondition for everything which in Wordsworth has been miscalled 'aesthetic' pleasure.[48] It is not that two must close in one, but that a false One – here, the evacuation of experience by the self-projections of thought in the service of necessity, self-preservation – must be *opened*.

In general, then, Wordsworth uses 'thought' and 'thinking' not as beginning Cartesianism does, but as lapsed Cartesianism does, to mean 'reflection'; yet despite this difference of vocabulary what is repeatedly at stake in Wordsworth's descriptions of experience is a thinking which is, not primarily a form for judgement or reflection, but affective substance. When another of the early blank-verse fragments begins by telling us that

> There is creation in the eye,
> Nor less in all the other senses: powers
> They are that colour, model and combine
> The things perceived with such an absolute
> Essential energy that we may say
> That these most godlike faculties of ours
> At one and the same moment are the mind
> And the mind's minister: ... [49]

we should resist the attempt rapidly to mis-assimilate this to the usual
focus of interest (the activity, or creativity of the subject or the mind). We
should resist this because if Wordsworth were saying merely that the
mind is creative, he would only be repeating a commonplace of ontologies of mind in the philosophy of the century and a half leading up to
his writing. What makes the position distinctive is the emphasis given to
what is understood by mind. These faculties *are* the mind *and* the mind's
minister. They are 'the mind's minister' to the extent that we understand
mind or thinking, in the usual way as reflection upon what the senses
bring it. But, first of all, they *are* the mind, not merely an accompaniment
of, addition to, or instrument of, the mind. First of all comes this
'absolute / Essential energy', the affective, the bodily, nature of thinking.

SLEEP-THINKING

The quotations which Wordsworth copied into his notebook are not the
only trace of his engagement with Descartes. Another is the dream of the
Arab related in book 5 of the 1805–6 *Prelude*. In 1956 Jane Worthington
Smyser demonstrated its links with the third of the dreams that Descartes
dreamed in 1619 in connection with the inauguration of his own philosophical programme. Descartes's record of his dreams, which he entitled
the *Olympica*, was made in a notebook subsequently lost. But an
inventory of it made by Hector-Pierre Chanut in 1650; excerpts from it
copied by Leibniz in 1676, published in a defective edition in 1859 (after
which Leibniz's notes were in turn lost); and a paraphrase/translation of
the *Olympica* in a 1691 life of Descartes, all survive.[50] The dreams were by
no means a passing incident, but rather the experience of a conversion
and choice of life in which the foundations of Descartes's philosophical
breakthrough were laid.

The discovery has been greeted with universal acceptance. Yet little has
been done with it. Few of the readings made of the dream of the Arab
have really wanted to ask why a dream of *Descartes's* should be a source at

this point of the poem.[51] At the same time, Descartes's dream itself has been little commented upon in those readings. The impression has been given that whatever difficulties of interpretation Descartes's dream might raise, they are not of any urgent significance for a reading of the dream of the Arab. There may be several reasons for this. It is hard enough to interpret Wordsworth's dream without adding the task of interpreting its source-dream too; Cervantes has sometimes seemed to usurp Descartes in the course of the dream of the Arab, which has little about it that is recognizably 'Cartesian'; and a good many of the readings which this passage of this book has received since 1956 have wanted to read it in ways not assisted by the memory that Descartes is the source. Smyser's speculation that Beaupuy was the source for Wordsworth's knowledge of the dream is now usually set aside; Coleridge is the more plausible candidate preferred. This has offered a further reason – as in the case of the quotations copied into the notebook – for not paying too much attention to the link with Descartes here.

Descartes dreams that he finds two books, a dictionary and a compendium of classical poetry. He opens the latter and chances upon a poem by Ausonius, 'What Way in Life Shall I Follow?' An unknown man then appears and gives him a further poem by Ausonius, 'Yes and No'. Descartes recognizes the poem as by Ausonius and offers to find it for the man in the compendium. He fails but tells the man that he can find him a better poem, and begins looking for 'What way in life . . . ?' He does not find it, but happens upon some engravings which lead him to tell the man that this is not the edition with which he is familiar; he still has not found it by the time both the books and the man disappear. Despite this, Descartes does not wake up, but (still asleep) proceeds to interpret his dream:

It is a most remarkable thing that, wondering whether what he had seen was a dream or a vision, he not only decided that it was a dream while he was still asleep but also interpreted it before he was fully awake. He judged that the *Dictionary* could only mean all the Sciences gathered together and that the anthology of the poets entitled the *Corpus Poetarum* represented in particular and in a more distinct way the union of Philosophy and Wisdom.

For he did not believe that we should be too surprised to see that the poets, even the most mediocre, were full of maxims that were more serious, more sensible, and better expressed than anything in the writings of the philosophers. He attributed this marvel to the divinity of Enthusiasm and the strength of Imagination [in the poets], which bring out the seeds of wisdom that are found in all men's minds – like the sparks of fire in [flint] stones – much more easily and much more brilliantly than can the Reason of the philosophers. Monsieur Descartes continued to interpret his dream while asleep, thinking that the piece of verse on the uncertainty of what sort of life one should choose, beginning 'What way in life shall I follow,' represented the good advice of a wise person or even of Moral Theology.

Thereupon, uncertain whether he was dreaming or thinking, he awoke and calmly continued to interpret the dream in the same sense. By the poets collected in the anthology, he understood Revelation and Enthusiasm, for the favors of which he did not despair at all. By the verse 'Yes and No,' which is the Yes and the No [in Baillet's margin: 'nai kai ou'] of Pythagoras, he understood Truth and Falsehood in human understanding and the profane sciences. Seeing that the interpretation of all these things succeeded so well to his liking, he was bold enough to persuade himself that it was the Spirit of Truth that had wanted to open unto him the treasures of all the sciences by this dream. There remained to explain only the little portraits in copperplate that he had found in the second book. He sought no further explanation for them after an Italian painter paid him a visit on the next day.[52]

The interpretation is notable for the fact that a good part of it is delivered whilst still asleep. For this reason several key elements of the dream are interpreted more than once. When asleep the anthology of poetry is interpreted as a union of philosophy and wisdom, as distinct from the knowledge of the particular sciences; when awake, the poets collected in the anthology are understood as 'Revelation and Enthusiasm'. The individual poems mentioned from it are then each given a further meaning: 'the advice of a wise person or even of Moral Theology' and 'Truth and Falsehood in human understanding and the profane sciences'. Still more striking than this multiplicity of interpretation is its coexistence with a more mundanely predictive decoding: once the Italian painter has visited, there is no need to seek a symbolic significance for the copperplate portraits.

In view of these features, it is not surprising that the significance of this dream is still as contested a matter as any concerning Descartes. (In part this is also a matter of the complexity of its textual transmission.[53]) Some of the interest in it is also typified by Jacques Maritain's reading. 'It is undeniably very annoying to find at the origin of modern philosophy a "cerebral episode," to quote Auguste Comte, which would call forth from our savants, should they meet it in the life of some devout personage, the most disquieting neuropathological diagnosis; and one can understand the dissatisfaction of those philosophical people in reading Baillet's account.'[54] As it happens, Maritain sounds more pleased than annoyed. Whether devotionally motivated or not, much reading is comparable to this one. Its focus of interest is the pleasing discovery that what is taken to be *the* rationalist project had roots in something so irrational as a series of dreams. Readings of this kind often take their cue from the suggestions of Descartes's possible contacts with Rosicrucianism; and from the striking way in which Baillet's 'Life' to Descartes's introduces the dreams, with an account of a mood of religious inspiration: 'He acquaints us, That on the Tenth of *November* 1619, laying himself down *Brimfull of his Enthusiasm*, and wholly possess'd with the thought of *having found that day the Foundations of the wonderful Science*, he had three Dreams one presently after another; yet so extraordinary, as to make him fancy that they were sent him from above'.[55] Georges Poulet's reading emphasizes the physiological aspects of this elation and subsequent dejection.[56] From a different position, this fascination is shared by Sophie Jama's recent 'ethnological' approach to Descartes's dreams, in which apparently incidental facts such as the dating of the dream on the eve of St Martin – a key date in the calendar of French popular superstition – open up an interpretation which understands the dreams as crystallizing for rationalist use a set of traditional and popular myths about dreams and their relation to knowledge.[57]

All the interpretations which are interested in unearthing in these dreams an irrationality subtending rationalism tend to take the precise nature of the rationalism of Descartes's mature philosophy rather for granted. One of the few readings to develop convincingly the proposition that the dreams may be of real importance to the interpretation of Descartes's mature thought is that by the phenomenologist and Descartes scholar Jean-Luc Marion. For Marion what is remarkable is not the 'enthusiasm' Descartes experiences before the dreams, or the suggestion that knowledge from above is revealed in a dream, but rather the reverse: the fact that, by contrast 'Nothing is revealed, either directly (inspired speech) or indirectly (deciphered text or authoritative hermeneut). Descartes is unique not because he experienced dreams – divinatory or otherwise – but because he perceived them, at first, as perfectly insignificant.'[58] Descartes not only takes himself for the best interpreter of his own dreams but does so as the interpreter of something which he has revealed to himself, rather than of a divine or any other external revelation. It is in this light that Marion interprets the most extraordinary – yet often neglected – feature of this dream. Descartes interprets it while he is still asleep. Marion points out that, far from representing an irrational clouding of the *cogito*, this is in fact strictly in line with what the *cogito* is going to mean in the *Meditations*. Indeed, for Marion, it is at this point that the distinctive sense of 'thinking' which we have explored earlier begins to emerge: 'The indifference of thought to the pair waking/ sleeping constitutes a decisive moment in the *Meditations* that, in a sense, simply pursues "along the same lines" a strict self-interpretation of *cogitatio* through the various dreams sent by an 'evil spirit' to the human mind.'[59] Indeed it is only if thinking be not primarily reflection, but instead primarily evidence, that it could intelligibly be said to be 'indifferent' to the pair waking/sleeping. Only if we take Descartes seriously when he insists that 'By the term "thought" I understand *everything* which we are aware of as happening within us, insofar as we have awareness of it'[60] can we make sense of this claim; and, conversely, this claim lays the ground for such a conception of thinking.

The reception of the third dream is thus marked by a division between Cartesian reading of it, in which the dream is considered primarily from the point of view of its significance for the later system, and symptomatic reading of it, in which it represents a point at which a dependence of Cartesian rationalism on all the irrationality it suppresses would surface. If the latter tendency is disfigured by a reductively rationalistic understanding of Descartes's thought, the former, in its lack of interest in the dream's extra-doctrinal paralipomena, risks missing much. The place of poetry within it is what, more than anything else, makes it difficult to understand Descartes's interpretation. Marion's sense that what is novel about this is that Descartes perceives his dreams 'at first, as perfectly insignificant' – that he bestows a meaning upon them which is his to decide upon – looks right for so long as we feel that there is no attempt to establish a real or necessary thematic connection between the dream-objects and their 'meanings'. But when we read that 'he did not believe that we should be too surprised to see that the poets, even the most mediocre, were full of maxims that were more serious, more sensible, and better expressed than anything in the writings of the philosophers', the grounds of interpretation shift: there is now argued to be something about the *Corpus Poetarum* which naturally fits it to represent a union of philosophy and wisdom. Poetry is no longer merely a vehicle of the dream but part of its meaning. It is not a matter of the quality of the poetry. Even the most mediocre poetry may contain maxims superior to anything in philosophy. This surprising situation is thought of by Descartes as a 'marvel'. It is explained from poetry's ability to bring out a wisdom which is, *in nuce*, always already there in any mind: 'He attributed this marvel to the divinity of Enthusiasm and the strength of Imagination, which bring out the seeds of wisdom that are found in all men's minds – like the sparks of fire in stones – much more easily and much more brilliantly than can the Reason of the philosophers.'

The supplementary status so often accorded poetry in relation to cognition is rejected here. The 'enthusiasm' and 'imagination' shown by the poets are important not because they offer a corrective to reason or an ornamental or sentimental or humanizing supplement to it, but because they 'bring out' a reason which is already present. This is most decisively shown in the conclusion to the interpretation. What the union of philosophy and wisdom signified by and participated in by poetry is supposed to open up is directly named as 'the treasures of all the sciences'.[61] The *Corpus Poetarum* is not in the event to lead us to a truth beside or above that of science, but to science itself. In a sense, then, Marion is right to reject the centrality which poetic 'enthusiasm' has been given in readings of this dream – for so long as enthusiasm is interpreted as the supplementary opposite of a 'thinking' interpreted to mean 'reflection': if enthusiasm be taken to mean, for example, the acceptance of 'whatever groundless Opinion comes to settle it self strongly' upon the enthusiast's 'Fancies'.[62] Once we take notice of the fact that poetic enthusiasm is understood as what enables us to see a thinking which is always already taking place – to notice what Berkeley called that light 'that irradiates every mind, but is not equally observed by all'[63] – it is no longer possible to place the emphasis on enthusiasm *rather than* reason, revelation *rather than* inquiry. Poetry, here, is thought of as fitted to stand for what makes us see our *thinking*: what makes us see our thinking, not as 'thinking that', 'judging that', 'knowing that', but as the irreducibly affective fact of experience.

WORDSWORTH HUMAN AND INHUMAN

In a speech given upon the occasion of the award of the Büchner Prize, Paul Celan drew attention to the following passage from Büchner's *Lenz*:

As I was walking in the valley yesterday, I saw two girls sitting on a rock. One was putting up her hair, and the other helped. The golden hair hanging down, and a pale, serious face, so very young, and the black dress, and the other girl so careful and attentive. Even the finest, most intimate paintings of the old German masters can hardly give you an idea of the scene. Sometimes one would like to be a Medusa's head to turn such a group to stone and gather the people round it.[64]

Celan comments:

> Please note, ladies and gentlemen: 'One would like to be a Medusa's head'
> to ... seize the natural as natural by means of art!
>
> *One* would like to, by the way, not: *I* would.[65]

The comment concisely draws attention to a cruel redundance in
Büchner's Lenz's surmised desire. 'One' might be willing to kill, to turn
these girls to stone. (*One* might wish, whereas *I* might not. Perhaps that's
so that the murderousness in the wish can be disowned.) Why? So as to
allow something which is already there to be seen, to be seen. It is as
though, despite its already being there, the scene would be invisible unless
art should intervene. Celan takes this intervention – apparently redundant, yet at once petrifying and revelatory – as telling us something
important about what art is like. It kills, as it were, in the service of life.
By a redundant intervention, it allows us to be shown what is already
there.

> Thou also, Man, hast wrought,
> For commerce of thy nature with itself,
> Things worthy of unconquerable life;
> And yet we feel, we cannot chuse but feel
> That these must perish.[66]

What is art for? For commerce of man's nature with itself. But why
should there be any need for such commerce? In what sense can commerce with itself really be spoken of as an exchange at all? Art, the
intermediary, adds nothing to man's nature, which is in no way dependent upon representation, and which, much rather, makes representation
itself possible; yet these 'things worthy of unconquerable life' are the
objects by which man's nature shows itself to itself. It is hard to keep hold
of the slippage in the last two and a half lines. By the time we have been
told, with an intensifying emphasis, that we must feel 'that these must
perish' we have unawares been almost persuaded that they are alive. But
that was not said; only that they are worthy of unconquerable life. So we
are dealing with a slippage in the sense of life: from the always affective
immediacy which I cannot doubt, to the half-figurative sense of the
persistence or survival of something the conviction of whose 'life' might
at any time begin to seem idolatrous, something which we project into
inanimate receptacles. The lament over what 'we' feel must perish thus

risks being false consciousness, our way of obscuring from ourselves that we have idolatrously confused the living with the non-living – and of obscuring from ourselves what we may have killed off in the process.

The passage immediately continues like this:

> Tremblings of the heart
> It gives, to think that the immortal being
> No more shall need such garments; and yet Man,
> As long as he shall be the Child of Earth,
> Might almost 'weep to have' what he may lose,
> Nor be himself extinguish'd; but survive
> Abject, depress'd, forlorn, disconsolate.
> A thought is with me sometimes, and I say,
> Should earth by inward throes be wrench'd throughout,
> Or fire be sent from far to wither all
> Her pleasant habitations, and dry up
> Old Ocean in his bed left sing'd and bare,
> Yet would the living Presence still subsist
> Victorious; and composure would ensue,
> And kindlings like the morning; presage sure,
> Though slow perhaps, of a returning day!
> But all the meditations of mankind,
> Yea, all the adamantine holds of truth,
> By reason built, or passion, which itself
> Is highest reason in a soul sublime;
> The consecrated works of Bard and Sage,
> Sensuous or intellectual, wrought by men,
> Twin labourers and heirs of the same hopes,
> Where would they be? Oh! why hath not the mind
> Some element to stamp her image on
> In nature somewhat nearer to her own?
> Why, gifted with such powers to send abroad
> Her spirit, must it lodge in shrines so frail?[67]

The lines are a bit obscure. It is hard to tell exactly how far the destruction is imagined to go. It appears to be suggested that even were the earth to dry up entirely, thus making all plant, animal and human life impossible, some kind of 'living presence' would subsist and would eventually recolonize the earth. This slight obscurity, though, diminishes to a minimum in face of the astonishing loss of perspective in what has been said. Granted, the entire population of the world might be wiped out. Certainly, in compensation, life of some kind would gradually return. All the books, though, would be lost forever. Think of that! The

judgement of the 'friend' on all this is exact. ''Twas going far to seek
disquietude.' With this the passage turns back on itself. The beginning of
this section, in fact, has already foregrounded the element of fancifulness
in these fears:

> Even in the steadiest mood of reason, when
> All sorrow for thy transitory pains
> Goes out, it grieves me for thy state, O Man,
> Thou paramount Creature! and thy race, while Ye
> Shall sojourn on this planet; not for woes
> Which thou endur'st; that weight, albeit huge,
> I charm away; but for those palms atchiev'd,
> Through length of time, by study and hard thought,
> The honours of thy high endowments; there
> My sadness finds its fuel.

A sadness which is looking around for 'fuel' already begins to look as
though it should join those other instances of deliberately stoked-up
feeling which Wordsworth identifies as one of the temptations of the
poetic vocation.[68] The admission that the poet can 'charm away' grief for
the entire weight of human suffering, in favour of grieving for a hypo-
thetical loss of its learning and letters, suggests that what is first of all
described as 'the steadiest mood of reason' may not be reason at all.
Reason at its steadiest can discount pains because of their 'transitory'
character. Yet even reason at its steadiest, it is said, cannot dispel this
fantasy of intellectual bereavement. The light irony, then, redounds not
only upon the poet who enjoys entertaining such far-fetched fears, but
also upon the kind of reason which can calmly discount (everyone else's)
pain on the grounds that it will pass.

Why *does* Wordsworth go so far to seek disquietude? If I imagine for a
moment that I were to try to reassure him by telling him that eventually
all such data would be imperishably stored in ineradicable databases, I
come to feel that the fear which he has mentioned is not the fear which is
really important.[69] Doubt about this fear is first raised by the apparent
redundance of the event in which it is feared that these labours will be
lost. Earlier, art and science allowed the self-reduplication of human
nature, its 'commerce with itself'. Now, they themselves undergo a still
more puzzling self-reduplication. They start out invulnerable, as 'adamantine holds of truth' (an earlier draft offers the less absolute-sounding
'adamantine holds of quiet thought'[70]). What they stamp themselves on,
however, is a more fragile element. It is strange that something already

secured in adamant should then attempt to preserve itself by going out
into frail shrines. Neil Hertz once suggested that apparent fears of
apocalyptic depopulation often look more like fantasies when examined
closely.[71] Isn't it possible that what gets represented here as lamentable
and deplorable – viz., the destruction of the entire human race; – a
destruction represented as less deplorable only than the loss of all
humanity's great books – might, instead, be just what is wished for? That
there is a murderousness inseparable from the cathexis of these person-
ating objects, these shrines, idols or fetishes, to which we transfer 'our'
hopes and fears?

A disquietude which has been fetched from so far away will not be
given up lightly, nor is it. After the dream has been narrated Wordsworth
returns to the same point:

> Full often, taking from the world of sleep
> This Arab Phantom, which my Friend beheld,
> This Semi-Quixote, I to him have given
> A substance, fancied him a living man,
> A gentle Dweller in the Desart, craz'd
> By love and feeling and internal thought
> Protracted among endless solitudes;
> Have shaped him, in the oppression of his brain,
> Wandering upon this quest, and thus equipp'd.
> And I have scarcely pitied him; have felt
> A reverence for a being thus employ'd,
> And thought that in the blind and awful lair
> Of such a madness reason did lie couch'd.
> Enow there are on earth to take in charge
> Their Wives, their Children, and their virgin Loves,
> Or whatsoever else the heart holds dear;
> Enow to think of these; yea, will I say,
> In sober contemplation of the approach
> Of such great overthrow, made manifest
> By certain evidence, that I methinks
> Could share that Maniac's anxiousness, could go
> Upon like errand. Oftentimes, at least,
> Me hath such deep entrancement half-possess'd,
> When I have held a volume in my hand,
> Poor earthly casket of immortal Verse!
> Shakespeare or Milton, labourers divine.[72]

Most startling in this passage is the outburst halfway through it: 'Enow
there are on earth...' It is startling because of its inconsequence. It

sounds like an answer to an objection, but it is an objection which readers are not really likely to have been thinking of. Before this point the passage is not talking about how wrong or irresponsible the preservative burial of western culture might be, but about how insanely deluded it might be. Now, though, the poet breaks out as though the charge which has been levelled is neglect of kith and kin. There is an undecidability of voice at this point, too. One way of reading the outburst is to take it as part of what Wordsworth 'has' felt but does not necessarily now endorse. But we cannot be certain of that, because a new sentence has begun here, and it later goes on to offer direct affirmations in the present ('yea, will I say, ... '). That suggests that Wordsworth is directly asserting that there are plenty of people to do the mundane job of fulfilling immediate obligation, so that there should also be some who are free to experiment with apparently surplus labours like precautionary book-burial (or like writing poetry).

The shape of this thought connects it to a context not often linked with this passage: Wordsworth's reflections on the specifically monastic tradition of reclusiveness. Both are concerned with a point of crisis in the choice of life. The appeal against destruction of the monastic shape of life takes just the same exceptionalist shape: 'Here, if here only!' Just as there are 'enough' people on earth to live in what is elsewhere called 'domestic selfishness', so there are 'enough' citizens to work at the production of capital. If the diligent idleness of monasticism is prohibited, the very idea of this particular shape of happiness will have been lost to the world altogether. The monastic connection could be thought irrelevant, because the dreamer's horseman is a Bedouin Arab. But he is an unusual one. Although it has been not incorrectly suggested that 'Wordsworth makes a point of calling him a Bedouin, a word which, as he would have known from reading Volney's *Travels through Egypt and Syria*, means "desert dweller" or "dweller in a country without habitation" ... As a nomad, the Bedouin, like the "vagrant dwellers in the houseless woods" of *Tintern Abbey*, personifies natural, unaccommodated existence at its most rudimentary, short of outright savagery',[73] this reminder by itself would give us a misleading impression of Volney's thought about the Bedouin. As important to Volney as their nomadic character is the way in which they exemplify a kind of noble solidarity which can to the outsider look like (although, Volney points out, it is not) communism:

Among themselves they are remarkable for a good faith, a disinterestedness, a generosity which would do honour to the most civilized people. What is there more noble than that right of asylum so respected among all the tribes? A stranger, nay, even an enemy, touches the tent of the Bedouin, and, from that instant, his person becomes inviolable. It would be reckoned a disgraceful meanness, an indelible shame, to satisfy even a just vengeance at the expence of hospitality ... his generosity is so sincere, that he does not look upon it as a merit, but merely as a duty: and he readily, therefore, takes the same liberty with others. To observe the manner in which the Arabs conduct themselves towards each other, one would imagine that they possessed all their goods in common. Nevertheless, they are no strangers to property; but it has none of that selfishness which the increase of the imaginary wants of luxury has given it among polished nations.[74]

In an unpublished essay of around 1800 so different a thinker from Volney as Hegel could write that

When an Arab has drunk a cup of coffee with a stranger, he has *eo ipso* made a bond of friendship with him. This common action has linked them, and in the strength of this link the Arab is bound to render him all loyalty and help. The common eating and drinking here is not what is called a symbol. The connection between symbol and symbolized is not itself spiritual, is not life, but an objective bond; symbol and symbolized are strangers to each other, and their connection lies outside them in a third thing; their connection is only a connection in thought. To eat and drink with someone is an act of union and is itself a felt union, not a conventional symbol. It runs counter to natural human feeling to drink a glass of wine with an enemy; the sense of community in this action would contradict the attitude of the parties to one another at other time.[75]

Although a certain kind of modern historiography might find it convenient to count these reflections as part of a 'myth' of noble savagery or some such, they well convey some features of the operations of reciprocity in a certain kind of non-contractual society.[76] The reciprocity has not been entered into *de jure* but *de facto*: or, rather, it is essential to the structure of a society in which no distinction between law and economy may be drawn that the *de jure/de facto* distinction makes no sense. Volney and Hegel both picture a society whose solidarity is, not a personal preference on the part of its members, but part of life. For their Bedouin Arabs, the idea that 'Enow there are on earth' to meet fundamental social obligations could only seem insane.

The dreamer's Arab, in contrast, is a maniac, if at all, partly because of the protraction of interior reflection in endless solitudes. This brings him, at first, closer to inspired or deranged desert ascetics than to anything recognizable from his possible source (Volney) for his ideas of Bedouin

life. The desert of this dream is linked to the 'desert' on which Wordsworth reflects in 'The Tuft of Primroses' when he asks what drove
St Antony and the other inventors of Christian monasticism out into the
desert in the first place; and most of all by the disregard of obligations to
kin which poetry and monasticism alike appear to risk.

This reclusive vein of reflection in Wordsworth's work towards 'The
Recluse' is the antitype to the vein in which Wordsworth later declared
that a deep distress had humanized and, implicitly, had socialized, his
soul. That line suggests that there was something inhuman about his soul
before. For so long as the idea of writing (and, in some sort, of being)
'The Recluse' remained effective, a deep longing for 'independent happiness', 'the life where hope and memory are as one', kept, as it were, re-
dehumanizing his soul. The poems associated with 'The Recluse' reach
for a possibly collective happiness through an unblinking awareness that
discrete living individuals and their experiences are the only imaginable
constituents of such felicity. That we cannot be absolutely certain whether
the outburst 'Enow there are on earth' is voiced as what the poet now
thinks or as what he has 'sometimes' thought well captures the antagonism between the human and inhuman Wordsworth. It is an antagonism critical to the projected poem. The figure of the Bedouin Arab
concentrates it. He is solitary to an extent which is possibly insane. Yet it
is also imaginable that were we merely to succeed in touching his tent; –
were we effectively to join this maniac on his errand – we might par-
ticipate in an unbreakable solidarity such as it has become almost
impossible for us to dream about.

LIFE BESIDE ITSELF

'The less of life remains, the more seductive it is for consciousness to take
the bare harsh remnants of the living for the appearance of the Absolute.
But nothing which does not promise something which transcends even
life can be experienced as truly alive; no labour of the concept can escape
from this.'[77] On this kind of account, there is a difference between the
bare harsh remnants of the living and being 'truly alive'. For that to
be true, the concept of life must be structured in a particular way. It
must be what this author elsewhere calls an 'emphatic' concept. What an
'emphatic' concept is may be explained by its contrast with 'cover-
concept'. A 'cover-concept' sorts and classifies the particulars which fall
under it. It thus says, not what those particulars (emphatically) *are*, but
what they *fall under*. An emphatic concept, by contrast, always does more

than classify particulars as the sorts of quiddity which do or do not belong to its set. It does more, because it is a concept which is, ineliminably, normative or evaluative as well as descriptive. A clearer example than 'life' is the concept of 'art'. To describe a given object as *art* is not merely to say that it fulfils in its physical properties the criteria for membership of a class; it is also at the same time to evaluate it, to set up a claim, however inconclusible, to the agreement of others to this judgement. In the quotation above, *life* is being understood as an 'emphatic' concept too; so that there might be certain kinds of life of which it could be said that 'life does not live'.

Perhaps this way of discriminating among senses of 'life' may be both illuminated and complicated if we consider a passage from the second book of the poem:

>   ... already I began
> To love the sun, a Boy I lov'd the sun,
> Not as I since have lov'd him, as a pledge
> And surety of our earthly life, a light
> Which while we view we feel we are alive;
> But, for this cause, that I had seen him lay
> His beauty on the morning hills, had seen
> The western mountain touch his setting orb,
> In many a thoughtless hour, when, from excess
> Of happiness, my blood appeared to flow
> With its own pleasure, and I breath'd with joy.[78]

The account of the young boy's pleasure here is one of the most striking illustrations in the authorship of the notion of the cognitive body. The blood appears to flow with its own pleasure. It does not feel as though sensuous data have been accumulated and sent to the mind to be processed into properly aesthetic feeling or to have cognitive significance bestowed on them. Instead it is as though it is impossible to distinguish between the cognitive-evaluative aspects of this feeling and the sheerly somatic aspect of it. In the simplest yet most striking expression imaginable, Wordsworth can now emphatically, rather than tropically, say 'I breath'd with joy'. The joy is not something put together out of conceptually processed sense-data; it is there in the breathing. Yet in the same passage we have a sense for 'life' which stands at a (complex) distance from this. The man's love of the sun is much stranger. It is partly symbolic: the sun has now become a 'pledge'. Yet, curiously, it is a pledge of something of which one might think one could hardly fail to be certain

of: 'a light / Which while we view we feel we are alive'. Couldn't the same
be said of anything that we view, of sherry or frontiniac or rope-dancing,
for examples? It appears not, and so this later, more mature or less intense
love of the sun, is shadowed by a darker implication: that much of the
time we do not feel we are alive at all, that we feel precisely as though we
do not have experience, and that it takes something quite intrusively
remarkable, such as an intolerably powerful light, to make us feel that we
are alive. And this reminds us that it is not in fact possible for the human
eye to look directly at the sun for long without becoming damaged.
When the sun succeeds in making us feel that we are alive it does so not
merely in the sense that we know that we have experience, but in the sense
which is (in an unspecified way) more than merely constative. When
Wordsworth says of the pre-linguistic infant (on whose behalf a great deal
of energy has sometimes been expended to show that it too is in fact
wholly textual) that 'Emphatically such a being lives'[79] – we should
consider the possibility that he might understand the sense of his own
adverb perfectly. *Emphatically,* in the sense that he or she does not live the
half-life of one in thrall to his or her own operative personification –
'labour itself', for example – but a life which is, normatively or evalua-
tively rather than only classificatorily, alive.

But the quotation with which we began this section suggests, also,
something potentially more troubling. If 'nothing which does not promise something which transcends even life can be experienced as truly
alive', then the possibility of a perfect plenitude of life is blocked in its
very interior; the experience of true or full aliveness would depend upon
the promise of something more than just life. The experience of being
'truly alive' would depend upon not being only alive, or upon not
investing everything in the mere fact of life. One way of understanding
this would be as a qualification to the kind of Cartesianism represented in
material phenomenology. The indubitable life championed there rests on
the willingness to bracket out everything transcendent. But if amongst my
indubitable experiences is, ineliminably, the continual feeling that, say,
the world is really there, then this promise of 'something which transcends
even life', something which – merely possibly, rather than certainly –
breaks the *Immanenzzusammenhang,* the context of immanence, is part of
what life, taken emphatically, means. When the defence of the difference
between life and death, the defence against fetishism, takes place in the
medium of representation, it deploys a particular fetish to prevent *pan-
fetishism.* 'This means going beyond what is human, stepping into a realm
which is turned towards the human, yet uncanny – the realm where the

monkey, the automatons and with them … oh, art, too, seem to be at home.'[80]

The dream framed by the unsociable fears or fantasies we have been looking at is further framed by the residues of the reading of Cervantes offered by the 'Friend' and of his meditations on poetry and geometry. The manner of that framing introduces a further motive for the way in which the fear of the destruction of the frail vessels sheltering the achievements of human intellect has been framed:

> On Poetry, and geometric Truth,
>   The knowledge that endures, upon these two,
> And their high privilege of lasting life,
> Exempt from all internal injury,
> He mused; upon these chiefly: … [81]

The worry about the *external* injury which the scripts of poetry and geometry may undergo allows their exemption from *internal* injury to be asserted in passing and without discussion. What it thus also allows to pass unelaborated is the yoking together of poetry and geometry as 'the knowledge that endures'. The atmosphere of the dream, and many of its details, could hardly be less like that of Descartes's dream. The opposed yet complementary books, however, are what make Smyser's comparison persuasive.

> … the Arab told him that the Stone,
> To give it in the language of the Dream,
> Was Euclid's Elements; 'And this,' said he,
> 'This other,' pointing to the Shell, 'this book
> Is something of more worth.' And, at the word,
> The Stranger, said my Friend continuing,
> Stretch'd forth the Shell toward me, with command
> That I should hold it to my ear: I did so;
> And heard that instant in an unknown Tongue,
> Which yet I understood, articulate sounds,
> A loud, prophetic blast of harmony,
> An Ode, in passion utter'd, which foretold
> Destruction to the Children of the Earth,
> By deluge now at hand. No sooner ceas'd
> The song, but with calm look, the Arab said
> That all was true; that it was even so
> As had been spoken; and that he himself
> Was going then to bury those two Books,

The one that held acquaintance with the stars,
And wedded man to man by purest bond
Of nature undisturb'd by space or time;
Th'other that was a God, yea many Gods,
Had voices more than all the winds, and was
A joy, a consolation, and a hope.[82]

The status of poetry in relation to cognition here is hardly less complicated than its status in Descartes's dream. What kind of 'book' this
might be is unclear. We discover that it is a book only when the Arab
proposes to bury it. Until that point it appears that Euclid's *Elements* is
instead contrasted with a 'song'. That the Ode is sounded in a language
which the dreamer does not know, but still understands, is of a piece with
the dream logic in which the horseman can be 'neither, and both' a
Bedouin and Quixote. Much stranger problems are to follow. It is a
prophecy and is thus associated with the denunciation of false idols.[83] Yet
at once other features of the description make this 'prophetic' character
seem strange. Most obviously, it is a prophecy of something which is
happening at the same time that it is prophesied. It is thus a poem
prophesying its own present destruction. This is what makes the Arab's
mission look especially maniacal. The poem is to be buried for the sake of
some possible future generation. Should it be retrieved, however, it will
be found to be the obsolete prophecy of an apocalypse which has already
happened. The other possibility is that this ode is only one of many
which the shell is capable of producing. In this case what is to be buried is
not this particular performance of this particular poem, but rather a
machine capable of producing many performances of many poems. This
looks more likely in view of the last three lines of the passage.

Yet those lines themselves introduce new difficulties. The shell now
appears not as a prophet but as 'a God, yea many Gods'. This phrase is at
the centre of what is troubling and opaque about the account of poetry
here. This is partly because it comes at such an unexpected angle to the
account of the apocalyptically prophetic Ode which we have just been
given. Any monotheistic readership is likely to associate destruction to the
children of the earth with their having worshipped false gods. But now
the messenger of that destruction is itself described as 'many gods'. The
Arab's account uses a fetish – the mere thing treated as a god – to
announce what feels like the punishment for fetishism. Here we may
recall Volney's tendentious remark that 'It is singular, also, that it should
be there that religion is the freest from exterior forms, insomuch that no

man has ever seen, among the Bedouins, the Turkmans, or Curds, either priests, temples, or regular worship.'[84] Volney's travels represent a people almost free of superstition, because free of a priestly monopoly upon truth; Wordsworth's Bedouin appears to be, much more troublingly and unclassifiably, at once monotheist prophet and polytheist fetishist.

The difficulty of determining whether the shell-book is single or multiple is confirmed by the final line of the description: 'A joy, a consolation, and a hope.' This is confusing. Why wouldn't it be enough for poetry to be 'joy'? Isn't joy as good as it gets? The need for bliss to contain both joy *and* consolation is oddly proleptic of those few lines which remain largely the same in each of the drafts of 'To the Same' (i.e. 'Lycoris') written between 1817 and 1820: the poet remarks there that 'We two have had such blissful hours together / That were power granted to replace them (fetched / From out the pensive shadows where they lie) / In the first warmth of their original sunshine, / Loth should I be to use it.' In other words, the memory is so sweet that it not only induces a reluctance to repossess the original, but (still more paradoxically) *that is what shows how blissful the original bliss was.*[85] Here it is, precisely, as though joy is not enough by itself: that the impossible requirement of poetic bliss is, as it were, for us *both* to have joy *and* at the same time to have the other pleasures which compensate us for the loss of it. The shell-book is both joy and consolation for the loss of joy. It thus participates in the range of paradisial contradictions which we find in other speculative passages of the authorship: that paradise should be a simple produce of the common day long before the promised hour arrives; that there should be a happiness in which hope and memory are as one. This idea of bliss is not 'aesthetic'. It is not, for example, about the sublation of directly sensuous pleasures in favour of disinterested pleasures. Its impossible wish is not for any old 'romantic undifferentiation', but for a blessedness not mismade in the image of aprioristic categorization.

The choice, and the difficulty, for philosophic song is not then whether to represent experience with perfect transparency or to represent it with opacifying enchancements. It is rather to know and choose between a fetish which attracts to truth and one which only fascinates to torpor. It might be, at a certain historical period, to attempt to know the sometimes indiscriminable difference between a shrine and an idol. Here, the great books of the world are 'shrines so frail' for spirits from geometers to poets; elsewhere, the artificers of philosophic systems are idolatrously adoring a waxen image. Here, the 'garment' you would weep to exchange even for immortal nudity; elsewhere, the poison shirt which, grotesquely,

becomes inseparable from your skin by sticking to it.[86] The centrality to
the whole idea of *The Recluse* of this intimate connection, and difficult
discrimination, between shrine and idol, can be glimpsed in the very last
fragment which Wordsworth managed towards it, the address to Nab
Well later entitled *Composed when a probability existed of our being obliged
to quit Rydal Mount as a residence.* The feeling which Wordsworth attaches to Nab Well and to streams in general is reflected upon thus:

> Millions of kneeling Hindoos at this day
> Bow to the watery element adored
> In their vast stream; and if an age hath been
> As books and haply votive Altars vouch
> When British floods were worshipped, some faint trace
> Of that idolatry, thro' Monkish rites
> Transmitted even to living memory,
> Might wait on Thee – . . . [87]

An idolatry which has become a 'faint trace' may be that 'outworn'
creed which we might prefer to the generalized superstition of 'getting
and spending'. The feeling which is here gently linked to idolatry has a
few lines earlier been linked to the reliquary:

> Who, hurrying on
> With a step quickened by November-cold,
> Shall pause, the skill admiring that can work
> Upon thy chance-defilements – wither'd twigs
> That, lodg'd within thy crystal depths, grow bright
> As if they from a silver tree had fallen;
> And oaken leaves, that, driven by whirling blasts
> Into thy cell, have sunk and rested there,
> Till, the more perishable parts consumed,
> Thou, by a crust of liquid beads, hast turned
> The Skeletons to brilliant ornaments?
> But should a luckless hand, from off the floor
> On which the gleaming relics lie, uplift them,
> However gently, into vulgar air,
> At once their tender brightness disappears,
> And the rash intermeddler steals away,
> Chiding his folly. Thus (I feel the truth)
> Thus with the fibers of these thoughts it fares;
> And O how much of all that Love creates
> Or beautifies like changes undergoes,

Suffers like loss when drawn out of the Soul,
Its silent laboratory.[88]

The description of the twigs as 'gleaming relics' has been developed in
a way which forces a more detailed recollection of actual reliquaries and
their encased or decorated bones upon us by the mention of skeletons
turned to brilliant ornaments. The startling turn that Wordsworth then
takes is to use this figure as a figure for the soul. The 'intermeddler' is the
one who classes the 'cabinet' of his 'sensations'.[89] The intermeddler takes
his sensations for things which he has, not is. The cabinet of curiosities is
an only partially secular descendant of the reliquary. Yet the final turn in
this passage is the most startling. This shrine is also a 'laboratory'. The
soul is a place where enchantment and knowledge are indiscriminable to
the extent that our knowledge is irreducibly affective. It is the place of
that bliss which is a simple produce of the common day. The 'faint trace'
of idolatry becomes a counter-poison to the generalized idolatry.

It was written on the front of Wordsworth's whole song that art was in
the service of life. Damaged life would mean damaged art. (For this
reason the very fact that Wordsworth's later poetry is not always as
powerful as the earlier poetry has in turn its own power and value. The
poems' loss is the authorship's gain.) This was written into its texture
also, in each of the many moments of revulsion at any pseudo-animation
of the unliving. There can be life without writing. There cannot be
writing without life. Yet at moments like this, Wordsworth makes himself
come up against the limit that an absolutely living plenitude cannot
exhaustively be written. 'Every phrase which speaks pure immanence
distances and alienates us from it, without this infinite discourse on life
ever being capable of offering a path towards it, since it is in the
renunciation of any path that the path lies.'[90] It is then just to the extent
that Wordsworth is not a poet of 'sheer language', that his work always
operates from the experience of a ('Cartesian', if you want) discontinuity
between experience and representation, a discontinuity which a collection
of *representations* cannot of course by itself ever forcibly open, that language and textuality can be made visible in his writing.

I feel that my life is wrong or broken. I still feel that my book may be
right or may live. In this there is an alibi: a faith or a fetishism. Yet this
faith or fetishism is itself in the service of an intimation that the idea of
'life', as an emphatic concept, already signifies more than a description of
the bare minimum. The text which believes or fetishizes is, in Celan's
words, 'uncanny, yet turned towards what's human'. The law of nature is

not self-preservation, even were it agreed from left to right that it be so, because life is always spilling over into the wish for more, and into the maniacal errands, renunciations, losses and works in which that wish issues. To think life a more mixed mode than does the theodicy of self-preservation need not be an esoteric position. '*Life* is a Term, none more familiar. Any one almost would take it for an Affront, to be asked what he meant by it. And yet if it comes in Question, whether a Plant, that lies ready formed in the Seed, have Life: whether the Embrio in an Egg before Incubation, or a Man in a Swound without Sense or Motion, be alive, or no, it is easy to perceive, that a clear distinct settled *Idea* does not always accompany the use of so known a Word, as that of *Life* is.'

CHAPTER 7

Light

'There was a time' in any given literary critic's life at which he or she was not a literary critic. When such a person comes to read Wordsworth and, say, to face the Ode ('There was a time'), perhaps with the intention of writing about it, he or she may, provided that the repressive apparatus generally in place to push such intimations back into the well have in it a small defect of any kind, stumble across a sense that their own activity, literary criticism, represents an instance of just the kind of loss which the poem is talking about. The tremblings or nausea with which such a person may turn to face the task of writing about this Ode arise not only from the usual causes (anxiety before the peer group or groups currently in possession of it; guilt at the likely prospect that the critic's words will merely burble or drone fluently and stupidly when set against the poem itself) but also from an awareness of how much energy of repression is about to be called upon, to shut down the 'purely subjective' features of the concrete history of the individual's experience of this poem in favour, perhaps, of the notional 'experience' of it supposedly had, and which would now in fact first be constructed, by the individual's paid persona, the critic. Just as, for the child, there may be certain pages of particular books which it dreads to open because of the monsters illustrated there, so there can be certain pages of collections of poetry which the critic finds that *he/she* hesitates to open, and in this case too because of the fear of what may be found there. The panic is over bliss. 'This glimpse of glory, why renewed?'

That is a line from Wordsworth's fine later poem 'Composed upon an Evening of Extraordinary Splendour and Beauty', a poem whose plain allusions to the great Ode ('There was a time') Wordsworth took the trouble further to underline with a note. In that poem it is *glory* which, it appears, feels intolerably painful. The allusions to that earlier ode make up a central part of the content of this one. The long struggles for consolation charted earlier are now made to feel, it is implied, almost like

wasted labour by a return of glory which is not merely unlooked-for but
had been definitely discounted ('I now can feel no more'). Despite this,
glory has in fact been glimpsed. Faced with this, the best recourse is to
deny that anything of the kind has happened:

> Had this effulgence disappeared
> With flying haste, I might have sent
> Among the speechless clouds a look
> Of blank astonishment;
> But 'tis endued with power to stay
> And solemnize one closing day
> That frail Mortality may see
> What is? – ah no – but what *can* be.[1]

If this effulgence *had* disappeared with flying haste, the poet implies, it
wouldn't have been quite comprehensible or wouldn't have needed to be
written about. That a look of *blank* astonishment could have been sent
implies that the astonishment would have been so complete as not to
allow the poet even to register that here was effulgence or glory, and
certainly so complete as not to force him to write an ode on the subject.
But it persists; it will not be hidden. The stanza then performs its remedy
for this distressing situation in the last two lines quoted. 'That frail
Mortality may see / What is? – ah no, but what *can* be.' Although it has
already been admitted that this effulgence *is*, and indeed that it endures
for a space of time which makes it impossible merely to blank it, it is
none the less now denied that it *is*, and instead it is converted into a sign
of something elsewhere. It is 'a presence which is not to be put by',
but which is put by anyway.[2] The appropriate complement of this
deferral is the reference to 'frail Mortality' which, more than any other
feature of this passage, marks it out as one which Wordsworth could
not have written in, say, 1804. The complement, that is, to the conversion
of present glory into a signifier is the recession to a variety of conventional
modern sub-Augustinianism.[3] That is a mode which Wordsworth
could wield in his later years with a peculiar resonance, one which does
not really have its like anywhere else: a resonance exemplified,
for instance, in a powerful couplet from the second of the *Evening
Voluntaries*:

> Care may be respited, but not repealed;
> No perfect cure lies on the bounded field.[4]

But here, in this Ode, it dwindles to a thinner appeal: 'O, let thy grace remind me of the light, / Full early lost and fruitlessly deplored.' Thin, because it is in this poem not really the *loss* which has been deplored at all, but rather the loss of the loss. Wordsworth does not in fact ask: 'Why lost?', but rather: 'Why renewed?'

That the poem despite this has a high value lies in the very openness with which the experience of this 'putting by' of glory is laid out in front of the reader:

> And, if there be whom broken ties
> Afflict, or injuries assail,
> Yon hazy ridges to their eyes,
> Present a glorious scale,
> Climbing suffused with sunny air,
> To stop – no record hath told where!
> And tempting fancy to ascend,
> And with immortal spirits blend!
> – Wings at my shoulder seem to play;
> But, rooted here, I stand and gaze
> On those bright steps that heaven-ward raise
> Their practicable way.[5]

The implications of this passage differ from those of a 'frail Mortality' awaiting a sheer gift of grace, because they suggest the existence of a 'practicable way' to heaven. The final line produces something of the same effect as the close of 'Stepping Westward', especially when thought together with the note indicating that this Jacob's ladder is not a merely arbitrary fancy but in part meteorologically produced;[6] except that here bliss does not lie in the way but at its end. At first it is said that no record has told where the ladder stops, but then the steps are confirmed to raise their way 'heaven-ward'. In such lines the poem exposes and thus qualifies the process which has taken place in its own first stanza, the process of pretending that a glory which is actually experienced is in fact a token or pledge of some other glory at some other time or place. The bliss seems to be there at my shoulder. Instead I choose to imagine the ascending mountain ridges as a kind of ladder to a bliss which I have displaced to heaven: a ladder which, for all its 'practicability', I do not climb but instead gaze at. Rooted to the spot: openly picturing its poet paralysed in the face of sheer possibility, the poem offers us the experience of the loss of experience.

THE GREAT ODE

This difficulty of bearing bliss is not merely a product of a late point in Wordsworth's course, a point at which bliss might have become inconvenient, say, to 'repose'. In an early draft of the very Ode which stands at once as the hymn to bliss and the elegy for its loss, we find, at the place later occupied by a jubilant co-celebration, 'The fullness of your bliss, I feel – I feel it all', this:[7]

> Even yet more gladness I can hold it all

The difficulty of 'holding' or containing bliss, the difficulty of bearing bliss, stands over the whole poem as much as the sorrow of losing it.

Whenever I think about the 'Ode ('There was a time')' I cannot not think (since I means I and not you here) about my first experience of it. However ignorant or inaccurate I may therefore come to think any of the interpretations which that experience produced, what I do when I wholly suppress it in favour of a more hermeneutically proper account is, from one point of view, to put away childish things, to relinquish one delight, to subject my interpretations to the scrutiny of peers which is alone supposed to determine its truth; from another, it is to imply as the basis of my writing, willingly or not, a more proper or approbable set of experiences of the poem which are, none the less, since I can in the event never wholly put by the memory of that first reading, only a simulacrum of the experiences which I have in the event had. If I force myself to recall to the extent that this is possible the real contours of my first experience of reading this poem, it is at once clear that much of what makes up the particular bliss of it is not properly speaking what may count either as part of literary criticism or as part of any of the new-philological replacements which have turned so determinedly to all the material particularity which such criticism has supposedly excluded. If the copy in which this poem was first read were printed on paper not quite of India fineness, yet thin enough to be reminscent of some of the Bibles which I had seen to that date, and if the mock-gilding on its edges confirmed this reminiscence; if the printer had pushed the Ode into pages of double-column, with the usual effect of squashing its more expansive lines up against the column and thus forcing their terminations into a smaller or larger coda on the next line, often competing for space with the next 'line' properly so called; my coloured experience of these facts would be relevant neither to a properly literary-critical treatment of the poem (and at best only to such a treatment of this particular printing of it) nor to an interpretation in which the implied and sedimented meanings of book production *c*. 1850, rather than of reading *c*. 1980, are to be considered. Then what I remember as the absolutely critical fact, that the line 'Shout round me, let me hear thy shouts, thou happy shepherd boy' not only was crammed into a line and a coda of this double-columned space, but also, the type being smaller, the characters in a smaller point and the ink less thickly applied than in any other edition of the type which I have seen, that defects in the printing had further resulted in the words of these lines being just barely legible, and in much of their punctuation disappearing entirely; – this fact will say nothing about this poem at all but will merely be an 'arbitrary' point in the contingent experience of a single individual; and it was of course with just the chastening knowledge of the insignificance of my own experience that the elation which I had experienced at reading this line, at the sense of a destruction of an apparently absolute, yet really arbitrary, obstacle to bliss, to which this line appeared to me to give utterance, and which had caused me to leap up from the ground and walk out of the door, faded (over months and years) into dejection as I became aware of how much of this bliss depended precisely upon what it was not supposed to depend upon: upon the defective printing; upon the colour of the cover, the feel of the paper; upon the fact that I had bought the book with my 'own' money; upon the comfortable interior, so close to the hills, which had been provided for my reading.

What survived that dejection was a strong memory of this line and of its importance to the poem, coupled with a troubling sense that none of the many reasons which might be brought up to explain the power which I felt in it could in fact do so. The contextualist answer seemed even worse. It would say that of course no line has glory in itself but only 'in relation' to whatever. The answer still leaves a reader asking why the glory seems to happen when this line happens. The attempt to say why must rely on analysis. A line is cut up into its different aspects. Yet each of these by itself has no set series of effects. Then comes the transubstantiation. Components with no inherent effects combine to produce an effect. In this case I quickly ruled out the defective printing. I had seen other texts defectively printed; they had not had this effect. The pattern of internal rhyme in this line, by which *ow ow ow ow* rang out along it like a series of cries of pain, rather than necessarily of joy; the sheer length of the line, emphatically underscored by the unusual dominance of monosyllables in it; these 'in combination with' (what in fact they could only be separated from 'for the purposes of analysis') the paraphrasable meaning and its strangeness: the apparently redundant imperative to the shepherd boy to do what he is already doing; the further redundance of asking the shepherd boy to allow the poet to 'hear' his shouts when, if he has obeyed the first imperative to shout, the poet must, unless deaf, already be hearing him; the cloudy compression of asking the shepherd boy to shout 'round' him, which transfers the preposition from an implied verb of *moving* around the poet to one of *shouting* around him (it not being clear in what literal sense one person may shout *around* another): all these appeared to suggest a loss of control, or a spontaneous overflow of powerful feelings, testifying to an experienced, rather than only to a mentioned, moment of bliss: to which I can now see that the defective printing in truth did add, in its effacement of punctuation, in the way that all the overflows present in the line had the good luck to be confirmed by the obliteration of the printed marks which would generally signify its end, the single 'accidental' element allowing me to lose control of my own feelings, that is, to be moved: moved off the floor and out into the street.

Some of the most attentive criticism of this poem has focussed on what has seemed to it like a vagueness in it, a resort to general terms. Hartman found in this poem and in the 'Ode to Duty' 'a certain vague or perhaps "philosophical" generality in some of Wordsworth's expressions':

> Why did the poet not specify of what nature, other than timely, the utterance was? He is keeping the experience at a certain level of generality. He does not specify, for the same reason, the content of the 'thought of grief'. Though he begins his Ode with a specific sentiment, it is still expressed in very general terms, and we learn nothing about the conditions in which it arose except that the season was spring . . . 'Fields of sleep' is another difficulty in the same stanza: what does it stand for? The West? The west wind that awakens nature yet recalls the region nearest the setting sun? A mingling of the themes of birth and death would not be inappropriate, but again one is uncertain as to whether the phrase has real mystery or is a periphrasis avoiding a more specific term.[8]

Hartman sounds more like Jeffrey here than he usually does, and his complaints that the poet has not provided more specific reportage about his own experience feel tactical, designed to get at what is important about the poem. It is not simply that the poem deals in universalities which are too general to carry conviction. Rather, something more troubling is the case. The poem seems to be no more in control of conceptual universality than it is of detailed particularity. Its printed utterance appears to *waver* towards vagueness, refusing either to subsume or to exemplify. A remark by Ferguson illuminates this point. She detected in the subtitle given to the poem from 1815 onwards an evasion of the usual philosophical modes of structuring the relation between universal and particular which she took to be exemplary for the poem's logic or illogic at large:

> the logical connections of the title – like the movements from stanza to stanza in the poem – have a curiously wavering quality, so that induction and deduction, the progress from particular to general and the progress from general to particular, never become distinct and opposite logical modes. For it is impossible to choose which is the general term and which might be the particular – the proposition of a future immortality or the recollections which might be of preexistence.[9]

These insights lay open the perhaps surprising possibility that this very wavering quality might be the source of what truth-content the poem has: of its truth to experience, despite 'keeping the experience at a certain level of generality'; of whatever philosophical truth it may claim, despite its refusal of either inductive or deductive modes of proceeding. What James Montgomery said of stanza 6, to which he was hostile for dogmatic reasons, that it consists of 'unwarranted speculations',[10] might be applied to the poem as a whole. To consider why unwarranted speculations might ever have either lyrical or philosophical power demands a closer attention to the particular course of their waverings.

Of the many shaded areas in the account above, the phenomenology of 'bliss' or 'glory' is the murkiest. It is so in the Ode too. 'Glory' and its cognates return repeatedly (5, 16, 18, 57, 64, 83, 181). What is Wordsworth talking about?

It has often been thought evident that from the start Wordsworth is primarily telling the personal story of this decline, as a loss of his own capacity to see. This results from reading back the narrative of child development written later into the first stanzas. It is said at an early point that 'The things which I have seen I now can see no more'; but it is not yet said whether this is because of a decline in the power of sight or because the things are no longer there. And the next stanza ends by saying that the poet *knows* 'That there hath pass'd away a glory from the earth.' In the light of what the poem later says, it is natural to read lines like these figuratively, as a projection on to the earth of a passing away of power in the soul. But an earlier line combines with this to suggest an under-sense which works differently. 'It is not now as it hath been of yore' is strange because 'of yore' is a strange expression to use about oneself.

Beneath the easiest reading, which assimilates such moments to the later personal-developmental narrative, is another one in which what they say, however strange, is listened to: that the earth itself has lost a glory or an enchantment which it once possessed. Later on, the relation between 'glory' and 'earth' remains complicated. In stanza 6 earth tries to make man 'Forget the glories he hath known.' At first this looks straightforward. Glory is in the soul and from heaven; earth confuses and obscures this glory. In what sense is it then *from the earth* that glory has passed away – when the earth is what in any case tries to make us forget this glory? The poem thus develops two currents of suggestion about 'glory' and 'earth' at once. In the current which the central stanzas promote to retrospective dominance, glory is all in the soul and lost by earthly muddying. In another current which remains present, glory was also once upon the earth and has passed away from it. Only if we hear both currents can we begin to understand the force of the word 'glory' in this poem.

'Glory' itself resists any other procedure. It is an awkward word to use simply to describe a mental state. Where such senses appear they generally imply that the glory is not really such: when Evelyn asks to be acquitted of glory, he is asking to be acquitted of what would later be called, precisely in order to distinguish it from glory, *vainglory*.[11] The most telling instance of this sense, *OED* 1a, is Hobbes's definition: 'Glory, or internal gloriation or triumph of the Minde', which suggests a more radical scepticism: that even what we think of as 'objective' glory (*OED* 2) is in reality only the sum of such subjective 'gloriations'. After Hobbes, *OED* 2 is 'objective' not usually in the sense that glory is thought of as being strictly the property of an object, but only in the sense that the sum total of subjective valuations is thought of as though it were objective. The objective sense proper of glory is largely reserved, in modern English, to theology: as when the souls of believers at their death 'do immediately pass into glory' (*OED* 7a). The history of the word glory, then (especially when considered also as a means for translating from older languages), is itself an epitome of enlightenment or disenchantment. When the priesthood go up to Sinai, what they see is not a sign, manifestation or effect of the glory of the Lord but that glory itself. It does not signify itself by means of light. It is light. 'And the glory of the LORD abode upon mount Sinai, and the cloud covered it six days: and the seventh day he called unto Moses out of the midst of the cloud. And the sight of the glory of the LORD *was* like devouring fire on the top of the mount in the eyes of the children of Israel.'[12] In such a context the question of whether the word *kavod* first signifies something 'quite secular' such as weight or power (or power growing with the weight) and so later comes 'figuratively' to be used for glory, or vice versa, relies on a cleaner distinction between the literal and the figurative than will really make sense of the texts.

In beginning to think about what 'glory' actually means in this poem, the extent to which even apparently simple substantive terms require attention, yet elude simple definition, becomes more visible. It is clear that at one time glory was not merely symbolized or otherwise signified by light, but *was* light, a sense which of course persists in the technical use of 'glory' for an aureole of light (*OED* 9c). The relationship between 'light' and 'glory' well instances on the lexical level what Ferguson notes on the syntactical: the refusal of the usual means for disciplining the relationship between universal and particular, or between abstract and concrete. When we come 'trailing clouds of glory' it is very hard not to read glory as the light which illuminates these clouds; when the 'gleam' is *itself* described as 'visionary', the phrase implies that this instance of light is itself endowed with a special cognitive power.

What is 'light', in this poem about its shining or fading? The opening lines already show how hard it is to answer this question:

> There was a time when meadow, grove, and stream,
> The earth, and every common sight,
>   To me did seem
> Apparell'd in celestial light,
> The glory and the freshness of a dream.

> (1–5)

But meadow, grove and stream *must* be apparelled in celestial light even to be seen. Because of this, the lines not only produce one of those moments in Wordsworth's verse at which heaven is seen in the quotidian. They impress this on readers by a reversal. The rhetorical organization ('There was a time') leads us to anticipate that an illusion is about to be dispelled. Once it seemed as though they were clothed in celestial light, and now I can see that they are not. Yet the event goes otherwise. Once they seemed to be – what they in fact really are, apparelled in celestial light. This in turn affects our understanding of glory. We mistake the situation if we think that when Wordsworth says 'The things which I have seen I now can see no more' he is talking merely about the loss of an especially intense state of feeling. That is to say, we mistake it if we think of this as 'only a feeling'. Take the line at its word. It does not say: 'The feelings I have felt I now can feel no more', but 'The things which I have seen I now can see no more.' What the stanza says is not that an emotional colouring (for example, 'the tone of the ideal world') has been lost, but that an experience of something which is presumably there has been lost. It leaves undecided whether loss of things, or loss of sight, is the cause.

Light disconcerts and awes in this poem because it so often refuses to be either figurative or literal. The notorious fourth stanza, whose narrative is all too easily telescoped or banalized in recollection, well instances this. ' "Fades into" does not *say* "fades out" ' (Cavell).[13] It is easy, that is, to remember the stanza as saying that light fades into darkness, whereas it actually says that light fades into light.

> Heaven lies about us in our infancy!
> Shades of the prison-house begin to close
>   Upon the growing Boy,
> But He beholds the light, and whence it flows,
>   He sees it in his joy;
> The Youth, who daily farther from the East
>   Must travel, still is Nature's Priest,
>   And by the vision splendid
>   Is on his way attended;
> At length the Man perceives it die away,
> And fade into the light of common day.
>   (66–76)

The prominence of narrative stages here – infant, boy, youth, man – gives the passage a deceptive easiness. The dominant strain is clear enough. A divine light in the soul is replaced by daylight. Yet the final line nevertheless feels surprising, because the expected completion of the gradual darkening which has begun when 'Shades of the prison-house begin to close' does not occur. Instead light fades into light. '[F]ade *into*' equivocates so far as to imply that the light of common day itself contains or is illuminated by celestial light. In the prospectus for 'The Recluse', the poet asks why paradise should not be 'a simple produce of the common day'.[14] Here common day is quite capable of producing, not merely the compensatory varieties of feeling which are awarded to us in place of joy, but bliss itself. The phrase 'common day' captures a singular innovation of Wordsworth's poetry: the steady observation of the quotidian in such a way as to see paradise. 'Common day' is the meeting point of bliss and disenchantment.

If we look again at this stanza in that light, the difficulty of finding a prism to separate daylight from soul-light is illuminated. The boy 'beholds the light, and whence it flows, / He sees it in his joy.' These lines too are difficult to fit into the simple narrative of the replacement of soul- by day-light, because it is hard to see in what sense the boy 'beholds' the light of his own soul, or 'sees' it. It is not that the boy beholds the light of his soul instead of daylight, but that what he sees when he sees sunlight is seen in joy. The passage, in fact, reads as a variant retelling of the passage about love of the sun in the second book of the prospectus to 'The Recluse'. As a man, he loved the sun as a pledge, that is to say as a certain kind of sign. As a boy 'he breathed with joy'. Light, in this line of the ode, shines undecidably over both figure and letter. The light which he sees in his joy is real light. He is also real who sees it. Were it taken for granted that the daylight is literal, soul-light only figurative, then figure and letter would wrongly have been marshalled in the service of a nihilated ontology.

But is there a light in the soul? Around this question had revolved much of the previous two centuries' psychology. One of the most important determinations and hence modifications of Descartes's sentient *cogito* found in subsequent theory of the mind (whose importance for British thought has been convincingly demonstrated[15]) is that provided by the Cartesian Nicolas Malebranche. Malebranche consistently presents himself as a follower of Descartes. His faithfulness to his own understanding of the *cogito*, however, leads to an important transformation of the meaning of that feature of Descartes's thought. Whereas, as we have seen earlier, for Descartes fear, pain and hunger may count among my *ideas*, for Malebranche 'It is certain that the soul sees in itself, *and without ideas*, all the sensations and passions that affect it at the moment – pleasure, pain, cold, heat, colors, sounds, odors, tastes, its love and hatred, its joy and sadness, and all the rest – because none of the soul's sensations and passions represent anything resembling them outside the soul, and are but modifications of which a mind is capable.'[16] This leads Malebranche to a strictly patristic treatment of light in the soul. Malebranche agrees with Descartes that the radical sentience in the *cogito* is indubitable. But this does not mean that the self has a clear *idea* of itself. ' "Say not that you are a light unto yourself," says Saint Augustine, for only God is a light unto Himself and can see all that He has produced and might produce by considering himself.'[17] With this we are taken back into the ancient roots of modern enlightenment. Augustine frequently repeats his warning not to confuse our *lumen illuminatum* with God's *lumen illuminans*. It plays a central role in one of the most distinctive and influential features of his theology, its anti-Pelagianism: its denial that humans can by their virtue compel God to reward them with salvation. And this anti-Pelagianism is then profoundly influential for modern epistemology and psychology, even, and perhaps especially, for its most sceptical tendencies.

Clearly much of the way in which Wordsworth connects 'light' with 'soul' can be understood in terms of this kind of Augustinianism. The soul is a light, but not a self-constituting or self-sufficient light: it comes trailing clouds of glory from God, who is its home. But there are few better examples than Augustine of the truth that just the most determined attempts to preserve the letter of a tradition may produce the most decisive shifts in its meaning.[18] Light, in Malebranche, is properly the object of optics. Other uses of the term will be figurative. In the doxography of 'light', along which Augustine is himself a relatively late point, that distinction is much less securely established. Werner Beierwaltes, in a splendid article on the subject, nevertheless too quickly imposes a clear rhetorical division when he comments that 'In pre-Socratic philosophy, light is preponderantly a metaphor for the intelligibility of being and truth (actuality as such) and for thinking's orientation towards meaning and the experience of self-evidence.'[19] Rather that intelligibility cannot be conceived apart from the idea of light. The danger and uncertainty of the boundary between literal and figurative light is still present in Augustine, despite the existence of a highly developed apparatus for figurative interpretation of scripture by this date:

> Don't put it to yourself that God is anything like what you see in the sky, whether sun or moon or stars or anything that shines and glitters in the sky. God is not that. But again, don't suppose that the reason why God is not the sun is that the sun is like a kind of wheel, not a boundless space of light, and so you say to yourself 'God is infinite and boundless light,' and you stretch the sun, as it were, and make it have no limits, neither this way nor that, neither upward nor downward – and you put it to yourself that this boundless light is what God is. God is not that either. God indeed *dwells in light inaccessible* (1 Tm 6:16). But such light does not rotate, nor can it be perceived with the eyes in your head.[20]

Here we are much closer to the way in which 'light' is often used in the Ode. From one point of view, the whole weight of the passage is a demythologizing one, a negative way. A series of sensuously perceptible light-analogues for God are presented and successively rejected, however much they try to generalize or demystify themselves in order to do the job. Yet at the end, it is agreed that God dwells in light inaccessible. He dwells in light itself – and not in something which is like light, or a purely conceptual glory for which light is a symbol or any other kind of representation. So that from another point of view the procedure is the reverse of what might be expected. It does not reject a series of literal myths about God's light in order to reinstate them at a merely symbolic or figurative level. It rather rejects a series of figures for God's light in order to insist on its reality and inaccessibility. The light inaccessible with which the passage closes cannot be rhetorically sorted.

These considerations are least of all intended to provide Wordsworth with a 'position' of any kind along the long trajectory of opinions about the physical or metaphysical nature of light. (Indeed, what an examination of the doxography of 'light in the soul' shows is the extreme difficulty of separating out in it strands which are often, and especially as 'background' to Wordsworth's poem, treated as neatly separated dry goods – Platonism, neo-Platonism, Cartesianism, Malebranchism; rationalist, empiricist, transcendental idealist, etc. One good instance of such a difficulty is provided by the thought of a Malebranchist Platonist such as Norris of Bemerton.[21]) They are rather intended to show how the poem's wavering over 'light' reanimates, in the territory of philosophic song, the equivocality of a history which lies buried beneath, yet profoundly shapes, apparently secular and disenchanted treatments of light in modern metaphysics (whether the metaphysics is acknowledged or not). Equivocality of a fundamental word of this kind in a philosophical poem raises central difficulties and opportunities for interpretation. In one good reading of Hölderlin's later hymns, attention is drawn to the importance in them of 'very general words for existing things [*Seiendes*], words which waver between existing things and abstraction, as does Hölderlin's pet word "Äther"'.[22] Words of this kind incurred the charge that these lyrics were 'formless, vague and remote'. But they also hold a double resistance. They fit no better into a didactic poetry of ideas than they do into a poetry directly recounting personal experience. (Hartman's and Ferguson's remarks suggest that something like this double resistance may also be at work in Wordsworth's Ode.) They thus form an obvious *point d'appui* for philosophical interpretation. This is why they present both eminent opportunities and critical dangers. In Hölderlin's case the equivocal status of such words, neither fully concrete nor properly conceptual, offered an elective affinity with a practice of thinking (Heidegger's) in which this separation itself was always at stake.

But dangers are also present in that part of the Ode which constitutes what we might think of as its dogmatic core, the stanza which Coleridge described as 'mental bombast' and the place where it offers us the direct statement of what makes up that glory which is supposed to have been lost.

> Thou, whose exterior semblance doth belie
> Thy Soul's immensity;
> Thou best Philosopher, who yet dost keep
> Thy heritage, thou Eye among the blind,
> That, deaf and silent, read'st the eternal deep,
> Haunted for ever by the eternal mind, –
> Mighty Prophet! Seer blest!
> On whom those truths do rest,
> Which we are toiling all our lives to find;
> Thou, over whom thy Immortality
> Broods like the Day, a Master o'er a Slave,
> A Presence which is not to be put by;
> To whom the grave
> Is but a lonely bed without the sense or sight
> Of day or the warm light,
> A place of thought where we in waiting lie;
> Thou little Child, yet glorious in the might
> Of untam'd pleasures, on thy Being's height,
> Why with such earnest pains dost thou provoke
> The Years to bring the inevitable yoke,
> Thus blindly with thy blessedness at strife?
> Full soon thy Soul shall have hear earthly freight,
> And custom lie upon thee with a weight,
> Heavy as frost, and deep almost as life!

'Best Philosopher' in what sense? Only one phrase is offered before the verse moves on to offer other related but not identical characterizations: eye among the blind, prophet, seer, &c. This phrase is 'who yet dost keep / Thy heritage'. The implication is that the philosophers proper, by contrast, lose it. In a further illustration of the torn character of the stem 'philosoph-' in Wordsworth's authorship, the child is the 'best Philosopher' precisely in so far as he does *not* have the 'philosophic Mind' which is appealed to at line 189. But what 'heritage' is meant? Presumably the clouds of glory which we trail when we come from God. We lose this through 'custom', the stanza as a whole implies, which soon lies upon us with a weight 'deep almost as life'. Custom, then, is not life, however much it may have come to feel like it. From within custom, we toil to find out truths about life; the child is the best philosopher in the sense that this child *grounds* the truths which we (for example, as philosophers) try to *find*. What are these truths? The poem cannot know, because it is written from the standpoint of one whose development into custom is almost complete. It cannot therefore state them. Instead it attempts to lay bare the ground of those truths in a conjectural description of the child's experience whose obscurity is, on the poem's own terms, wholly to be expected. The most difficult lines here are those which most directly concern what Wordsworth later came to represent or to clarify as the poem's central subject, immortality. Three separate direct characterizations of the child's sense of it are offered. The child's immortality broods over it like the day. In this extremely unclear characterization two separate comparisons are compressed. The child's immortality is to the child as is a mother bird to her egg. This brooding in general is like the day. The separate and conjoint unclarity of these comparisons is made more resonant, but no clearer, by allusion to the holy spirit: the spirit of heaven which descends upon John the Baptist 'like a dove' and abides upon him (John 1.32). If we thus accept that we do not need to follow the literal implications of 'broods' too closely, but rather take them as a summoning of a tradition of thought about the holy spirit, we are still left with 'broods like the day'. The expression refers us back to the 'common day' which has earlier been mentioned as the faded terminus at which the advance of custom leaves us. This light of this 'day', then, we must assume, is not faded, but brighter: but the actual words here give us no ground for thinking that: they rather suggest that this brooding is indeed something common or universal, like daylight: as the sun rises on the evil and the good alike (Matthew 5.45).

This may help us to read the initially equally puzzling claim that follows, that the child's immortality broods over it (so we must suppose in the absence of any further verb) like 'a Master o'er a Slave'. The forced, the involuntary character of the child's thought-feelings about immortality is crucial for Wordsworth. They are no more all our own work than is daylight. They are luck, the luck of being emphatically alive, for which we can take no credit at all. On this luck rest all the truths which we later toil to find, and for the supposed discovery of which we later precisely do take credit. They are, indeed, 'a Presence which is not to be put by'; and with this the poem appears to open one of the moments of open contradiction which litter its surface. The presence is not to be put by. But putting it by is just what the child is already at work to do, in a way which this very stanza is about to lament; and indeed, the stanza suggests, this putting by will finally triumph. In fact, though, the poem's concern seems oddly misplaced, because the 'Yoke' is 'inevitable'. It will come whether the child 'provokes' it or not. When it is said, then, that the child's immortality broods over it like the day, the comparison enforces the point that the celestial light which the poem is trying to remember or imagine is at the same time something absolutely quotidian.

Few passages have seemed to critics more to introduce wavering into the poem than this passage from its antepenultimate stanza:

> Not for these I raise
> The song of thanks and praise;
> But for those obstinate questionings
> Of sense and outward things,
> Fallings from us, vanishings;
> Blank misgivings of a Creature
> Moving about in worlds not realiz'd,
> High instincts, before which our mortal Nature
> Did tremble like a guilty Thing surpriz'd:
> But for those first affections,
> Those shadowy recollections,
> Which, be they what they may,
> Are yet the fountain light of all our day,
> Are yet a master light of all our seeing;
> Uphold us, cherish us, and make
> Our noisy years seem moments in the being
> Of the eternal Silence: truths that wake,
> To perish never;
> Which neither listlessness, nor mad endeavour,
> Nor Man nor Boy,
> Nor all that is at enmity with joy,
> Can utterly abolish or destroy!
>
> (142–63)

Puzzlement has often sprung from the idea that anything so shadowy could be 'a master light'. It would be wrong to pretend, and useless to demonstrate, that this difficulty can be dispelled. It would also be wrong just to write it off, as is so often done with problems in a poem's thinking, to poetical high spirits. What matters is to show why the difficulty is significant, rather than just confused. This does require showing what kind of sense the lines do make. First of all, it is clear that what is not at stake is a conventional opposition between the mind, understood as self-consciousness or self-reflection, and the world, understood as including everything affective. The 'obstinate questionings' are 'of sense and out-ward things', which already suggests that there are inward things which do the questioning. These inward things could hardly be less like self-consciousness or self-reflection. They are in the next line specified not as the activity or mastery of reflective spirit over itself and its objects but as just the reverse, as the loss of such mastery, as 'fallings from us, vanishings'. It is these lapses or lacunae which are then treated as the condition of the possibility of our experience, 'a master light of all our seeing'. They are later called 'affections'.

Some of the apparently paradoxical character of this passage is removed if we can keep hold of this without dissolving it into the usual opposition between self-consciousness and affectivity. Because the passage is not presenting us with a light of mental activity darkened by affectivity or sensing whether exterior or interior, the opposition between light and darkness does not have the same meaning as it has in, for example, Locke ('Light, true light in the Mind is, or can be nothing else but the Evidence of the Truth of any Proposition'[23]). When can 'shadowy recollection' become a master light of seeing, that is, become what makes seeing possible? When it preserves that 'first affection' which is the very element without which all our knowledge, reflective or otherwise, would be just nothing. The recollections are not 'shadowy' because they are of something which is a fantasy or whose unreality has been replaced by a more mature knowledge, but because they may be the object of a listless or madly endeavouring attempt to 'destroy' them. They are not 'utterly' abolishable or destructible, however, for a straightforward reason which the poem itself has already given. They are a master light of all our seeing. All our seeing: not just of glorious or ecstatic vision, but also of seeing daylight. These first affections are the condition of possibility even of that listlessness or mad endeavour which would like to destroy them. Wordsworth still means that this 'Presence' is 'not wholly to be put by'. When can dark recollection become 'a master light'? When light has been misidentified with the purifying deletion of affectivity.

This makes the poem's last turn all the more startling. When the poet exclaims 'O joy! that in our embers / Is something that doth live', he is not now speaking, as he will later, of the supplementing of intimations of immortality with consolations of various kinds, with 'years that bring the philosophic mind', &c., but rather with a still remaining element of the 'Presence which is not to be put by', that which is not to be sublated. Something that doth live is precisely not custom in the sense that custom is only 'deep *almost* as life'. The final two stanzas behave, by contrast, as though their predecessors have surrendered something which has not in fact so far been surrendered at all. They give up bliss by telling the story of how it has already been given up. This is a sleight of hand in the poem's logic. It is a sleight of hand in getting to an ending; a counterpart to the *Prelude*'s sleight of hand in getting started. It is most clearly detectable in these lines:

> I only have relinquish'd one delight
> To live beneath your more habitual sway.
> (193–4)

This sounds like a sacrifice. I have given up *x* so that I can have *y*. But what reason is there to think that giving up *x* should secure *y*? Far from summarizing what has happened, the lines in fact introduce two quite new moves. They suggest that bliss not only decays, but that in certain respects it is better that it should do so, because the best is the enemy of the good. Equally importantly, they transmute something which has been regarded so far as outside the poet's control into a symbolic act. 'I have relinquish'd': this retrospective performative turns a loss which has so far been represented not only as involuntary, but as incomplete and in fact incompletable, into a willed sacrifice.

How tempting it is to run off with this last and worst loss – the loss of self-knowledge which consists in congratulating oneself on one's loss – as though it were what the poem meant! Yet if it is not what the poem means, this is for a surprising reason. We might expect to object to any such interpretation along the lines that the poem is to be interpreted in its whole process rather than simply in its result. What is curious here, though, is that the unsatisfactoriness of that reading (that is, to take the sacrifice of bliss as the result of the poem) becomes evident not through considering how some dialectical or other progressive argument in the poem is wilfully ignored by this result-taking, but rather through the way the final stanza lays bare the *lack* of process or development in the poem. Recall how quite forlorn these lines sounded in the first stanza:

> The Rainbow comes and goes,
> And lovely is the Rose
> (10–11)

The dejection comes from the fact that the lines are supposed to cheer us up. From their position in apposition to the lament that a glory is gone from the earth, they are implied to say what is not so bad after all. Yet the best that can be said is that the rainbow – comes and goes. It is as though the poet has already reached the point at which, should it ever come, he asks to die in 'My heart leaps up', a point at which the rainbow simply comes and goes, shuttling back and forth without any particular significance being applied to this fact. Now, here, 'The innocent brightness of a new-born Day / Is lovely yet', just as, there, 'lovely is the Rose'.

No progress has been made. No sublation has occurred. The poem is not dialectic but 'fluctuations of generous feeling'.[24] It is pathos of repetition. With all of melancholia's inability to progress, it yet has mourning's open grief. Echo gives the lie to the retrospective gesture of having-sacrificed. Even as it tells a story about how bliss was given up, the poem sounds longing for bliss.

Conclusion: imagination

Where, then, have we arrived? If this is really *philosophic* song, to what philosophical, rather than merely lyrical, results (if any) has it led?

This book has been tracing, not the doxa of a philosophical system happening to have been subsequently clothed in verse, but rather a peculiar kind of thinking which happens to have happened *in* verse. Accordingly its focus has been not upon the many and well-documented aspects of Wordsworth's writing which repeat or work within some pre-existing ontological lexicon, but rather with moments at which, under the pressure of steady attention to some particular subject, such vocabularies break down, and the possibility of new thinking is glimpsed. For this reason, the truth-contents of Wordsworth's poetry do not provide us a philosophical system, a machinery of propositions standing in a mutually supportive and finally non-contradictory relation to each other. Indeed, the readings in this book have tended to locate poetic thinking just at those points where some contradiction is openly exposed and felt in its full force as the trace of a real antagonism.

Yet it is possible at this point to gather together thoughts which have so far been pursued mainly in isolation from each other. Wordsworth's response to the enlightenment critique of religion is not primarily restorationist. Instead it dwells on the way in which that very critique continues to bear a religious character. This paradox can be figured either comically, as a kind of Quixotism, or tragically, as a kind of Rivers-ism. This response provides a framework for Wordsworth's response to the much wider question of disenchantment in general. In technical philosophy that disenchantment works through a double manoeuvre: the phenomenalization of the object, the evacuation of the subject. The period preceding Wordsworth is one in which a lapsed-Cartesian ontology (chapter 6) is continually eaten away at by sceptical questioning. The notion that objects might have qualities and meanings of their own independent of those which are conferred on them by subjects becomes ever more certainly mythical; yet at the same time the idea that such subjects might have any being of their own independent of that which is conferred on them by objects is equally remorselessly erased: all of which culminates in a nihilated ontology in which, somehow, nothing plus nothing is supposed to equal something.

In this context some of the traditional preoccupations of interpretation of the philosophical content of Wordsworth's poetry perhaps look less significant. If both subject and object have been hollowed out by disenchantment, then adding them up (for example by 'overcoming' 'Cartesian' dualism) makes no difference at all. Just because Wordsworth was not a philosopher, but a poet who wished to write philosophic song, the mere question of the world's *number* (say, of 1, 2, 3 or 4: of monism, dualism, speculative idealism or 'fourfold' mythmaking) is not the pivot of his poetic thinking. Likewise, the question of 'whether' Wordsworth is a poet of Nature or a poet of transcendental individual vision perhaps no longer makes the same kind of sense – not so much for the old reason, that he would supposedly be some kind of instinctive dialectician, but because the perfectibility of *both* forms of disenchantment, the nihilation *both* of Nature and of the soul, are simultaneously contested, *precisely by keeping open the difference between them.* His verse fights tooth and lung against these nothings which we are supposedly to accept as the very substance of our lives: the phenomenalized object, the evacuated subject; the total then made of this no-subject and no-object.

But this *loss of experience* is by no means a problem only for philosophy. It is felt wherever we allow some idol of emptiness (an illimitable walk, a dead letter, a vacant commerce) to govern our thinking and doing. It is faced in Wordsworth's verse, not by a fabulated retreat to myth, but by attention to experience. The truth-content of Wordsworth's poetry, then, were we forced to contract it to a pulse of an artery, would lie in this resistance. Such resistance lives in what I described earlier as the speculative element of Wordsworth's verse, an element in which collide the nostalgic and utopian wish for efficacious magic – the wish to change this world with poetry – and the steadily attentive, the phenomenological, look at a subject.

In one of the later fragments intended for his never-completed long poem, 'The Recluse', Wordsworth writes of a moment in the city which seemed to offer him repose. He has come full of anxiety and foreboding from a meeting with Coleridge.

Press'd with conflicting thoughts of love and fear,
I parted from thee, Friend! and took my way
Through the great City, pacing with an eye
Down cast, ear sleeping, and feet masterless,
That were sufficient guide unto themselves,
And step by step went pensively. Now, mark!
Not how my trouble was entirely hush'd.
(That might not be) but how by sudden gift,
Gift of Imagination's holy power!
My Soul in her uneasiness received
An anchor of stability. It chanced
That, while I thus was pacing, I raised up
My heavy eyes and instantly beheld,
Saw at a glance in that familiar spot
A visionary scene: a length of street
Laid open in its morning quietness,
Deep, hollow, unobstructed, vacant, smooth,
And white with winter's purest white, as fair,
As fresh and spotless as he ever sheds
On field or mountain. Moving Form was none,
Save here and there a shadowy Passenger,
Slow, shadowy, silent, dusky, and beyond
And high above this winding length of street,
This noiseless and unpeopled avenue,
Pure, silent, solemn, beautiful, was seen
The huge majestic Temple of St. Paul
In awful sequestration, through a veil,
Through its own sacred veil of falling snow.[1]

Here the whole creative powers of man have been laid to sleep not by any 'spectacle', but by anxiety. The walk is illimitable, automatic, until Wordsworth should recover some control over it. Yet what brings him up short is nothing of his own work, but the 'chance' that he should look up. Although this is a 'sudden gift', help from elsewhere, it is then at once glossed, remarkably, as the 'Gift of Imagination's holy power!' In the first full draft of the poem this interjection is not set apart in any way. In the fair copy made later, however, it was clearly at first omitted and then later squeezed in between the surrounding lines, an effect which Kishel's transcription of DC MS 65, 119[r] aptly represents thus:

Now, mark!
Not how my trouble was entirely hush'd,
(That might not be) but how by sudden gift

> Gift of imagination holy power
> My Soul in her uneasiness received
> An anchor of stability.

It is natural enough to conjecture, with Kishel, that the omission was 'probably inadvertent', but also to wonder why the line might have slipped the mind in transcription.[2] The 'sudden gift' from elsewhere, a gift of the apparently quite contingent fact that it has started snowing, becomes, it seems, a gift from the self, a gift of the imagination: unless it be the case that here 'imagination' might stand precisely for what is *not* all your own work, for an experience of meaning which is undergone, and which is distinguished from fancy or fantasy by not being the voluntary assignment of meaning to a helpless vehicle. Hence it may be no paradox to say that in this 'Gift of imagination', the 'Soul' 'received', rather than bestowed, a 'sudden gift'. The sudden gift interrupts the perpetual flow of exchange. A wooden placard expresses the wish of many children: 'Let it snow!'[3] – and perhaps not only because of the possible release from school. When it snows you can be sure that something is actually happening. That the apparently unstoppable flow of timetabled non-events can in fact be stopped; – that the second weather which impels 'depressions', 'surges' and 'erosions' of financial confidence should be interrupted by weather, can be an intimation of bliss, and in any case feels like an experience at once meaningful and real. None other than this is 'imagination'. Imagination is the capacity for experience.

The description of what it was that Wordsworth actually saw, and which partially relieved his uneasiness, forms in several ways a counterpoint to the experience of the London streets addressed in the 'poem to Coleridge'. The redundance of 'look' and 'aspect' which introduced that account is echoed here. The instant at which Wordsworth looks up cannot be as instantaneously described but is strikingly extended: the poet 'raised up' his 'heavy eyes', 'beheld' and 'saw', 'at a glance'. Yes, it happened at a glance; but it is described four times. The poem partly relies on several repetitions to create its sense of a real duration suddenly donated within a perpetual flow of punctual presences: the occasional figures in the street are twice described as 'shadowy'; they are 'silent' and the cathedral is 'silent'; the 'veil' of snow before it is named twice in two lines. The listing shape of many lines in book 7 of *The Prelude* reappears here, but with a difference. The draft is built around three lines which become focal by the echoes in their shapes:

Deep, hollow, unobstructed, vacant, smooth,
Slow, shadowy, silent, dusky, and beyond
Pure, silent, solemn, beautiful, was seen

Putting these lines next to each other at once shows a difference. In the
first of them all the words are adjectives, but not in the second and third.
The second of these lines can come as an exhilarating surprise or sudden
gift, because the flow of adjectives to which readers may have got used is
interrupted, and attention is thrown forward, a propulsion which is not
in fact stilled until the very end of the poem, when we read the word
which has until then been held back, and which we may have been
longing to read as though it were the name for the whole experience of
interrupting beauty which is described in the poem: 'snow'.

The redundance which expresses the wish for an unconscious reciprocity of excess appears in the verse itself at moments of imaginative
power; that is, at moments when something significant is actually
experienced. Even the 'awful sequestration' of the cathedral is animated
by such a wish. What makes the episode of the cathedral an experience is
not the emptiness of the empty streets – which were empty before, when
Wordsworth was treading mechanically through them – but the interruption of chancing to look up, its suddenness: by which a difference is
opened up. This 'sequestration' is strongly linked to the much-discussed
episode in which Wordsworth, lost in the phantasmagoria, the 'second-
sight procession', sees a blind beggar with a placard in book 7 of the
'poem to Coleridge'. There too ''twas my chance / Abruptly to be smitten
with the view', and it is this abrupt interruption which gives the sight
almost the weight of a conversion: 'My mind did at this spectacle turn
round, / As with the weight of waters ... / ... I look'd / As if admon-
ish'd from another world.'[4] The blind beggar is no less awfully sequestered than the cathedral. The societarian objection – why does he gaze at
the beggar rather than helping him? – only partially hits its target, because
this character of the city as a spectacle rather than as a possible sphere of
action, and most a spectacle when activity is most repetitiously frenetic, is
just Wordsworth's subject. The writing is trying to detach those spectacles
which wake us up from those which send us to sleep.[5] It is on this note, in
fact, that Wordsworth's reversion to London in book 8 closes:

'Twas a Man
Whom I saw sitting in an open Square
Close to the iron paling that fenced in

The spacious Grass-plot: on the corner-stone
Of the low wall in which the pales were fix'd
Sate this one Man, and with a sickly Babe
Upon his knee, whom he had thither brought
For sunshine, and to breathe the fresher air.
Of those who pass'd, and me who look'd at him
He took no note; but in his brawny Arms
(The Artificer was to the elbow bare
And from his work this moment had been stolen)
He held the Child, and bending over it,
As if he were afraid both of the sun
And of the air which he had come to seek,
He eyed it with unutterable love.

(viii. 844–59)

The instant is again an interruption in that it has been 'stolen' from those who own it. In the epoch of pseudo-experience, the 'vacant commerce' among personified commodities,[6] possible experiences come to take the form of gifts or thefts. The encounter is a failure or an absence of reciprocity. The worker takes no notice of the poet, who stands and gazes at this 'scene'. The writing is open to being blamed for the absence of transparency which is its subject. Yet the 'awful sequestration' of the cathedral, the unknowability of the blind beggar, the failure of encounter between poet and artificer may be kinds of counter-magic. Instead of viewing the 'mystery' of the unintelligible aspects of the city from a willed vantage of pretended clear sight, they place mystery against mystery, the mysteriousness of an interruption (an interruption, for example, which allows the unprecedented achievement of getting out a line like 'Of the low wall to which the pales were fix'd' without the least sense of bathos) to the prevailing and systematic mystery. And for this reason trying to distinguish these kinds of mystery – to distinguish the mysteriousness of experiencing something from the mystification of failing to experience anything – is not like dividing sheep from goats, but like groping around in a cave.

If any of DC MS 38 1^v (discussed above, chapter 6) is drafting for 'the "Higher Mind" material' in book 13, it is striking to see how different was the solution which Wordsworth eventually adopted to the difficulties evident there.

With forehead bent
Earthward, as if in opposition set
Against an enemy, I panted up

With eager pace, and no less eager thoughts.
Thus might we wear perhaps an hour away,
Ascending at loose distance each from each,
As I, as chanced, the foremost of the Band,
When at my feet the ground appear'd to brighten,
And with a step or two seem'd brighter still,
Nor had I time to ask the cause of this,
For instantly a Light upon the turf
Fell like a flash: I look'd about, and lo!
The Moon stood naked in the Heavens, at height
Immense above my head, and on the shore
I found myself of a huge sea of mist,
Which meek and silent, rested at my feet:
A hundred hills their dusky backs upheaved
All over this still Ocean, and beyond,
Far, far beyond, the vapours shot themselves,
In headlands, tongues, and promontory shapes
Into the Sea, the real Sea, that seem'd
To dwindle and give up its majesty,
Usurp'd upon as far as sight could reach.
Meanwhile the Moon look'd down upon this shew
In single glory, and we stood, the mist
Touching our very feet: and from the shore
At distance not the third part of a mile
Was a blue chasm, a fracture in the vapour,
A deep and gloomy breathing-place thro' which
Mounted the roar of waters, torrents, streams
Innumerable, roaring with one voice.
The universal spectacle throughout
Was shaped for admiration and delight,
Grand in itself alone, but in that breach
Through which the homeless voice of waters rose,
That dark deep thorough-fare had Nature lodg'd
The Soul, the Imagination of the whole.

Just now I suggested that imagination was the capacity for experience.
If the claim were intended to stand as a definition, for example, adequately covering all Wordsworth's uses of the word, it would have to
be withdrawn right now in the face of a passage such as this. The words
are an affront to common reason. It is hard enough that 'Imagination',
here, is nothing at all in Wordsworth but is actually out there in what he
sees. It is much harder that this Imagination is actually lodging in a
particular bit of this landscape. There it is: there, in that break in the mist:
there: Imagination! I now see that in this book I have been gradually

developing the idea that the difference between imagination and idolatry is both the most vital difference in the authorship, and the hardest accurately to discriminate. There is no method, tool or machine which can guarantee us in advance that we may know delusion from meaning (chapter 1), shrine from idol (chapter 6), 'illimitable walk' from 'endless way' (chapter 5), mystification from mystery (conclusion). This passage raises that difficulty to a further power, in that it is an account of Imagination which is itself cast in terms which must raise disturbingly idolatrous echoes. In fact, when we look more closely, the passage both suggests and complicates such connections. Imagination is given a particular spot in the spectacle. That allocation appears to ignore centuries of the enlightened de-substantialization of Imagination, which for technical philosophy is not only quite obviously not out there in the world, but which also is not in any substantive sense 'in here' either. To this extent, the words are idolatrous. They house divine powers in a particular bit of matter. Except that that particular bit of matter where imagination is lodged turns out to be not a bit of matter at all, but the absence of one. It is a cut, a gap, a 'chasm' or 'breach'. Why is this absence at the centre of the experience described? The voice of waters seems homeless in the sense that, whilst it can be heard, its source or home cannot be seen. If there is a deity here, it is a speaking and not a visible or idolized one; and yet there is an idolatry in making this voice appear (albeit as 'homeless') from a particular site, or from a particular cut in a particular site.

The passage in fact offers us three separate moments of sudden revelation. The moon's emergence from the clouds reveals the sea of mist; the sea of mist gives way far in the distance to 'the real sea'; it also opens internally to [allow] the homeless voice of waters to ascend. The second of these moments makes explicit something which is fundamental to each. The shock of the real is at the heart of what imagination means in this passage. This shock is administered in the phrase 'the Sea, the real Sea'. The phrase tells us what to take for figure and what to read by the letter. The sea of mist is a figure at whose edge the literal sea can be seen.

Imagination has little to do with 'the aesthetic'. In the passage we have just read, the fact of placing imagination in a particular spot in the landscape is so startling that we are likely to miss another, equally important feature of the passage: the paratactic equivalence established in the line 'The Soul, the Imagination of the whole'. For no tradition of philosophical or half-philosophical 'aesthetics' could imagination be understood as anything like a 'soul' at all. 'Imagination' is one of those words, in fact, whose treatment by Wordsworth most sharply marks off whatever 'philosophic Song' may do from what philosophy does. Wherever he tries in verse to say what imagination is, Wordsworth becomes more than usually cataloguing or paratactic. Even when the sentence starts as though about to offer us the definition, it ends otherwise. Later in book 13, for instance, Wordsworth explains how 'fear and love' have helped to preserve him from 'a universe of death' – fear and love, but especially love, and of love, especially that 'love more intellectual' of which he then says that imagination is the necessary condition:

> This love more intellectual cannot be
> Without Imagination, which in truth
> Is but another name for absolute strength
> And clearest insight, amplitude of mind,
> And reason in her most exalted mood.[7]

If 'but another name' encourages readers to hope for definition, the length of the list at once makes it clear that the passage is rather a refusal of a definition. Not only are some of the items on the list themselves barely intelligible – when a quality so particular as 'strength' is qualified as 'absolute' it is hard to know what meaning to continue to attach to the substantive – but they overlap and differ in ways that make the passage less a clarification than a further diffusion of the term's meaning. 'But another name' significantly signals, none the less, that no esoterically technical significance is attached to the word. If imagination is 'absolute strength' *and* 'clearest insight' *and* 'amplitude of mind' *and* 'reason in her most exalted mood', perhaps the only thing that does begin to become clear is that imagination cannot possibly be a philosophical name for a clearly defined faculty, power or ontological region. Indeed we perhaps begin to suspect that what imagination describes is not even a kind of capacity for experience but a kind of experience. So that even when Wordsworth goes on to describe imagination as a 'faculty' which 'has been the moving soul of our long labour', the description of that faculty, it at once becomes clear, has had to take a narrative course rather than an analytic or synthetic form, a course which is here, like that planned in Coleridge's unwritten epic, compared to that of a river now visible, now unseen:

> lastly, from its progress have we drawn
> The feeling of life endless, the one thought
> By which we live, Infinity and God.

We need to see what is lost if we paraphrase these lines as meaning something like 'imagination, finally, is the source of our hope of immortality, the one idea which keeps us going, the idea of infinity and God'. Such a paraphrase would miss almost everything of interest here. It misses the paratactic identification of or equivocation between 'feeling' and 'thought'. This makes a critical difference: without that identification or equivocation, the thought by which we live might easily be just another 'thought' in a sense like Kant's: a state which (precisely, indeed, as Kant does in fact treat the topic of the possible immortality of the soul) we think but in principle cannot experience.[8] Because 'thought' and 'feeling' are paratactically undifferentiable, this thought is also an experience which we already have, is also a 'feeling of life endless'. It is not a conjecture but rather an extension of the life which is already in thinking. In this sense is it 'the one thought By which we live': not the one conjectural consolation which makes it possible for us to go on, but the one thought which makes our life possible as life. And that, finally, makes all the difference to how *Imagination* is imagined here: never as what you may at will *decide* to imagine or not to imagine, nor as a purely trans-cendental 'condition of the possibility of experience', but rather as what is indubitably real and lived in experience, as what we experience when the 'universe of death' or 'counter-spirit' to which we become comfortably habituated is interrupted. Imagination happens to us at that instant when we are brought emphatically to affirm that we live.

Notes

INTRODUCTION

1 *Thirteen-Book Prelude*, vol. I, pp. 112–13 (i. 229–39); 'favourite' appears as 'favorite' in Reed's text. Book and line numbers in parentheses without further reference always refer henceforth (unless stated otherwise) to Reed's 'AB-stage reading text' of the *Thirteen-Book Prelude*.

2 David Bromwich, *Disowned by Memory: Wordsworth's Poetry of the 1790s* (Chicago: University of Chicago Press, 1998), p. 4. For a sharply contrasting view, see Alan Bewell, *Wordsworth and the Enlightenment: Nature, Man, and Society in the Experimental Poetry* (New Haven and London: Yale University Press, 1989), p. x: 'The working thesis of this study is that Wordsworth's major objective as a poet was to write a series of poems that together would constitute a general history of the imagination, of the forms that it has taken over the course of human history and the role that it has played in the genesis and development of social institutions such as language, poetry, religion, property, and civil government.'

3 S. T. Coleridge, *Table Talk recorded by Henry Nelson Coleridge (and John Taylor Coleridge)*, ed. Carl Woodring (2 vols., Princeton: Princeton University Press, 1990), vol. I, pp. 307–8 (21 July 1832).

4 Stanley Cavell, *In Quest of the Ordinary: Lines of Skepticism and Romanticism* (Chicago and London: Chicago University Press, 1988), p. 42. Cavell, of course, is looking back at Wordsworth through Emerson, and through a meditation on what it means to be a philosopher in America; his account of Wordsworth sees how much we must lose were we to think of Wordsworth's impulse to 'philosophic Song' as merely adventitious.

5 '*Essay on morals*' (title editorial), in William Wordsworth, *Selected Prose*, ed. John O. Hayden (London: Penguin Books, 1988), pp. 104–6, p. 105.

6 For a development of this view about poetry more broadly, and about prosody in particular, see S. Jarvis, 'Prosody as cognition', *Critical Quarterly* 40.3 (Autumn 1998), pp. 1–14. This article attempts to rejoin and renew a long (and, as I hope to show, in part a *Wordsworthian*) tradition of treating metre and rhythm as matters indissociably connected with thinking. For a recent development of this case from the discipline of discourse analysis,

see Ann Wennerstrom, *The Music of Everyday Speech: Prosody and Discourse Analysis* (Oxford: Oxford University Press, 2001).

7 Samuel Taylor Coleridge, *Biographia Literaria*, ed. Nigel Leask (London: Everyman, 1997), p. 191.

8 Jean-Luc Marion, *Étant donné: essai d'une phénoménologie de la donation* (2nd, corrected edition, Paris: Presses Universitaires de France, 1998), rear endpaper (my translation). For my view of Marion's phenomenology of this gift, see S. Jarvis, 'Problems in the phenomenology of the gift', *Angelaki: Journal of the Theoretical Humanities* 6.2 (August 2001), pp. 67–77.

9 'Philological' is used here not in the emphatic sense recently developed by Keston Sutherland ('J. H. Prynne and philology', unpublished Ph.D. thesis, University of Cambridge, 2004) but to denote a practice of reading which remains immanently within a constructed notion of the totality of an author's self-understandings.

10 Exceptions are made only for allusions and epigraphs, in cases where precise reference would destroy the interest of these modes.

11 Max Horkheimer, 'Schopenhauer today' (1961), in *Critique of Instrumental Reason: Lectures and Essays since the End of World War II*, trans. Matthew J. O'Connell and others (New York: Seabury Press, 1974), pp. 63–83, p. 66.

12 *Poems, in Two Volumes*, p. 107.

13 Immanuel Kant, 'Critique of practical reason', in *Practical Philosophy*, ed. and trans. Mary J. Gregor (Cambridge: Cambridge University Press, 1996), pp. 137–271, p. 269.

14 Immanuel Kant, *Critique of Pure Reason*, trans. Norman Kemp Smith (London: Macmillan, 1933), p. 295 (B345). 'Stray' does not capture the full force of *ausschweifen*, which means both 'to digress' (of a speaker) and 'to run riot' (say, of someone's imagination).

15 Francis Jeffrey, review of *Poems, in Two Volumes* (1807), *Edinburgh Review*, 11 (October 1807), pp. 214–31, p. 221; repr. in Reiman, vol. II, pp. 429–38, p. 433.

16 'Reflective judgement' is here used in Kant's sense, to denote a case where 'only the particular is given and the power of judgement is to find the universal for it' (Kant, *Kritik der Urteilskraft*, ed. Gerhard Lehmann (Stuttgart: Philipp Reclam Jun., 1963), p. 34 [26]; see Kant, *Critique of Judgement*, trans. Werner S. Pluhar (Indianapolis: Hackett, 1987), pp. 18–19) and, in particular, to denote that type of reflective judgement, the pure aesthetic judgement of taste, which is subjectively universal (Kant, *Kritik der Urteilskraft*, §31, p. 192ff.; Pluhar, p. 143ff.). For my contention that this structure of subjective universality need not entail a commitment to Kant's own understandings of subjectivity and universality, see S. Jarvis, 'An undeleter for criticism', *diacritics* 32.1 (Spring 2002), pp. 3–18.

17 Brennan O'Donnell, *The Passion of Meter: A Study of Wordsworth's Metrical Art* (Kent, Ohio, and London: Kent State University Press, 1995).

18 Reed, *Middle Years*, p. 36, comments that the Ode was '[p]robably basically composed, except first stanza ... early 1804 by Mar 6'.

19 (*EY*, p. 434); quoted in O'Donnell, *The Passion of Meter*, p. 27.

20 Quoted in O'Donnell, *The Passion of Meter*, p. 40.
21 Ibid., p. 54; Matthew Prior, *The Literary Works*, ed. H. Bunker Wright and Monroe K. Spears (2 vols., Oxford: Clarendon Press, 1971), vol. I, pp. 230–44.
22 Roger Lonsdale, ed., *Gray, Collins and Goldsmith: The Complete Poems* (London: Longman, 1969), p. 73.
23 Matthew Prior, 'Ode', in *Literary Works*, vol. I, p. 235, line 80. See Prior, *Poems on Several Occasions* (London, 1709), p. 283.
24 E.g. *Thirteen-Book Prelude*, viii. 432: 'By the dead letter, not the spirit of things'.
25 'However, it is not inadvisable to recollect that in all the free arts something constraining, or, as it is called, a *mechanism*, is nevertheless required; a mechanism without which the *spirit* which, in art, must be *free*, and which alone animates the work, would have no body at all and would quite evaporate (such, for example, in poetry, are correct and rich diction, together with prosody and metre), since many of our recent educators think that a free art is best advanced by removing all compulsion from it, and by converting it from work into mere play.' Kant, *Kritik der Urteilskraft*, §43, p. 231 [176] (my trans.); see Pluhar, p. 171.
26 David Simpson, in one of the best-judged series of remarks on Wordsworth's 'Ode' to date, has argued that Wordsworth must have been aware of Schiller's account of the 'beautiful soul': Simpson, *Wordsworth's Historical Imagination: The Poetry of Displacement* (London: Methuen, 1987), pp. 39–40. Friedrich Schiller, *On the Aesthetic Education of Man. In a Series of Letters*, ed. and trans. Elizabeth M. Wilkinson and L. A. Willoughby (Oxford: Clarendon Press, 1967), p. 215: 'The dynamic State can merely make society possible, by letting one nature be curbed by another; the ethical State can merely make it (morally) necessary, by subjecting the individual will to the general; the aesthetic State alone can make it real, because it consummates the will of the whole through the nature of the individual.' The implication, however, is that political rights are to be withheld until subjects have shown themselves fit to enjoy them: 'as a need [the Aesthetic State] exists in every finely attuned soul; as a realized fact, we are likely to find it, like the pure Church and the pure Republic, only in some chosen few circles, where conduct is governed, not by some soulless imitation of the manners and morals of others, but by the aesthetic nature we have made our own' (p. 219). Today, however, '[a]mong the lower classes we are confronted with crude, lawless instincts, unleashed with the loosening of the bonds of civil order, and hastening with ungovernable fury to their animal satisfactions' (p. 25).
27 *Thirteen-Book Prelude*, i. 107–8 (ll. 17–19; 31–2).
28 'Preface' to *Lyrical Ballads*, p. 756.
29 'Reply to Mathetes', in Wordsworth, *Selected Prose*, pp. 107–26, p. 126. The 'following words' are the final stanza of the poem, whose last two lines are emphasized typographically.
30 Quoted in *Poems, in Two Volumes*, p. 428.
31 George Dyer, 'Prefatory essay. On lyric poetry', in *Poems* (2 vols., London, 1802), vol. I, p. xvi.

32 Gianvincenzo Gravina, *Della Ragione Poetica* [Venice, 1731], repr. in *Opere Italiane. Della Ragione Poetica e della Tragedia* (Cosenza: Brenner, 1992).

33 John Brown, *A Dissertation on the Rise, Union, and Power, the Progressions, Separations, and Corruptions, of Poetry and Music. To which is prefixed, The Cure of Saul. A Sacred Ode.* (London, 1763), p. 39; Dyer, vol. I, p. xii.

34 'Essays upon epitaphs', in Wordsworth, *Selected Prose*, pp. 322–71, p. 326.

35 'The secret of Kant's philosophy is the impossibility of fully conceiving despair.' Theodor W. Adorno, *Negative Dialektik* (Frankfurt am Main, 1966), p. 378 (my translation).

36 This is the translation given in G. S. Kirk, J. E. Raven and M. Schofield, *The Presocratic Philosophers*, (2nd edn, Cambridge: Cambridge University Press, 1983), p. 118. The interpretation of this passage is contested; I follow that of Hermann Schmitz, *Anaximander und die Anfänge der griechischen Philosophie* (Bonn: Bouvier, 1988), pp. 31–5.

37 'Legal and/or moral' because the separation between law and ethics is itself historically particular.

38 Schmitz, p. 22.

39 Kant, *Critique of Pure Reason*, p. 113.

40 Marcel Detienne, *The Masters of Truth in Archaic Greece*, trans. Janet Lloyd (New York: Zone Books, 1996), p. 52.

41 'Preface' to *Lyrical Ballads*, p. 748.

42 'Essay on morals', in Wordsworth, *Selected Prose*, p. 105.

43 *Salisbury Plain*, p. 38. see chapter 1, 'Stocks and stones', below.

44 Bewell, *Wordsworth and the Enlightenment*.

45 To John Wilson, 7 vi. 1802, in *EY*, p. 355.

46 Hugh Sykes Davies, *Wordsworth and the Worth of Words*, ed. John Kerrigan and Jonathan Wordsworth (Cambridge: Cambridge University Press, 1986), p. 3.

47 Friedrich Schlegel, 'Athenäums-Fragmente', in *Werke in einem Band*, ed. Wolfdietrich Rasch (Vienna: Carl Hanser, 1971), pp. 25–88, p. 31 (my translation).

48 See Jeffrey, review of *Poems, in Two Volumes (1807)*, p. 216; repr. in Reiman, vol. II, p. 430.

49 *Monthly Repository*, 2nd series, ix (1835), pp. 430–4, repr. in Reiman, vol. I, pp. 699–700, p. 700.

50 Quoted in *Shorter Poems 1807–1820*, p. 24.

51 John Wyatt, *Wordsworth and the Geologists* (Cambridge: Cambridge University Press, 1995), p. 98: 'Whewell had argued that Hare adopted the philosophy of certain writers because he admired their poetry. Hare replied, emphasizing every word, "But poetry is philosophy, philosophy is poetry."'

52 See John Wilkinson, 'Cadence', *Reality Studios* 9 (1987), pp. 81–5, p. 82.

53 Reiman, vol. II, p. 430.

54 Ibid., p. 431.

55 Ibid.

56 See the discussion of the way in which fundamental philosophical problems are converted in some main currents of twentieth-century thought into 'illusory' or 'pseudo-problems', in Adorno, *Negative Dialektik*, pp. 211–13.

57 'Prospectus' to 'The Recluse', in William Wordsworth, *The poems*, ed. John O. Hayden (2 vols, London: Penguin: 1977), vol. II, pp. 38–9.

58 Such prohibitions often occur through definition, e.g.: 'to be is to be the value of a bound variable'. W. V. O. Quine, quoted in Michael J. Loux, *Metaphysics: Contemporary Readings* (London: Routledge, 2001), p. 13; cf. Quine, 'On what there is', *Review of Metaphysics* 2 (1948), pp. 21–48.

59 William and Dorothy Wordsworth to Mary and Sara Hutchinson, 14 vi. 1802, in *EY*, p. 366. I was first brought to think about this passage by a lecture course given by J. H. Prynne in the Faculty of English, University of Cambridge, 1984.

60 'Preface' to *Lyrical Ballads*, p. 759.

61 Quoted in *Poems, in Two Volumes*, p. 35.

62 *Lyrical Ballads*, p. 309.

63 See chapter 6, 'Life'.

1. OLD IDOLATRY

1 *Thirteen-Book Prelude*, vol. I, pp. 323–4 (xiii. 428–52). The phrase 'old Idolatry' also occurs in the later 'Effusion, in the pleasure-ground on the banks of the Bran, near Dunkeld': *Shorter Poems 1807–1820*, pp. 133–7, p. 136.

2 See chapter 6, 'Life'. For the importance of the figure of the shrine in Wordsworth's poetic, see Forrest Pyle, 'Wordsworth: the poetry of enshrinement', in *The Ideology of Imagination: Subject and Society in the Discourse of Romanticism* (Stanford, Calif.: Stanford University Press, 1995), pp. 59–93. This book takes an approach to the relationship between 'ideology' and 'imagination' which differs from that in Pyle's subtle account.

3 *Thirteen-Book Prelude*, vol. I, pp. 296–7 (xi. 74–92).

4 *Ruined Cottage*, p. 465.

5 Ibid., p. 467.

6 William Wordsworth, *Poetical Works*, ed. E. de Selincourt and H. Darbishire (5 vols., Oxford: Clarendon Press, 1940–9), vol. I, p. 316. *The Poems*, ed. John O. Hayden (2 vols., Harmondsworth: Penguin, 1977), vol. I, p. 243.

7 *Thirteen-Book Prelude*, vol. I, p. 138 (iii. 121–9); *Fourteen-Book Prelude*, p. 168 (iii. 127–35); *Ruined Cottage*, p. 46.

8 Jonathan Lamb, 'Hartley and Wordsworth: philosophical language and figures of the sublime', *Modern Language Notes* 97.5 (1982), pp. 1964–85.

9 William Wordsworth, *Selected Prose*, ed. John O. Hayden (London: Penguin, 1988), pp. 381–2.

10 Robert Lowth, *Isaiah. A New Translation* (London, 1779); Benjamin Blayney, *Jeremiah and Lamentations. A New Translation* (Oxford, 1784).

11 There is no evidence that Wordsworth knew Blayney's work; he offered Francis Wrangham some 'bulky old Commentaries on the Scriptures' in 1812,

but Blayney's work was neither especially bulky, nor, in 1812, especially old. Lowth's volume he may well have known through Coleridge, who used it in his *Lectures on Revealed Religion*, and who according to Henry Nelson Coleridge 'used to call Isaiah his ideal of the Hebrew prophet'. S. T. Coleridge, *Lectures 1795 on Politics and Religion*, ed. Lewis Patton and Peter Mann (Princeton: Princeton University Press, 1971), p. 153n.

12 *Salisbury Plain*, p. 35.
13 William Stukeley, *Stonehenge. A Temple Restor'd to the British Druids* (London, 1740), pp. 2, 34.
14 *Salisbury Plain*, p. 35.
15 Lucan, *The Civil War*, ed. and trans. J. D. Duff (London: Heinemann, 1969), p. 145.
16 [Daniel Eaton], *Politics for the People, or A Salmagundy for Swine* (4th edn, London, 1794), p. 10. William Blake, *Complete writings*, ed. Geoffrey Keynes (Oxford: Oxford University Press, 1972), pp. 489, 491.
17 *Salisbury Plain*, p. 38.
18 Ibid., p. 27.
19 Coleridge, *Lectures 1795 on Politics and Religion*, p. 18.
20 'Essays upon epitaphs', in Wordsworth, *Selected Prose*, p. 361.
21 John Toland, *Letters to Serena* (London, 1704), p. 127; p. 72. See, later, Joseph Priestley, *An History of the Corruptions of Christianity* (2 vols., Birmingham, 1782), vol. I, p. 20.
22 Thomas Paine, 'Common sense', in *Political Writings*, ed. Bruce Kuklick (Cambridge: Cambridge University Press, 1989), p. 9.
23 Ibid., pp. 8–9.
24 Paine, 'The Age of Reason, Part First', in *Political Writings*, pp. 249–56.
25 Thomas Paine, *The Age of Reason. Part the Second. Being an Investigation of True and Fabulous Theology* (London, 1795), p. 9.
26 Baron d'Holbach, *Examen Critique de la Vie & des Ouvrages de Saint-Paul* ('Londres' (probably Amsterdam), 1770). See also d'Holbach, *L'Esprit du Judaisme, ou Examen Raisonné de la Loi de Moyse, & de son influence sur la Religion Chrétienne* ('Londres' (probably Amsterdam), 1770), p. viii.
27 Constantin Volney, *The Ruins: or a Survey of the Revolutions of Empires* (2nd edn, London, 1795), p. 237ff., p. 362; Condorcet, *Outlines of an Historical View of the Progress of the Human Mind* (London, 1795), p. 65. For an account of the importance of studies of archaic Egyptian society and writing to this theory of religion, see Patrick Tort, *La Constellation de Thot* (Paris: Aubier-Montagne, 1981).
28 Volney, *The Ruins*, p. 244.
29 Jacob Bryant, *A Treatise Upon the Authenticity of the Scriptures, and the Truth of the Christian Religion* (London, 1792), pp. 238, 239; Joseph Priestley, *An Answer to Mr Paine's Age of Reason* (London, 1795); Gilbert Wakefield, *An Examination of the Age of Reason* (London, 1794).
30 Priestley, *An Answer to Mr Paine's Age of Reason*; Wakefield, *An Examination of the Age of Reason*.

31 Paine, *The Age of Reason. Part the Second,* p. 2. See Richard Watson, *An Apology for the Bible, in a series of letters addressed to Thomas Paine* (London, 1796), pp. 16, 18–19.

32 An exception is John Prior Estlin, *Evidences of Revealed Religion, and particularly Christianity, stated, with reference to a pamphlet called The Age of Reason* (Bristol, 1796), p. 17; Estlin also draws on Lowman, however (p. 15), and Coleridge himself may have had a hand in this pamphlet: see Coleridge, *Lectures 1795 on Politics and Religion,* p. 152n.

33 Coleridge, *Lectures 1795 on Politics and Religion,* p. 126.

34 Ibid., pp. 87, 113n. Nigel Leask, 'Pantisocracy and the politics of the 'Preface' to *Lyrical Ballads*', in Allison Yarrington and Kelvin Everest, eds., *Reflections of Revolution* (London: Routledge, 1993), pp. 39–57.

35 Coleridge, *Lectures 1795 on Politics and Religion,* p. 127. Coleridge admitted that although 'An abolition of individual Property is perhaps the only infallible preventive against accumulation' there was property in the ancient Hebrew polity because the ancient Jews were incapable of 'so exalted a state of society' (p. 128).

36 Coleridge, *Lectures 1795 on Politics and Religion,* p. 143.

37 Ibid., p. 18.

38 Ibid., p. 116.

39 Ibid., pp. 116–17.

40 Ibid., p. 117.

41 Moses Lowman, *A Dissertation on the Civil Government of the Hebrews* (London, 1740), pp. 18–19.

42 Coleridge, *Lectures 1795 on Politics and Religion,* p. 136.

43 Ibid., p. 137.

44 Ibid., p. 128.

45 *Borderers,* p. 815.

46 Ibid.

47 Ibid., p. 65.

48 *Thirteen-Book Prelude,* vol. I, p. 222 (viii. 435–6); *Fourteen-Book Prelude,* p. 299 (viii. 299–300).

49 *Borderers,* p. 66.

50 G. W. F. Hegel on Abraham in 'The spirit of Christianity and its fate', in *Early Theological Writings,* trans. T. M. Knox (Philadelphia: University of Pennsylvania Press, 1975), pp. 182–301, p. 185.

51 *Borderers,* p. 178 (II. iii, 400–1), p. 176 (II. iii, 381–2).

52 Ibid., p. 180 (II. iii, 427–8, 423–5). The later text reads 'in open day Shall Nature be avenged': p. 181 (ll. 1122–3).

53 William Wordsworth, *Lyrical Ballads and Other Poems, 1797–1800,* ed. James Butler and Karen Green (Ithaca: Cornell University Press, 1992), p. 304.

54 *Borderers,* p. 63.

55 There is also of course an allusion to Milton's sonnet on the massacre of the Piedmontese, 'Even them who kept thy truth so pure of old / When all our Fathers worshipped stocks and stones.' John Milton, *Complete Shorter Poems,* ed. John Carey (London: Longman, 1971), p. 409.

56 *Thirteen-Book Prelude*, vol. I, pp. 323–4 (xiii. 442, 431–2, 441); *Fourteen-Book Prelude*, pp. 270–1 (xiv. 446, 435–6, 445). The fourteen-book text reads 'deliverance' for 'redemption'.

57 *The Excursion, being a portion of The Recluse, a Poem* (London, 1814), p. 367; 'Humanity', in *Last Poems*, pp. 210–13, p. 213, ll. 90–1.

58 See Duncan Wu, 'Editing intentions', *Essays in Criticism* 41.1 (January 1991), pp. 1–10.

59 *Ruined Cottage*, p. 54, ll. 215–17.

60 Ibid., p. 121.

61 Condorcet, pp. 61–8; Volney, *The Ruins*, pp. 363–4.

62 Wordsworth, *Selected Prose*, p. 328.

63 Blayney, *Jeremiah and Lamentations*, pp. 70–1. Lowth, *Isaiah*, p. 206, praises Horace for a similar thought in commenting on Isaiah's denunciation of idol-worship.

64 For the possibility of thinking a new kind of humanism, see in particular Adorno, 'On the classicism of Goethe's *Iphigenie*', *Notes To Literature*, trans. Shierry Weber Nicholsen (2 vols., New York: Columbia University Press, 1992), pp. 153–70.

65 *Ruined Cottage*, p. 46, ll. 87–9.

66 Ibid., p. 46, p. 48, ll. 94–103.

67 Wordsworth, 'Essay on morals', in *Selected Prose*, pp. 104–6, 105.

68 See Emmet Kennedy, *A Philosophe in the Age of Revolution: Destutt de Tracy and the Origins of 'Ideology'* (Philadelphia: American Philosophical Society, 1978), pp. 47–9, 68.

69 M. Le Comte Destutt de Tracy, *Élémens d'Idéologie* (5 vols., Paris, 1824), vol. I, pp. xviij–xix.

70 James Chandler, *Wordsworth's Second Nature: A Study of the Poetry and Politics* (Chicago: University of Chicago Press, 1984), pp. 216–34; p. 229. Wordsworth, 'Essay on morals', p. 104.

71 Jon P. Klancher, *The Making of English Reading Audiences, 1790–1830* (Madison, Wis.: University of Wisconsin Press, 1987), p. 150, takes issue with the phrase 'Romantic ideology' for essentializing the concept of Romanticism but concedes that 'Wordsworth, among others, successfully established the terms for that subliming of the historical in the ideal'. Marjorie Levinson refers to 'the material that "Tintern Abbey" so consummately sublimes' in *Wordsworth's Great Period Poems* (Cambridge: Cambridge University Press, 1986), p. 56.

72 Wordsworth to James Webbe Tobin, 6 March 1798: *EY*, p. 212.

73 This idea of materialism as a 'critical thinking without transcendental method' is argued for in Simon Jarvis, *Adorno: A Critical Introduction* (Cambridge: Polity Press, 1998), pp. 148–231.

2. FROM IDOLATRY TO IDEOLOGY

1 Karl Marx, *Die Frühschriften*, ed. Siegfried Landshut (Stüttgart: Alfred Kroener Verlag, 1971), pp. 341–2 (my translation).

2 See Valerie I. H. Flint, *The Rise of Magic in Early Medieval Europe* (Oxford: Clarendon Press, 1991), pp. 18–20.

3 A term I borrow from Patrick Tort's subtle account of Marx's theory of ideology. Tort, *Marx et le problème de l'idéologie. Le modèle Égyptien* (Paris: Presses Universitaires de France, 1988), pp. 9–47, p. 25.

4 Theodor W. Adorno and Max Horkheimer, *Dialektik der Aufklärung* [1944] in Adorno, *Gesammelte Schriften*, ed. Rolf Tiedemann (23 vols., Frankfurt am Main: Suhrkamp, 1970–), vol. III (1981). For my reading of this work, see Simon Jarvis, *Adorno: A Critical Introduction* (Cambridge: Polity Press, 1998), pp. 20–43.

5 Karl Marx and Friedrich Engels, 'Die Deutsche Ideologie', in *Werke*, vol. III (Berlin: Dietz, 1962), pp. 9–530, p. 31.

6 I offer a more extended development of this view in 'Adorno, Marx, materialism', in *The Cambridge Companion to Adorno*, ed. Tom Huhn (Cambridge: Cambridge University Press, 2004).

7 Robert Kaufman, 'Red Kant, or the persistence of the third critique in Adorno and Jameson', *Critical Inquiry* 26.4 (Summer 2000), pp. 682–724, p. 697. In this and other articles (for example, 'Negatively capable dialectics: Keats, Vendler, Adorno and the theory of the avant-garde', *Critical Inquiry* 27.2 (Winter 2001), pp. 354–84; 'Everybody hates Kant: Blakean formalism and the symmetries of Laura Moriarty', *Modern Language Quarterly* 61.1 (March, 2001), pp. 131–55), Kaufman has been pursuing an important line of enquiry into British Romanticism through Adorno's aesthetic theory.

8 This is a connection which can readily be appreciated upon consulting Constantin Volney's *Law of Nature, or Catechism of French Citizens* (London, 1796), p. 10: '*Q. Explain to me the principles of the law of Nature with relation to man?* A. They are simple; all of them are comprised in one fundamental and simple precept. *Q. What is that precept?* A. It is *self-preservation*.'

9 Thomas Hobbes, *Leviathan*, ed. Richard Tuck (Cambridge: University Press, 1991), p. 270.

10 Ibid.

11 Ibid., pp. 24–31.

12 Ibid., p. 455.

13 Ibid., pp. 418–19.

14 *A True Ecclesiastical History, from Moses to the Time of Martin Luther, in Verse. By Thomas Hobbes of Malmesbury. Made English from the Latin Original* (London: Printed for E. Curll in the Strand, 1722), p. 48. For the (mistaken) view that the philosophy of the Fathers was Aristotelian, see ibid., p. 53; Hobbes, *Leviathan*, p. 418. For an illuminating reconsideration of theses about the corruption of the apostolic church in the patristic period, see Daniel H. Williams, 'Constantine, Nicaea, and the "Fall" of the Church', in *Christian Origins: Theology, Rhetoric and Community*, ed. Lewis Ayres and Gareth Jones (London and New York: Routledge: 1998).

15 Hobbes, *Leviathan*, pp. 455–7.

16 Ibid., p. 45. Naturally this is a familiar Protestant trope. See Henry More, 'An antidote against idolatry', in *The Theological Works* (London, 1707), pp. 771–802, p. 783; James Owen, *The History of Images and Image-Worship. Shewing, The Original and Progress of Idolatry among* Pagans, Jews, and Christians: *with A Refutation of the Second Council of Nice, and of other Advocates for Idolatry* (London, 1709), p. 37, p. 141.

17 Augustine, *The City of God against the Pagans* (7 vols., Cambridge, Mass.: Harvard University Press, and London: William Heinemann, 1988), vol. III, pp. 121–3 (viii. 24).

18 See Flint, *The Rise of Magic*, p. 18.

19 Augustine, *The City of God*, vol. IV, p. 123 (iv. 32).

20 [Blount, Charles,] *Great is Diana of the Ephesians: or, The Original of Idolatry, Together with the Politick Institutions of the Gentiles Sacrifices* (n.p., n.d.).

21 Thomas Paine, 'The Age of Reason, Being an Investigation of True and of Fabulous Theology, Part First [1794]', in *Political Writings*, ed. Bruce Kuklick (Cambridge: Cambridge University Press, 1989), p. 211.

22 Henry More, *Divine Dialogues* (2 vols., London, 1668), vol. I, p. 411; quoted in Harrison, p. 57.

23 Robert Boyle, *A Free Enquiry into the Vulgarly Received Notion of Nature* [1686], ed. Edward B. Davis and Michael Hunter (Cambridge: Cambridge University Press, 1996), pp. 40–1.

24 *Thirteen-Book Prelude*, vol. I, p. 222 (viii. 428–36).

25 Here are some examples of the kind of characterization I have in mind. Marjorie Levinson writes of her sense that 'Wordsworth's most generalized representations owed their pronounced ideality to some disturbing particular and to the need to efface or elide it.' *Wordsworth's Great Period Poems: Four Essays* (Cambridge: Cambridge University Press, 1996), pp. 1–2. Antony Easthope suggested that '*The Prelude* and most of Wordsworth's early writing can confidently relocate the transcendent from faith in an object to faith itself, to subjective experience as a domain of transcendence.' *Wordsworth now and then: Romanticism and contemporary culture* (Buckingham and Philadelphia: Open University, 1993), p. 33. On a more expansive scale, Anne K. Mellor argues that 'Precarious indeed is this unique, unitary transcendental subjectivity, for Wordsworth's sublime self-assurance is rendered possible, as many critics have observed, only by the arduous repression of the Other in all its forms: of the mother, of Dorothy, of other people, of history, of nature, of "unknown modes of being", of that very gap or "vacancy" which divides his present from his past ideality.' *Romanticism and Gender* (New York and London: Routledge, 1993), p. 148. It has by no means been necessary, of course, to find Wordsworth's stance in any strict sense idealist in order to apply the rubrics of 'ideology' to him.

26 Louis Althusser, 'Ideology and ideological state apparatuses (notes towards an investigation)', in *Essays on Ideology* (London: Verso, 1984), pp. 1–60, p. 51.

27 Ibid., p. 56.

28 Ibid., pp. 41–2.

29 Ibid., p. 49.

30 G. W. F. Hegel, *Phenomenology of Spirit*, trans. A. V. Miller (Oxford: Oxford University Press, 1977), pp. 119–38.

31 Althusser, 'Ideology and ideological state apparatuses', p. 50.

32 See Gillian Rose, 'A note on Althusser', in *Hegel Contra Sociology* (London: Athlone, 1981), pp. 37–9.

33 Karl Marx and Friedrich Engels, *The Holy Family; or, Critique of Critical Criticism*, trans. Richard Dixon and Clemens Dutt, in *Collected Works*, vol. 4 (London: Lawrence and Wishart, 1975), p. 7. The view that this appeal to a materialist humanism of 'the real individual human being' is a survival from an 'early' period of Marx's thought is mistaken. See Michel Henry, 'Le lieu de l'idéologie', in *Marx* (2 vols., Paris: Gallimard, 1976), vol. I, pp. 368–479.

34 Marx and Engels, *The Holy Family*, p. 79.

35 Althusser, 'Ideology and ideological state apparatuses', pp. 49–50.

36 'Now, while the thesis I wish to defend formally speaking adopts the terms of *The German Ideology* ("ideology has no history"), it is radically different from the positivist and historicist thesis of *The German Ideology*.'

37 Althusser, 'Ideology and ideological state apparatuses', p. 34.

38 Cf. J. H. Prynne, 'Questions for the time being', in 'The White Stones', *Poems* (Newcastle upon Tyne: Bloodaxe, 1999), pp. 37–126, p. 113.

39 Martin Heidegger, 'Die Aufgabe einer Destruktion der Geschichte der Ontologie', in *Sein und Zeit* (16th edn, Tübingen: Max Niemeyer Verlag, 1986) §6, pp. 19–27; *Being and Time*, trans. John Macquarrie and Edward Robinson (Oxford: Blackwell, 1962), pp. 41–9. For the genesis of the project of a 'destruction of the history of previous ontology', see Theodore Kisiel, *The Genesis of Heidegger's 'Being and Time'* (Berkeley, Los Angeles and London: University of California Press, 1993), especially pp. 249–51, 494. For 'deconstruction' as an attempt to render *Destruktion* and *Abbau*, see Simon Critchley, *The Ethics of Deconstruction: Derrida and Lévinas* (Oxford: Blackwell, 1992), p. 27.

40 Paul de Man, 'Phenomenality and materiality in Kant', in *Aesthetic Ideology*, ed. Andrzej Warminski (Minneapolis and London: University of Minnesota Press, 1996), p. 72.

41 G. W. F. Hegel, 'Limitation and the ought' and 'Remark on the ought', in *Science of Logic*, trans. A. V. Miller (London: George Allen and Unwin, 1969), pp. 131–6.

42 Immanuel Kant, *Critique of Pure Reason*, trans. Norman Kemp Smith (London: Macmillan, 1933), p. 300 (A 298/B 355).

43 Quoted by de Man thus (from Immanuel Kant, *Critique of Judgement*, trans. J. H. Bernard (New York: Hafner Press, 1951), pp. 110–11), in 'Phenomenality and materiality', p. 80.

44 De Man, 'Phenomenality and materiality', p. 82.

45 Immanuel Kant, *Kritik der Urteilskraft*, ed. Gerhard Lehmann (Stuttgart: Philipp Reclam Jun., 1963), §25, p. 144 [85].

46 For a subtle commentary on and defence of these aspects of de Man's thought, see Nigel Mapp, 'History and the sacred in de Man and Benjamin', in *Between the Psyche and the Polis: Refiguring History in Literature and Theory*, ed. Michael Rossington and Anne Whitehead (Aldershot: Ashgate, 2000), pp. 38–58.

47 Theodor W. Adorno, 'Beitrag zur Ideologienlehre', in *Gesammelte Schriften*, vol. VIII (1972), pp. 457–77.

48 I am here deploying to a rather different end a formulation used by Marilyn Strathern to title her powerful rethinking of social-scientific uses of the nature/culture opposition. See Strathern, 'No nature, no culture: the Hagen case', in *Nature, Culture and Gender*, ed. Strathern and Carol MacCormack (Cambridge: Cambridge University Press, 1980), pp. 174–222.

49 This was seen early by Marx: '*Real humanism* has no more dangerous enemy in Germany than *spiritualism* or *speculative idealism*, which substitutes '*self-consciousness*' or the '*spirit*' for the *real individual man*.' Marx and Engels, *The Holy Family*, p. 7. But for a non-idealist sense of 'speculative' thinking, see Simon Jarvis, 'What is speculative thinking?', *Revue Internationale de Philosophie* 227 (2004), pp. 69–83.

50 Theodor W. Adorno, *Vorlesung zur Einleitung in die Erkenntnistheorie 1957–58* (Frankfurt am Main: Junius, n.d.), p. 215.

51 Marx and Engels, *The Holy Family*, p. 128.

52 Wordsworth takes the motto for his polemic on the Convention of Cintra from Bacon. For his readings in Bacon see Wu, *1770–1799* and *1800–1815*.

3. MATERIALISM OF THE BEAUTIFUL

1 Friedrich Pollock makes this blunt intervention in the course of a seminar held in exile in America by members of the Frankfurt School to discuss a paper by Ludwig (not Herbert) Marcuse on 'longing'. See 'Diskussions-protokolle', in Max Horkheimer, *Gesammelte Schriften* (15 vols., Frankfurt am Main: Fischer, 1985–), vol. XII: *Nachgelassene Schriften 1931–49*, pp. 563–70, p. 568.

2 E. P. Thompson, *Customs in Common* (London: Penguin, 1993), pp. 183–258, p. 183.

3 There is further discussion of 'economism' in the context of a discussion of the thought of Pierre Bourdieu below. But since 'economism' and 'economistic' will be important terms in this book, it is worth setting out at this stage what I do and do not understand them to mean. They do not refer simply to the discipline of economics, or political economy, or political arithmetic; nor to any idea that these disciplines might, quantitatively, have 'too much' influence on some other subject or way of thinking. (Philip Connell has shown the difficulty of seeing Wordsworth as a simple opponent *of these disciplines* in his *Romanticism, Economics, and the Question of 'Culture'* (Oxford: Oxford University Press, 2001)). Their sense here is, instead, quite limited. I use them to refer to the belief, whether examined or taken for

granted, that the separation between the political and the economic spheres of social action – a separation which is by no means a feature of all contemporary societies, let alone of all historical ones – is simply a natural feature of social action itself. In a commodity society, my legal and political status is not placed in question when I make an exchange. When I buy a loaf of bread, no one considers that the transaction has any consequences for my status as a citizen. But exchange is not always like this. In particular circumstances my failure to match your gift may make me and mine your debt-slaves. For a powerful account of the genesis of economism, see Louis Dumont, *Essays on Individualism: Modern Ideology in Anthropological Perspective* (Chicago and London: University of Chicago Press, 1986) and From *Mandeville to Marx: the genesis and triumph of economic ideology* (Chicago: University of Chicago Press, 1977), although note that Dumont's argument to the effect that Marx himself is an economistic thinker would need correction in the light of Michel Henry, *Marx* (2 vols., Paris: Gallimard, 1976). I develop a fuller consideration of 'economism' and the possible exits from it in 'The gift in theory', *Dionysius* 17 (December 1999), pp. 201–22.

4 *Lyrical Ballads*, pp. 85–8, p. 86.
5 Ibid., p. 762.
6 Ibid., p. 87, ll. 81–90.
7 *Ruined Cottage*, p. 54.
8 *Lyrical Ballads,* pp. 307–8. For a more extensive discussion of this fragment, see chapter 7 below.
9 Maurice Blanchot, 'On one approach to communism', in *Friendship*, trans. Elizabeth Rottenberg (Stanford, Calif.: Stanford University Press, 1997), Meridian: Crossing Aesthetics, pp. 93–7, p. 94.
10 Karl Marx, *Capital, Volume 1*, trans. Ben Fowkes (Harmondsworth: Penguin Books, 1976), Part 3, 'The production of absolute surplus value', esp. pp. 289–90, 315, 342.
11 Jacques Derrida, *Specters of Marx*, trans. Peggy Kamuf (London: Routledge, 1994), p. 170.
12 Marx, *Capital, Volume 1*, p. 343.
13 G. W. F. Hegel, *Phenomenology of Spirit*, trans. A. V. Miller (Oxford: Oxford University Press, 1977), p. 49.
14 'Labour is *not the source* of all wealth. *Nature* is just as much the source of use-values (and it is indeed of such that material wealth consists!) as labour, which is itself only the manifestation of a natural force, human labour power.' Karl Marx, 'Kritik des Gothaer Programms', in Marx and Friedrich Engels, *Werke* (42 vols. in 44, Berlin: Dietz, 1960–83), vol. XIX, pp. 15–32, p. 15 (my translation).
15 Karl Marx, *Theories of Surplus Value*, trans. Emile Burns (3 vols., London: Lawrence and Wishart, 1969), vol. I, pp. 50–1.
16 David Simpson, *Wordsworth and the Figurings of the Real* (London: Macmillan, 1982).

17 Jon P. Klancher, *The Making of English Reading Audiences, 1790–1832* (Madison, Wis.: University of Wisconsin Press, 1987), pp. 137–47.
18 In Pierre Bourdieu, *Meditations Pascaliennes* (Paris: Éditions du Seuil, 1997).
19 Pierre Bourdieu, *The Logic of Practice*, trans. Richard Nice (Cambridge: Polity Press, 1990), pp. 112–13.
20 Pierre Bourdieu, 'The work of time', in *The Logic of Practice*, pp. 98–111.
21 For an example of such an identification, see Annette Weiner, *Inalienable Possessions: The Paradox of Keeping-While-Giving* (Berkeley, Los Angeles and London: University of California Press, 1992), pp. 28–33.
22 Pierre Bourdieu, *Outline of a Theory of Practice*, trans. Richard Nice (Cambridge: Cambridge University Press, 1977), pp. 176–7.
23 'A factory in which the workers were really and literally cogs in the machine, blindly executing the orders of management, would come to a stop in a quarter of an hour. Capitalism can function only by continually drawing upon the genuinely *human* activity of those subject to it, while at the same time trying to level and dehumanize them as much as possible.' Cornelius Castoriadis, *The Imaginary Institution of Society* (Cambridge: Polity Press, 1987), p. 16.
24 Pierre Bourdieu, 'The field of cultural production, or: the economic world reversed', in *The Field of Cultural Production*, ed. Randal Johnson (Cambridge: Polity Press, 1993), pp. 29–73, p. 35.
25 Bourdieu, *Outline of a Theory of Practice*, p. 177.
26 Bourdieu, 'Flaubert's point of view', in *The Field of Cultural Production*, pp. 192–211, p. 192. The emphasis is Bourdieu's.
27 Anne Robert Jacques Turgot, 'Reflections on the formation and distribution of wealth', in *Turgot on Progress, Sociology and Economics*, ed. and trans. Ronald L. Meek (Cambridge: Cambridge University Press, 1973), pp. 119–82, p. 158.
28 Wordsworth to William Mathews, 8 June 1794: *EY*, p. 125.
29 Turgot, pp. 123, 126.
30 Luke 6.35. Turgot cites the text as it was most often cited by scholastic commentators on usury: see Jacques Le Goff, *Your Money or Your Life: Economy and Religion in the Middle Ages*, trans. Patricia Raum (New York: Zone Books, 1990), pp. 21–2. The most recent edition of the German Bible Society's text, however, reads: 'mutuum date nihil desperantes' ('despairing of no man'). *Biblia Sacra Iuxta Vulgatam Versionem*, ed. Roger Gryson (Stuttgart: Deutsche Bibelgesellschaft, 1994), p. 1618. 'Love your enemies and do good to them, and lend without any hope of return': *The New Jerusalem Bible* (London: Darton, Longman and Todd, 1990).
31 Jerome on Ezekiel 18.6, quoted in Le Goff, *Your Money or Your Life*, p. 26.
32 Edmund Burke, *Thoughts and Details on Scarcity, originally presented to the Right Hon. William Pitt, in the month of November 1795* (London, 1800), p. 18.
33 Ibid.
34 Ibid., p. 32.
35 Adam Smith, *An Enquiry into the Nature and Causes of the Wealth of Nations* (2 vols., London, 1776), vol. I, p. 17.

36 Marx, *Theories of Surplus Value*, trans., vol. I, pp. 44–68. In this context it is therefore significant that instead of rejecting the very idea of the 'gift of nature' as, for example, an 'ideology', Marx, consistent with his repeated insistence on the role of nature in the production of real wealth, regarded it as a *real* gift, but one which had been misappropriated. 'The property therefore which labour-power in action, living labour, possesses of preserving value, at the same time that it adds it, is a gift of nature which costs the worker nothing, but is very advantageous to the capitalist since it preserves the existing value of his capital. As long as trade is good, the capitalist is too absorbed in making profits to take notice of this gratuitous gift of labour. Violent interruptions of the labour process, crises, make him painfully aware of it.' *Capital, Volume 1*, p. 315. The gift of nature is a gift of labour, but the gift of labour is a gift of nature. It is a gift of the difference between the living and the non-living.

37 *Home at Grasmere*, p. 52, MS B, ll. 254–6.

38 Ibid., p. 78, MS B, ll. 649–63.

39 *Lyrical Ballads*, p. 304.

40 *The Fourteen-Book Prelude*, p. 268 (xiv. 355).

41 'To the memory of Raisley Calvert', in *Poems, in Two Volumes*, pp. 151–2.

42 *Home at Grasmere*, pp. 78, 80, ll. 667–92.

43 Theodor W. Adorno, *Ästhetische Theorie* (Suhrkamp: Frankfurt am Main, 1970), p. 347.

44 William Paley, *Reasons for Contentment; addressed to the labouring part of the British public* (London, 1793).

45 Bourdieu, *Outline of a Theory of Practice*, pp. 176–7.

46 See Jonathan Parry, '*The gift*, the Indian gift, and the *"Indian gift"*', *Man*, NS. 21 (1986), pp. 453–73.

47 Bourdieu, *The Field of Cultural Production*, p. 193. For two important accounts of the problems consequent upon any such separation, see Henry, *Marx*, vol. I, pp. 368–479; Theodor W. Adorno, 'Beitrag zur Ideologienlehre', in *Gesammelte Schriften*, vol. VIII (Frankfurt am Main: Suhrkamp, 1972), pp. 457–77, p. 461.

48 *Home at Grasmere*, p. 40, MS B, l. 54.

49 *Poems, in Two Volumes*, pp. 232–3. The following resounding description of such a mill can be found in A. Rees, ed., *The Cyclopaedia; or Universal Dictionary of Arts, Sciences, and Literature (1810)*, vol. 38, 'Water': 'Floating-Mill with undershot Wheels.–A large floating water-mill, to be worked by the tides or currents, was stationed some years ago in the river Thames, between London and Blackfriars bridge, by permission of the Board of Navigation. Such permission having been granted with the view of reducing, if possible, the price of flour in the metropolis, and contributing to a constant supply of that necessary article of subsistence. The simplicity of this invention renders a long description superfluous, as it consists in merely applying the force of two large undershot water-wheels to each side of a barge, or any other vessel calculated to contain the interior part of the machinery; the float-boards are disposed in a proper manner to be acted on by the tide or current, so as to

give the wheels a rotatory motion, and by connecting them with proper machinery, to answer the purpose for which the mill is intended.' Such a mill could operate either at anchor or while moving. However 'it is only the performance of a small mill, although the wheels are of large dimensions, and it would require enormous wheels to make an effective floating mill in the River Thames. This machine is now removed from the river, because it was found to do so much injury to the vessels which continually ran against its floating frame, and the repairs of the damages frequently done to the mill by ice and the craft took away all the advantage of the mill.' In view of its size this may not have been the particular mill Wordsworth saw.

50 The phrase is Thomas Pfau's: *Wordsworth's Profession: Form, Class, and the Logic of Early Romantic Cultural Production* (Stanford, Calif.: Stanford University Press, 1997), p. 378. Pfau himself goes on to show that the matter is more complicated than might be thought.

51 'Preface' to *Lyrical Ballads*, p. 745.

52 Fenwick note; quoted in *Poems, in Two Volumes*, p. 421. 'Charles Lamb was with me at the time' of seeing the London mill 'and I thought it remarkable that I should have to point out to him, an idolatrous Londoner, a sight so interesting as the happy group dancing on the platform.'

4. HAPPINESS

1 Edward Gibbon, *The History of the Decline and Fall of the Roman Empire*, ed. David Womersley (3 vols., London: Penguin Books, 1994), vol. II, p. 411.

2 Gibbon, *Decline and Fall*, vol. II, p. 412.

3 Ibid., vol. II, p. 424.

4 Edmund Burke, *Reflections on the Revolution in France*, ed. Conor Cruise O'Brien (Harmondsworth: Penguin Books, 1969), pp. 270–1.

5 Joshua Lucock Wilkinson, *The Wanderer: or anecdotes and incidents, the result and occurrence of a ramble on foot, through France, Germany and Italy, in 1791 and 1793* (2 vols., London, 1798), vol. I, pp. 152–3.

6 Ibid., vol. I, p. 285.

7 Pierre Bayle, *A General Dictionary, Historical and Critical*, trans. John Peter Bernard, Thomas Birch and John Lockman (10 vols., 1734–41), vol. I, p. 28n.

8 Bayle, *General Dictionary*, p. 27n.

9 Joseph Bingham, *Origines Ecclesiasticae: or, the Antiquities of the Christian Church* (10 vols., London, 1711), vol. III, p. 7. For Bingham's significance as a patristic scholar, see L. W. Barnard, 'Patristic study in England in the early eighteenth century', *Studia Patristica* 23 (1989), pp. 211–14.

10 *Tuft of Primroses*, p. 47, ll. 280–93.

11 Gibbon, *Decline and Fall*, vol. II, p. 416.

12 'A Journey Through Egypt ... By M. Granger. Translated from the French, by John Reinhold Forster, F. R. S.', in *Travels through Sicily and that part of Italy formerly called Magna Graecia ... translated from the German by J. R. Forster, F. R. S.* (London, 1773), p. 338.

13 Francis Wrangham, *Rome is Fallen! A Sermon; preached at the Visitation held at Scarborough, June 5, 1798* (York, 1798), p. 30.

14 Francis Wrangham, *A Poem on the Restoration of Learning in the East* (Cambridge, 1805), p. 7.

15 Thomas Dudley Fosbrooke, *The Economy of Monastic Life, (As it Existed in England), A Poem, with Philosophical and Archaeological Illustrations* (Gloucester, n.d.), p. 1. A manuscript note in the Cambridge University Library collection of pamphlets amongst which Fosbrooke's is found, classmark Zz. 17. 29, dates Fosbrooke's poem '1795'.

16 Ibid., pp. 11–12.

17 Constantin Volney, *The Law of Nature; or, catechism of French citizens* (London, 1796), p. 10; *The Ruins: or a survey of the revolutions of empires* (London, 1795), p. 73.

18 Joseph Milner, *The History of the Church of Christ* (4 vols., Cambridge, 1795–1809), vol. II, p. 290. For a brief discussion of Milner, see Gareth Vaughan Bennett, 'Patristic tradition in Anglican thought, 1660–1900', in *Tradition in Luthertum und Anglikanismus*, ed. Günther Gassmann and Vilmos Vajta (Strasbourg: Gütersloher Verlagshaus Gerd Mohn, 1972), pp. 63–87. I thank Neil Hitchen for drawing my attention to this article.

19 Milner, *History of the Church of Christ*, vol. II, p. 294.

20 Ibid., p. 292.

21 *Tuft of Primroses*, p. 21ff.

22 Gibbon, *Decline and Fall*, vol. II, p. 29, n.29. For these passages from Nazianzen's poem, see Gregory of Nazianzus, *Autobiographical Poems*, trans. and ed. Carolinne White (Cambridge: University Press, 1996), pp. 45–7.

23 Gibbon, *Decline and Fall*, vol. II, p. 29.

24 *Tuft of Primroses*, p. 21; Chester L. Shaver and Alice C. Shaver, *Wordsworth's Library: A Catalogue* (New York: Octagon Books, 1979), p. 109.

25 See Abbie Findlay Potts, ed., *The Ecclesiastical Sonnets of William Wordsworth: A Critical Edition* (New Haven: Yale University Press, 1922), p. 24.

26 Wordsworth to James Webbe Tobin, 6 iii. 1798: *EY*, p. 212.

27 Samuel Taylor Coleridge, *Shorter Works and Fragments*, ed. H. J. Jackson and J. R. de J. Jackson (2 vols., Princeton: Princeton University Press, 1995), p. 1046. The remarks were made in 1823.

28 See Meredith Hanmer, *The Auncient Ecclesiasticall Histories of the First Six Hundred Years after Christ* (London, 1585), p. 334, where the role of Basil and Nazianzen in establishing the formula of 'one substance' is emphasized.

29 Louis Dumont, *Essays on individualism: modern ideology in anthropological perspective* (Chicago: University of Chicago Press, 1986), pp. 23–59.

30 Milner, *History of the Church of Christ*, vol. II, pp. 289–90.

31 Augustine, *Retractationes*, I, i, 1; cited in Peter Brown, *Augustine of Hippo: A Biography* (London: Faber and Faber, 1967), p. 115.

32 For an account of this connection, see David Brakke, *Athanasius and the Politics of Asceticism* (Oxford: Clarendon Press, 1995).

33 Gregory Nazianzen, Oration 21, in *Discours 20–23*, ed. Justin Mossay (Paris: Editions du Cerf, 1980), pp. 148–50.
34 Condorcet, *Outlines of an Historical View of the Progress of the Human Mind* (London, 1795), p. 27; Volney, *The Ruins*, pp. 310–12.
35 Volney, *The Ruins*, p. 73.
36 Adam Smith, *An Inquiry into the Nature and Causes of the Wealth of Nations*, ed. Edwin Cannan (2 vols. in 1, Chicago: University of Chicago Press, 1976), vol. II, pp. 315–16.
37 St Jerome, letter 18, paraphrased in Bingham, *Antiquities*, vol. I, p. 259.
38 Gibbon, *Decline and Fall*, vol. II, p. 422.
39 Immanuel Kant, *Critique of Pure Reason*, trans. Kemp Smith (London: Macmillan, 1933), p. 93 [B75/A51].
40 St Basil, letter 2 in Basil, *The Letters*, trans. Roy J. DeFerrari (4 vols., Cambridge, Mass.: Harvard University Press, 1926–34), pp. 6–25, p. 13.
41 Basil, letter 2, p. 15.
42 Ibid., p. 11.
43 Ibid., p. 10. The letter is rapidly summarized, but not paraphrased, in William Cave, *Apostolici* (London, 1733), pp. 478–9.
44 Thomas West, *The Antiquities of Furness* (London, 1774), p. 21.
45 Ibid., p. 4.
46 Ibid., p. 21.
47 In the opinion of Arnaldo Momigliano. See his essay 'Marcel Mauss and the quest for the person in Greek biography and autobiography', in *The Category of the Person*, ed. Michael Carrithers, Steven Collins and Steven Lukes (Cambridge: Cambridge University Press, 1986), pp. 83–92, p. 90.
48 G. W. F. Hegel, *Phenomenology of Spirit*, trans. A. V. Miller (Oxford: Oxford University Press, 1977), pp. 339–40.

5. INFINITY

1 Walter Benjamin, *The Arcades Project*, trans. Howard Eiland and Kevin McLaughlin (Cambridge, Mass.: Harvard University Press, 1999), p. 806.
2 G. W. F. Hegel, *Werke* (20 vols., Frankfurt am Main: Suhrkamp, 1969), vol. V, *Wissenschaft der Logik, I*, p. 155 (my translation). All further references are to this edition. Here and throughout provision of my own translation need not imply a criticism of existing versions.
3 Immanuel Kant, *Critique of Pure Reason*, ed. and trans. Paul Guyer and Allen Wood (Cambridge: Cambridge University Press, 1998), p. 484.
4 Hegel, *Werke*, vol. VIII, *Enzyklopädie der philosophischen Wissenschaften im Grundrisse (1830). Erster Teil: Die Wissenschaft der Logik mit den mündlichen Zusätzen*, p. 199 (§94, Zusatz) (my translation).
5 Hegel, *Werke*, vol. V, p. 168 (my translation).
6 Ibid., p. 172.
7 I do not think that we can follow S. Žižek's illuminating work in regarding *Vernunft* as *only Verstand* which has come to understand its own limitedness.

The need to show that Hegel 'already' knows what deconstructive readers of him might have to tell us results in an approbable Hegel freed in advance from metaphysical commitments. A philologically superior interpretation can be found in M. Theunissen, *Sein und Schein. Die kritische Funktion der Hegelschen Logik* (Frankfurt am Main: Suhrkamp, 1980). It is instead worth considering the extent to which Hegel's insight into social experience is only made possible by those speculative elements in his logic which much contemporary thought finds merely archaic. See Theodor W. Adorno, *Hegel: Three Studies*, trans. Shierry Weber Nicholsen (Cambridge, Mass.: MIT Press, 1993). For a careful critique of Žižek's anti-metaphysical Hegel, see Peter Dews's essay 'The tremor of reflection: Slavoj Žižek's Lacanian dialectic', in *The Limits of Disenchantment* (London: Verso, 1996), pp. 236–58.

8   Hegel, *Werke*, vol. VII: *Grundlinien der Philosophie des Rechts oder Naturrecht und Staatswissenschaft im Grundrisse*, pp. 359–60.

9   Ibid., p. 200 (§94, Zusatz) (my translation).

10 For instances of the former, and the use of the structure of this motif against critical theory, see Rolf Ahlers, 'Endlichkeit und absoluter Geist in Hegels Philosophie', *Zeitschrift für philosophische Forschung* 29 (1975), pp. 63–80, and Ahlers, 'The overcoming of critical theory in the Hegelian unity of theory and practice', *Clio* 8.1 (1978), pp. 71–96; for a more complex use of this aspect of Hegel's thought, see Gillian Rose, 'From speculative to dialectical thinking', in *Judaism and Modernity: Philosophical Essays* (Oxford: Blackwell, 1993), pp. 3–63.

11 *Thirteen-Book Prelude*, vol. I, p. 226: 'And all the long Etcetera of such thought'.

12 But not always. 'I begin to wish much to be in town; cataracts and mountains, are good occasional society, but they will not do for constant companions.' Wordsworth to William Mathews, 7. xi. 1794, *EY*, p. 136.

13 S. T. Coleridge, *Table talk recorded by Henry Nelson Coleridge (and John Taylor Coleridge)*, ed. Carl Woodring (2 vols., Princeton: Princeton University Press, 1990), vol. I, pp. 307–8 (21 July 1832).

14 R. D. Stock, ed., *Samuel Johnson's Literary Criticism* (Lincoln: University of Nebraska Press, 1974), p. 270.

15 See Kant, *Critique of Pure Reason*, p. 494.

16 A point noted by John Plotz, 'The necessary veil: Wordsworth's "Residence in London" ', in *The Crowd: British Literature and Public Politics* (Berkeley, Calif.: University of California Press, 2000), pp. 15–42, p. 34. I thank Neil Hertz for drawing my attention to this work.

17 A good deal has at some times turned on the figure of the dead letter in Wordsworth's writing; it will be discussed in more detail in a later chapter of the book. I shall suggest that there is a materialist current in Wordsworth's writing, but that instead of being a materialism of ultimate literalness, such as Paul de Man finds in Kant's *Critique of Judgement* ('Phenomenality and materiality in Kant', in *Aesthetic ideology*, ed. Andrzej Warminski (Minneapolis and London: University of Minnesota Press, 1996) pp. 70–90), it is a current which runs in opposition to the phenomenalization of soul and world in modern philosophy.

18 Mary Jacobus, *Romanticism, Writing, and Sexual Difference: Essays on* The Prelude (Oxford: Clarendon Press, 1989), p. 111.

19 Thomas Pfau, *Wordsworth's Profession: Form, Class, and the Logic of Early Romantic Cultural Production* (Stanford, Calif.: Stanford University Press, 1997), p. 370.

20 'Self-perficient scepticism' is John Raffan's rendering, as reported by Gillian Rose: *Hegel Contra Sociology* (London: Athlone, 1981), p. 241. G. W. F. Hegel, *Phänomenologie des Geistes*, ed. Johannes Hoffmeister (Hamburg: Felix Meiner, 1952), p. 67; *Phenomenology of Spirit*, trans. A. V. Miller (Oxford: Oxford University Press, 1977), p. 49, p. 50. For a long time it has not been at all widespread actually to read Wordsworth as an instinctive Hegelian. It is possible, in fact, that it was never widespread, because although a diagram of Hegel's thoughts was often at stake in such readings, their content was more rarely so. But this does not mean that the spell of the analogy is broken. Its power persists in the way that it has shaped a variety of sceptical responses to Wordsworth's poetry since. The attacks, McGann's and others, on Wordsworth's 'romantic ideology' derived from a foreshortened idea of Marx's critique of Hegel, having taken the Hegelian reading of Wordsworth (as well as the Romanticist reading of Hegel: for a careful dismantling of McGann on Hegel, see David Ferris, *Silent Urns: Romanticism, Hellenism and Modernity* (Stanford, Calif.: Stanford University Press, 2000), pp. 57–61) at its own word and failing to consider how little Wordsworth resembled Hegel. The analogy retains its power even where it is denied. Paul de Man's writing about Wordsworth is too complicated to exhaust in a note, but there is a sense in which, in de Man's late work, having rescued Hegel from a chiasmic logic, de Man then finds that logic instead in aspects of Wordsworth: so that Wordsworth, carefully distinguished from Hegel, takes on the rejected characteristics, those of the Hegel for whom, for example, difference is supposedly always bound back into an economy of exchange (see the account of 'Tintern Abbey' in de Man, 'Phenomenality and materiality', p. 82, where it is claimed with respect to the passage of the poem there quoted that 'Wordsworth's sublime is an instance of the constant exchange between mind and nature, of the chiasmic transfer of properties between the sensory and intellectual world that characterizes his figural diction'). Even where Hegel's name is entirely absent, where Hegel has not been mentioned or even perhaps read, his thinking may be powerfully at work in the insistence that the logic of modernity is irreversible. Thus in a reading so little concerned with metaphysics as Jon Klancher's subtle *Making of English Reading Audiences*, and in which the most significant lines of thought are developed from Pierre Bourdieu, the certainty that Wordsworth's anxiety before commodity exchange represents a form of nostalgia is significantly shaped by Hegel's understanding of modernity as fate (Klancher, *The Making of English Reading Audiences, 1790–1832* (Madison, Wis.: University of Wisconsin Press, 1987), p. 143). Finally the analogy has its last victory in the wish it induces to tear Wordsworth away from philosophy altogether: as in David Bromwich's wish

to regard the philosophical aspects of Wordsworth's verse as an alien Coleridgean growth (Bromwich, *Disowned by Memory: Wordsworth's Poetry of the 1790s* (Chicago: University of Chicago Press, 1998)). That the names above represent some of the most significant writing about Wordsworth in the last thirty years indicates why it remains to detach Wordsworth from Hegel in the right way; – if there be any such.

21 It is thus only partly true to repeat what has by now become the reflex characterization of Hegel's thought as 'sacrificial'. It is a characterization which been important to reading Wordsworth, especially where interpretation has rightly attended to moments of uncontainable excess in his verse, moments which cannot be brought back into 'the phenomenological, incarnational (sacrificial, resurrectional), dialectical model of language' (Andrzej Warminski, 'Facing language: Wordsworth's first poetic spirits', in 'Wordsworth and the production of poetry', ed. Warminski and Cynthia Chase, special issue of *diacritics* 17.4 (Winter 1987), pp. 18–31, p. 28): where it attends, for example, to 'a blind, arbitrary and violent power of sheer linguistic positing' (ibid., p. 23). Yet perhaps it is not inevitable that this wish for a gift which is more than a chiasmus be made in the image of blindness, arbitrariness or violence. For a commentary on (among other matters) the role of a certain melodrama in the thought of Paul de Man, see Neil Hertz, 'Lurid figures', in *Reading de Man Reading*, ed. Lindsay Waters and Wlad Godzich (Minneapolis: University of Minnesota Press, 1989), Theory and History of Literature, 59, pp. 82–104.

22 S. Jarvis, 'The "unhappy consciousness" and conscious unhappiness: on Adorno's critique of Hegel and the idea of an Hegelian critique of Adorno', in *Hegel's Phenomenology of Spirit: A Re-Appraisal*, ed. G. K. Browning (Amsterdam: Kluwer Academic Publishers, 1997), pp. 57–72.

23 *Poems, in Two Volumes*, pp. 185–6.

24 William Wordsworth, 'Essay on morals', in *Selected Prose*, ed. John O. Hayden (London: Penguin, 1988), pp. 104–6. As Alan Bewell has pointed out, the title is not Wordsworth's and is not well chosen (Bewell suggests 'Against moral enquiry', but I would prefer 'Against moral theory').

6. LIFE

1 John Locke, *An Essay Concerning Human Understanding*, ed. P. H. Nidditch (Oxford: Clarendon Press, 1974), p. 503.

2 Quoted in Wu, *1800–1815*, p. 261.

3 Cf. 'What de Man has made of Wordsworth', in Don H. Bialostosky, *Wordsworth, Dialogics, and the Practice of Criticism* (Cambridge: Cambridge University Press, 1992), p. 6ff.

4 Paul de Man, 'Wordsworth and the Victorians', in *The Rhetoric of Romanticism* (New York: Columbia University Press, 1984), pp. 83–92, p. 85.

5 Rodolphe Gasché, *The Wild Card of Reading: On Paul de Man* (Cambridge, Mass.: Harvard University Press, 1998), p. 5.

6 Andrzej Warminski, 'Facing language: Wordsworth's first poetic spirits', in 'Wordsworth and the production of poetry', ed. Andrzej Warminski and Cynthia Chase: special issue of *diacritics* 17.4 (Winter 1987), pp. 18–31, p. 23. Marx's critique of critical criticism, though addressed to so different a subject, remains pertinent. 'For abstraction, love is the "maid from a foreign land" who has no dialectical passport and is therefore expelled from the country by the Critical police ... What Critical Criticism combats here is not merely love but everything living, everything which is immediate, every sensuous experience, any and every *real* experience, the "Whence" and the "Whither" of which one never *knows* beforehand.' Karl Marx and Friedrich Engels, *The Holy Family; or, Critique of Critical Criticism*, in *Collected Works*, vol. IV (London: Lawrence and Wishart, 1975), p. 23.

7 Paul de Man, 'Time and history in Wordsworth', in 'Wordsworth and the production of poetry', ed. Warminski and Chase, special issue of *diacritics* 17.4 (Winter 1987), pp. 4–17, p. 15.

8 David Bromwich, *Disowned by Memory: Wordsworth's Poetry of the 1790s*, (Chicago: University of Chicago Press, 1998), pp. 20–1.

9 Ibid., p. 14.

10 Immanuel Kant, *Critique of Pure Reason*, trans. and ed. Paul Guyer and Allen W. Wood (Cambridge: Cambridge University Press, 1998), pp. 412–13 [typography modified].

11 René Descartes, 'Author's replies to the sixth set of objections', in *The Philosophical Writings of Descartes*, trans. John Cottingham, Robert Stoothoff, Dugald Murdoch (3 vols., Cambridge: Cambridge University Press, 1984), vol. II, p. 285.

12 René Descartes, 'Principles of philosophy. Part one', in *Philosophical Writings*, vol. I, p. 195.

13 Gilbert Ryle, *The Concept of Mind* (Chicago: University of Chicago Press, 1984), p. 11, pp. 15–16. Jacques Maritain, *Le songe de Descartes* (Paris: Editions R.A. Corréa, 1932), p. 275.

14 Martin Heidegger, *Nietzsche*, Gesamtausgabe 6.2 (2 vols., Frankfurt am Main: Vittorio Klostermann, 1997), vol. II, p. 133 (my translation).

15 Quoted in Michel Henry, *Genealogy of Psychoanalysis*, trans. Douglas Brick (Stanford, Calif.: Stanford University Press, 1993), p. 72.

16 Henry, *Genealogy of Psychoanalysis*, p. 74.

17 Descartes, *Philosophical Writings*, vol. II, p. 382 (quoted in *Genealogy of Psychoanalysis*, p. 15).

18 Martin Heidegger *Einführung in die phänomenologische Forschung*, Gesamtausgabe 17 (Frankfurt am Main: Vittorio Klostermann, 1994), p. 284.

19 Henry, *Genealogy of Psychoanalysis*, p. 15.

20 Martin Heidegger, 'Die Abhebung der Analyse der Weltlichkeit gegen die Interpretation der Welt bei Descartes' [Contrast between our analysis of world-ness and the interpretation of the world in Descartes], in *Sein und Zeit* (Frankfurt am Main: Vittorio Klostermann, 1993), pp. 89–101.

21 'Humanism is thought against here because it does not set the *humanitas* of human beings high enough.' Martin Heidegger, *Über den Humanismus* (Frankfurt am Main: Vittorio Klostermann, 1991), p. 21 (my translation).

22 Descartes 'Sixth set of replies', in *Philosophical Writings*, vol. II, p. 298.

23 Descartes 'Second set of replies', in *Philosophical Writings*, vol. II, p. 113. See Henry, *Genealogy of Psychoanalysis*, pp. 50–1.

24 Henry, 'The decline of phenomenological absolutes', in *Genealogy of Psychoanalysis*, pp. 41–69.

25 Jean-Luc Marion, 'Générosité et phénoménologie. Remarques sur l'interprétation du *cogito* cartésien par Michel Henry', *Les Etudes Philosophiques* 51.1 (1988), pp. 51–72, p. 58 (my translation).

26 See also 'Auguries of innocence', *Complete Poetry and Prose of William Blake*, ed. David V. Erdman (Berkeley: University of California Press, 1982), pp. 493–96, p. 495, ll. 125–6. Descartes, 'Optics', in *Philosophical Writings*, vol. I, pp. 152–75, p. 172. Emphasis mine.

27 William Blake, 'A descriptive catalogue of pictures, poetical and historical inventions', in *Complete Writings*, ed. Geoffrey Keynes (Oxford: Oxford University Press, 1972), pp. 563–86, p. 585.

28 Nevertheless, it is contended here that Henry's material phenomenology represents the most philosophically advanced treatment of many problems which have been allowed almost to disappear altogether from reflection in the English-speaking human sciences. In particular no current 'materialism' can afford to ignore his work. Much of the most important discussion of Henry's work to date can be found in a special issue of *Les Etudes Philosophiques* devoted to him (51.1 (1988)), in which especially important are Marion, 'Générosité et phénoménologie', and Jean-Louis Chrétien, 'La vie sauve' (pp. 37–49). Also important is Michel Haar, 'Michel Henry entre Phénoménologie et Métaphysique', *Philosophie* 14 (1987), pp. 30–54. The Anglophone reception has been thin, but note the special issue of *Continental Philosophy Review* (32, 1999) devoted to his work and containing a useful bibliography. I thank the students (from whom I learnt much) who worked through Henry and Adorno with me on a course on 'Rethinking Materialism' at the Society for the Humanities, Cornell University, Winter 2000.

29 Henry, 'Le monisme ontologique', in *L'Essence de la Manifestation* (2nd edn, Paris: Presses Universitaires de France, 1990), pp. 39–164.

30 Henry, *Genealogy of Psychoanalysis*, p. 47.

31 See Jonathan Swift, *A Tale of A Tub and Other Works*, ed. Angus Ross and David Woolley (Oxford: Oxford University Press, 1986), p. 36.

32 See, especially, Michel Henry's account of Hegel in 'Mise en Lumière de l'essence originaire de la révélation par opposition au concept Hégélien de manifestation (Erscheinung)', in *L'Essence de la Manifestation*, pp. 863–906.

33 Heidegger, *Über den Humanismus*, p. 32.

34 See Stephen Menn, *Descartes and Augustine* (Cambridge: Cambridge University Press, 1998).

35 Wu, *1800–1815*, p. 74.
36 Jane Worthington Smyser, 'Wordsworth's dream of poetry and science: *The Prelude*, V', *Publications of the Modern Language Association* 71.1 (March 1956), pp. 269–75.
37 Samuel Taylor Coleridge, *The Letters of Samuel Taylor Coleridge, 1785–1806*, ed. E. L. Griggs (2 vols., Oxford: Oxford University Press, 1956), vol. II, p. 683. See Descartes, *Philosophical Writings*, vol. I, pp. 127–8.
38 As quoted by Coleridge, *Letters of Coleridge*, vol. II, pp. 683–84. Coleridge's quotation is in fact a slightly edited composite of two widely separated passages from Locke's *Essay*. See Locke, *An Essay Concerning Human Understanding*, p. 127, p. 288.
39 *Letters of Coleridge*, vol. II, p. 684.
40 Descartes, *Philosophical Writings*, vol. I, pp. 303–4.
41 Transcription of MS W (DC MS 38), 1ᵛ, Reed ii. 262.
42 *Thirteen-Book Prelude*, vol. I, p. 315.
43 Ibid., vol. II, p. 262n.
44 Transcription of MS W (DC MS 38), 1ᵛ, *Thirteen-Book Prelude*, vol. II, p. 262 ('immortaity' stands thus in the text).
45 *Thirteen-Book Prelude*, vol. I, p. 163 (v. 42).
46 Ibid., p. 316 (xiii. 113).
47 *Lyrical Ballads*, pp. 307–8.
48 *Thirteen-Book Prelude*, vol. I, p. 122 (i. 592)
49 *Lyrical Ballads*, pp. 323–4.
50 John R. Cole, *The Olympian Dreams and Youthful Rebellions of René Descartes* (Urbana and Chicago: University of Illinois Press, 1992), pp. 19–58.
51 But for exceptions, see J. Hillis Miller, 'The stone and the shell: the problem of poetic form in Wordsworth's Dream of the Arab', in *Mouvements Premiers: Etudes critiques offertes à Georges Poulet* (Paris: Librairie Jose Corti, 1972), pp. 125–47; Timothy Bahti, 'Figures of interpretation, the interpretation of figures: a reading of Wordsworth's "Dream of the Arab"', *Studies in Romanticism* 18 (Winter 1979), pp. 601–27.
52 Cole, *Olympian Dreams*, pp. 36–8. Some of the translator's glosses have been removed.
53 See Geneviève Rodis-Lewis, 'Le premier registre de Descartes', *Archives de Philosophie* 54.1 (1991), pp. 353–77; 54.2, (1991), pp. 639–57.
54 Jacques Maritain, *The Dream of Descartes, together with Some Other Essays*, trans. Mabelle L. Andison (New York: Philosophical Library, 1944), pp. 15–16.
55 [Adrien Baillet], *The Life of Monsieur Des-cartes, Containing the History of His Philosophy and Works: As Also, The most Remarkable Things that befell him during the whole Course of his Life* (London, 1693), p. 35. Paul Arnold claimed ('Le 'songe' de Descartes', *Cahiers du Sud* 35 (1952), pp. 272–91) that Descartes's 'dreams' were dependent on Rosicrucian sources; for an attack on this view, see Cole, *Olympian Dreams*, pp. 214–26.

56 Georges Poulet, 'The dream of Descartes', in *Studies in Human Time*, trans. Elliott Coleman (Baltimore: Johns Hopkins University Press, 1956), pp. 50–73, pp. 52–3.

57 Sophie Jama, *La nuit de songes de René Descartes* (Paris: Aubier, 1998).

58 Jean-Luc Marion, 'Does thought dream? The three dreams, or the awakening of the philosopher', in *Cartesian Questions. Method and Metaphysics* (Chicago: University of Chicago Press, 1999), p. 7.

59 Ibid., p. 15.

60 Descartes, *Philosophical Writings*, vol. I, p. 195.

61 See Gilbert Boss, 'Le songe d'une poétique philosophique (Les rêves de Descartes)', *Dialectica* 47.2–3 (1993), pp. 199–216, p. 208.

62 Locke, *Essay Concerning Human Understanding*, p. 699.

63 George Berkeley, 'A Letter to Sir John James, Bart. on the Differences between the Roman and Anglican Churches', in *The Works of George Berkeley*, ed. Alexander Fraser (4 vols., Oxford: Clarendon Press, 1901), vol. IV, p. 527.

64 Paul Celan, 'The Meridian. Speech on the occasion of receiving the Georg Büchner Prize, Darmstadt, 22 October 1960', in *Collected Prose*, trans. Rosmarie Waldrop (Manchester: Carcanet, 1986), pp. 37–55, p. 42.

65 Celan, 'The Meridian', p. 42.

66 *Thirteen-Book Prelude*, vol. I, p. 163 (v.17–21).

67 Ibid., p. 163 (v. 21–48).

68 See ibid., p. 234 (ix. 234) where Wordsworth describes himself 'Affecting more emotion than [he] felt' at the ruins of the Bastille, or x. 61–9 (vol. I, p. 269) where he distinguishes a 'substantial dread' from that which was 'conjured up from tragic fictions / And mournful Calendars of true history' (x. 66–8).

69 See Kathryn Sutherland, 'Revised relations? Material text, immaterial text, and the electronic environment', *Text. Transactions of the Society for Textual Scholarship* 11 (1998), pp. 16–39, p. 36.

70 *Thirteen-Book Prelude*, vol. II, p. 274.

71 In a paper given to the Society for the Humanities at Cornell University's seminar on The City, April 2001.

72 *Thirteen-Book* Prelude, vol. I, p. 166, (v. 140–65).

73 Ernst Bernhardt-Kabisch, 'The stone and the shell: Wordsworth, cataclysm, and the myth of Glaucus', *Studies in Romanticism* 24 (Spring 1985), pp. 455–90, p. 472. Duncan Wu discovered that brief extracts from Volney's *Travels* were copied out in DC MS 28. Wu, *1800–1815*, 'Volney'.

74 Constantin Volney, *Travels through Syria and Egypt in the Years 1783, 1784 and 1785* (2 vols., London, 1788), vol. II, pp. 412–13.

75 G. W. F. Hegel, 'The spirit of Christianity and its fate', in *Early Theological Writings*, trans. T. M. Knox (Philadelphia: University of Pennsylvania Press, 1975), pp. 182–301, pp. 248–9.

76 And, one might add, reflection on sharing food or drink with a stranger can well capture the *fact* of reciprocity even in a society which has concealed the

persistence of gift-exchange from itself by believing its own propaganda about the absoluteness of the commodity's triumph: see Claude Lévi-Strauss, *The Elementary Structures of Kinship*, trans. James Harle Bell, John Richard von Sturmer and Rodney Needham (Boston: Beacon Press, 1969), pp. 58–9.

77 Theodor W. Adorno, *Negative Dialektik* (Frankfurt am Main: Suhrkamp, 1966), p. 368. The phrase 'labour of the concept' is an allusion to the preface to Hegel's *Phenomenology of Spirit*.

78 *Thirteen-Book Prelude*, vol. I, p. 129 (ii. 184–93).

79 Ibid., p. 130 (ii. 265).

80 Celan, 'The Meridian', pp. 42–3.

81 *Thirteen-Book Prelude*, vol. I, p. 164 (v. 64–8).

82 Ibid., pp. 164–5 (v. 86–109).

83 See chapter 1 above.

84 Volney, *Travels through Syria and Egypt*, p. 418.

85 'To the same', *Shorter Poems 1807–1820*, p. 251. The poem derives with much addition and alteration from a poem which Wordsworth had read to him repeatedly in bed on 4 May 1802.

86 'Essays up on epitaphs', in William Wordsworth, *Selected Prose*, ed. John O. Hayden (London: Penguin Books, 1988), p. 361.

87 *Tuft of Primroses*, p. 88.

88 'Composed When a Probability Existed Of Our Being Obliged To Quit Rydal Mount' [early version], in *Tuft of Primroses*, pp. 78–82 (ll. 27–48).

89 *Thirteen-Book Prelude*, vol. I, p. 130 (ii. 228–9).

90 Jean-Louis Chrétien, 'La vie sauve', *Les Études Philosophiques* 51 (1988), pp. 37–49, p. 45 (my translation). That this point is offered from the ground of a doctrinally orthodox position on the necessity of losing one's life in order to save it, a position the answers to which would be contained in Henry's appendix on the Hegelian concept of appearance to *The Essence of Manifestation*, does not destroy its pertinence.

7. LIGHT

1 *Shorter Poems 1807–1820*, p. 255.

2 Is it worth noting in passing that 'put by' is a close English equivalent to a German verb which has given a great deal of trouble to philosophical translators: *aufheben*? Put by: at once 'superseded' and 'preserved'.

3 'Modern', and 'sub-', in the light of Henri De Lubac's outstanding 1965 study *Augustinianism and Modern Theology*, ed. Louis Dupré, trans. Lancelot Sheppard (New York: Crossroad Publishing Co., 2000). De Lubac shows how, precisely in the name of perfect fidelity to this father, central emphases of his thinking about the problem of divine grace are simplified by all sectors of the controversial spectrum. In particular Augustine's emphasis on the need for the gift of grace to be received, rather than irresistibly efficacious, is submerged.

4 'Not in the lucid intervals of life', *Last Poems*, p. 238, ll. 24–5.
5 *Shorter Poems 1807–1820*, p. 260.
6 The allusion to Jacob's ladder was at first part of the poem itself and was then removed to the notes. 'The multiplication of mountain-ridges, described, at the commencement of the third stanza of this Ode, as a kind of Jacob's Ladder, leading to Heaven, is produced either by watery vapours, or sunny haze, – in the present instance by the latter cause.' *Shorter Poems 1807–1820*, p. 260n.
7 DC MS 44, 78^r, l. 41, reproduced and transcribed in *Poems, in Two Volumes*, pp. 360–73, pp. 362–3. In the printer's copy, this is corrected in Dorothy Wordsworth's hand to read 'The fullness of your bliss – I feel it all.' It is assumed that the alteration to the line as it appeared in the first printed text – 'The fullness of your bliss, I feel – I feel it all' was made by Wordsworth in the proof (now lost).
8 Geoffrey H. Hartman, *Wordsworth's Poetry 1787–1814* (New Haven and London: Yale University Press, 1964), pp. 282–3.
9 Frances Ferguson, *Wordsworth: Language as Counter-Spirit* (New Haven and London: Yale University Press, 1977), p. 101.
10 James Montgomery on Wordsworth, *Poems, in Two Volumes* (1807), in *Eclectic Review* 4 (Jan 1808), pp. 35–43, repr. in Reiman, vol. I, pp. 333–5.
11 *OED* 1a.
12 Exodus 24.16–17.
13 Stanley Cavell, *In Quest of the Ordinary: Lines of Skepticism and Romanticism* (Chicago and London: Chicago University Press, 1988), p. 75.
14 'Prospectus' to 'The Recluse', in William Wordsworth, *The Poems*, ed. John O. Hayden (2 vols., London: Penguin, 1977), vol. II, p. 39.
15 Charles J. McCracken, *Malebranche and British Philosophy* (Oxford: Clarendon Press, 1983).
16 Nicolas Malebranche, *The Search after Truth*, trans. Thomas M. Lennon and Paul J. Olscamp (Cambridge: Cambridge University Press, 1997), p. 228. My emphasis.
17 Malebranche, *The Search after Truth*, p. 229. I am indebted to Nicholas Jolley, 'Malebranche on the soul', in *The Cambridge Companion to Malebranche*, ed. Steven Nadler (Cambridge: Cambridge University Press, 2000).
18 See de Lubac, *Augustinianism and Modern Theology*.
19 Werner Beierwaltes, 'Licht', in *Historisches Wörterbuch der Philosophie*, ed. Joachim Ritter and Karlfried Gründer (11 vols., Basel: Schwabe & Co., 1980–), vol. V, pp. 282–9, p. 282.
20 Augustine, *Sermons 1–19*, trans. Edmund Hill (Brooklyn, N.Y.: New City Press, 1990), Sermon 4, pp. 185–213, p. 187.
21 See McCracken, *Malebranche and British Philosophy*, pp. 156–79.
22 Theodor W. Adorno, 'Parataxis. Zur späten Lyrik Hölderlins', in *Noten zur Literatur* (Frankfurt am Main: Suhrkamp, 1990), p. 464.
23 John Locke, *An Essay Concerning Human Understanding*, ed. P. H. Nidditch (Oxford: Clarendon Press, 1974), p. 703.

24 Gordon Kent Thomas, ed., *Wordsworth's Convention of Cintra: A Facsimile of the 1809 Tract* (Provo, Utah: Brigham Young University Press, 1983), p. 9.

CONCLUSION

1 *Tuft of Primroses*, p. 59. The title 'St Paul's' is Ernest De Selincourt's and is not used here, especially since it pre-empts the poem's shock.
2 First full draft: *Tuft of Primroses*, p. 56; later fair copy: ibid., pp. 330–1.
3 Honness La., Ithaca, N.Y., opposite 'Little Feet' daycare centre, November 2000.
4 *Thirteen-Book Prelude*, p. 208, ll. 610–11, ll. 615–23
5 'Societarian' is a word invented by Charles Lamb. 'A complaint of the decay of beggars in the metropolis', in *Elia and the Last Essays of Elia*, ed. J. Bate (Oxford: Oxford University Press, 1987), pp. 130–7, p. 130. Lamb's view of begging should not be thought of as having been endorsed by this theft of his word.
6 *Home at Grasmere*, p. 88 (l. 810), p. 89 (l. 595).
7 *Thirteen-Book Prelude*, vol. I, p. 317 (xiii. 166–70).
8 Immanuel Kant, 'The paralogisms of pure reason', in *Critique of Pure Reason*, trans. Kemp Smith (London: Macmillan, 1933), pp. 328–83.

Bibliography

Adorno, Theodor W., *Negative Dialektik* (Frankfurt am Main: Suhrkamp, 1966)
 Ästhetische Theorie (Frankfurt am Main: Suhrkamp, 1970)
 Noten zur Literatur (Frankfurt am Main: Suhrkamp, 1990)
 'On the classicism of Goethe's *Iphigenie*', in *Notes to literature*, trans. Shierry
  Weber Nicholsen (2 vols., New York: Columbia University Press, 1992),
  pp. 153–70
 'Beitrag zur Ideologienlehre', in *Gesammelte Schriften* (23 vols., Frankfurt am
  Main: Suhrkamp, 1970–), vol. VIII, pp. 457–77
Adorno, Theodor W., and Max Horkheimer, *Dialektik der Aufklärung* [1944], in
  Adorno, *Gesammelte Schriften*, ed. Rolf Tiedemann (23 vols., Frankfurt am
  Main, Suhrkamp, 1970–), vol. III (1981)
 Vorlesung zur Einleitung in die Erkenntnistheorie 1957–58 (Frankfurt am Main:
  Junius, n.d.)
 Hegel: Three Studies, trans. Shierry Weber Nicholsen (Cambridge, Mass.: MIT
  Press, 1993)
Ahlers, Rolf, 'Endlichkeit und absoluter Geist in Hegels Philosophie', *Zeitschrift
  für philosophische Forschung* 29 (1975), pp. 63–80
 'The overcoming of critical theory in the Hegelian unity of theory and
  practice', *Clio* 8.1, (1978), pp. 71–96
Althusser, Louis, *Reading capital*, trans. Ben Brewster (London: Verso, 1979)
 'Ideology and ideological state apparatuses (notes towards an investigation)',
  in *Essays on Ideology* (London: Verso, 1984), pp. 1–60
Arnold, Paul, 'Le "songe" de Descartes', *Cahiers du Sud* 35 (1952), pp. 272–91
Augustine, *The city of God against the pagans* (7 vols., Cambridge, Mass.:
  Harvard University Press, and London: William Heinemann, 1988)
 Sermons 1–19, trans. Edmund Hill (Brooklyn, N.Y.: New City Press, 1990)
Bahti, Timothy, 'Figures of interpretation, the interpretation of figures: a
  reading of Wordsworth's "Dream of the Arab"', *Studies in Romanticism* 18
  (Winter 1979), pp. 601–27
[Baillet, Adrien], *The Life of Monsieur Des-cartes, Containing the History of His
  Philosophy and Works: As Also, The most Remarkable Things that befell him
  during the whole Course of his Life* (London, 1693)

Barnard, L. W., 'Patristic study in England in the early eighteenth century', *Studia Patristica* 23 (1989), pp. 211–14

Barrell, John, *English literature in history, 1730–1780: an equal, wide survey* (London: Hutchinson, 1983)

Basil of Caesarea, *The letters*, trans. Roy J. DeFerrari (4 vols., Cambridge, Mass.: Harvard University Press, 1926–34)

Bayle, Pierre, *A General Dictionary, Historical and Critical*, trans. John Peter Bernard, Thomas Birch and John Lockman (10 vols., 1734–41)

Beierwaltes, Werner, 'Licht', in *Historisches Wörterbuch der Philosophie*, ed. Joachim Ritter and Karlfried Gründer (11 vols., Basel: Schwabe and Co., 1980–), vol. V, pp. 282–89

Benjamin, Walter, 'Fate and character', in *Reflections*, ed. Peter Demetz, trans. Edmund Jephcott (New York: Schocken Books, 1986), pp. 304–11

 'Capitalism as religion', in *Selected writings 1913–1926*, ed. Marcus Bullock and Michael W. Jennings (Cambridge, Mass., and London: Harvard University Press, 1996), pp. 288–91

 The Arcades project, trans Howard Eiland and Kevin McLaughlin (Cambridge, Mass.: Harvard University Press, 1999)

Bennett, Gareth Vaughan, 'Patristic tradition in Anglican thought, 1660–1900', in *Tradition in Luthertum und Anglikanismus*, ed. Günther Gassmann and Vilmos Vajta (Strasbourg: Gütersloher Verlagshaus Gerd Mohn, 1972), pp. 63–87

Berkeley, George, 'A letter to Sir John James, Bart. on the differences between the Roman and Anglican churches', in *The works of George Berkeley*, ed. Alexander Fraser (4 vols., Oxford: Clarendon Press, 1901), vol. IV, pp. 521–34

Bernhardt-Kabisch, Ernst, 'The stone and the shell: Wordsworth, cataclysm, and the myth of Glaucus', *Studies in Romanticism* 24 (Spring 1985), pp. 455–90

Bewell, Alan, *Wordsworth and the Enlightenment: nature, man, and society in the experimental poetry* (New Haven and London: Yale University Press, 1989)

Bialostosky, Don H., *Wordsworth, dialogics, and the practice of criticism* (Cambridge: Cambridge University Press, 1992)

Biblia Sacra Iuxta Vulgatam Versionem, ed. Roger Gryson (Stuttgart: Deutsche Bibelgesellschaft, 1994)

Bingham, Joseph, *Origines Ecclesiasticae: or, the Antiquities of the Christian Church* (10 vols., London, 1711)

Blake, William, *Complete writings*, ed. Geoffrey Keynes (Oxford: Oxford University Press, 1972)

Blanchot, Maurice, 'On one approach to communism', in *Friendship*, trans. Elizabeth Rottenberg (Stanford, Calif.: Stanford University Press, 1997), Meridian: Crossing Aesthetics, pp. 93–7

Blayney, Benjamin, *Jeremiah and Lamentations. A New Translation* (Oxford, 1784)

[Blount, Charles,] *Great is Diana of the Ephesians: or, The Original of Idolatry, Together with the Politick Institutions of the Gentiles Sacrifices* (n.p., n.d.)

Boss, Gilbert, 'Le songe d'une poétique philosophique (Les rêves de Descartes)',
    Dialectica 47.2–3 (1993), pp. 199–216
Bourdieu, Pierre, *Outline of a theory of practice*, trans. Richard Nice (Cambridge:
    Cambridge University Press, 1977)
    The logic of practice, trans. Richard Nice (Cambridge: Polity Press, 1990)
    The field of cultural production, ed. Randal Johnson (Cambridge: Polity Press,
    1993)
    Méditations Pascaliennes (Paris: Editions du Seuil, 1997)
Boyle, Robert, *A Free Enquiry into the Vulgarly Received Notion of Nature* [1686], ed.
    Edward B. Davis and Michael Hunter (Cambridge: Cambridge University
    Press, 1996)
Brakke, David, *Athanasius and the politics of asceticism* (Oxford: Clarendon Press,
    1995)
Bromwich, David, *Disowned by memory: Wordsworth's poetry of the 1790s*
    (Chicago: University of Chicago Press, 1998)
Brown, John, *A Dissertation on the Rise, Union, and Power, the Progressions,
    Separations, and Corruptions, of Poetry and Music. To which is prefixed, The
    Cure of Saul. A Sacred Ode* (London, 1763)
Brown, Peter, *Augustine of Hippo: a biography* (London: Faber and Faber, 1967)
Bryant, Jacob, *A Treatise Upon the Authenticity of the Scriptures, and the Truth of
    the Christian Religion* (London, 1792)
Burke, Edmund, *Thoughts and Details on Scarcity, originally presented to the Right
    Hon. William Pitt, in the month of November 1795* (London, 1800)
    Reflections on the revolution in France, ed. Conor Cruise O'Brien
    (Harmondsworth: Penguin Books, 1969)
Castoriadis, Cornelius, *The imaginary institution of society* (Cambridge: Polity
    Press, 1987)
Cave, William, *Apostolici* (London, 1733)
Cavell, Stanley, *In quest of the ordinary: lines of skepticism and Romanticism*
    (Chicago and London: Chicago University Press, 1988)
Caygill, Howard, *Walter Benjamin: the colour of experience* (London: Routledge,
    1999)
Chandler, James, *Wordsworth's second nature: a study of the poetry and politics*
    (Chicago: University of Chicago Press, 1984)
Chrétien, Jean-Louis, 'La vie sauve', *Les Etudes Philosophiques* 51.1 (1988),
    pp. 37–49
Celan, Paul, 'The Meridian. Speech on the occasion of receiving the Georg
    Büchner Prize, Darmstadt, 22 October 1960', in *Collected prose*, trans.
    Rosmarie Waldrop (Manchester: Carcanet, 1986), pp. 37–55
Cole, John R., *The Olympian dreams and youthful rebellions of René Descartes*
    (Urbana and Chicago: University of Illinois Press, 1992)
Coleridge, Samuel Taylor, *The letters, 1785–1806*, ed. E. L. Griggs (2 vols.,
    Oxford: Oxford University Press, 1956)
    Lectures 1795 on politics and religion, ed. Lewis Patton and Peter Mann
    (Princeton: Princeton University Press, 1971)

Table talk recorded by Henry Nelson Coleridge (and John Taylor Coleridge), ed. Carl Woodring (2 vols., Princeton: Princeton University Press, 1990)

Shorter works and fragments, ed. H. J. Jackson and J. R. de J. Jackson (2 vols., Princeton: Princeton University Press, 1995)

Biographia Literaria, ed. Nigel Leask (London: Everyman, 1997)

Condorcet, *Outlines of an Historical View of the Progress of the Human Mind* (London, 1795)

Connell, Philip, *Romanticism, economics, and the question of 'culture'* (Oxford: Oxford University Press, 2001)

Critchley, Simon, *The ethics of deconstruction: Derrida and Lévinas* (Oxford: Blackwell, 1992)

Davidson, Edward, and William J. Scheick, *Paine, scripture and authority: the Age of Reason as religious and political idea* (Bethlehem: Lehigh University Press, 1994)

de Lubac, Henri, *Augustinianism and modern theology*, ed. Louis Dupré, trans. Lancelot Sheppard (New York: Crossroad Publishing Co., 2000)

de Man, Paul, *The rhetoric of Romanticism* (New York: Columbia University Press, 1984)

'Time and history in Wordsworth', in 'Wordsworth and the production of poetry', ed. Andrzej Warminski and Cynthia Chase: special issue of *diacritics* 17.4 (Winter 1987), pp. 4–17

Aesthetic ideology, ed. Andrzej Warminski (Minneapolis and London: University of Minnesota Press, 1996)

Derrida, Jacques, *Specters of Marx*, trans. Peggy Kamuf (London: Routledge, 1994)

Descartes, René, *The philosophical writings*, trans. John Cottingham, Robert Stoothoff and Dugald Murdoch (3 vols., Cambridge: Cambridge University Press, 1984)

Detienne, Marcel, *The masters of truth in archaic Greece*, trans. Janet Lloyd (New York: Zone Books, 1996)

de Tracy, M. Le Comte Destutt, *Elémens d'Idéologie* (5 vols., Paris, 1824)

Dews, Peter, *The limits of disenchantment* (London: Verso, 1996)

d'Holbach, Baron, *Examen Critique de la Vie & des Ouvrages de Saint-Paul* ('Londres' (probably Amsterdam), 1770)

L'Esprit du Judaisme, ou Examen Raisonné de la Loi de Moyse, & de son influence sur la Religion Chrétienne ('Londres' (probably Amsterdam), 1770)

Dumont, Louis, *From Mandeville to Marx: the genesis and triumph of economic ideology* (Chicago: University of Chicago Press, 1977)

Essays on individualism: modern ideology in anthropological perspective (Chicago and London: University of Chicago Press, 1986)

Dyer, George, 'Prefatory essay. On lyric poetry', in *Poems* (2 vols., London, 1802)

Easthope, Antony, *Wordsworth now and then: Romanticism and contemporary culture* (Buckingham and Philadelphia: Open University, 1993)

[Eaton, Daniel], *Politics for the People, or A Salmagundy for Swine* (4th edn, London, 1794)

Estlin, John Prior, *Evidences of Revealed Religion, and particularly Christianity, stated, with reference to a pamphlet called The Age of Reason* (Bristol, 1796)

Ferguson, Frances, *Wordsworth: language as counter-spirit* (New Haven and London: Yale University Press, 1977)

Ferris, David, *Silent urns: Romanticism, Hellenism and modernity* (Stanford, Calif.: Stanford University Press, 2000)

Flint, Valerie I. H., *The rise of magic in early medieval Europe* (Oxford: Clarendon Press, 1991)

Forster, John Reinhold, trans., 'A Journey Through Egypt ... By M. Granger. Translated from the French ... ', in *Travels through Sicily and that part of Italy formerly called Magna Graecia ... translated from the German* (London, 1773)

Fosbrooke, Thomas Dudley, *The Economy of Monastic Life, (As it Existed in England), A Poem, with Philosophical and Archaeological Illustrations* (Gloucester, n.d.)

Gasché, Rodolphe, *The wild card of reading: on Paul de Man* (Cambridge, Mass.: Harvard University Press, 1998)

Gibbon, Edward, *The history of the decline and fall of the Roman Empire*, ed. David Womersley (3 vols., London: Penguin Books, 1994)

Gravina, Gianvincenzo, *Della Ragione Poetica* [Venice, 1731], repr. in *Opere Italiane. Della Ragione Poetica e della Tragedia* (Cosenza: Brenner, 1992)

Gregory of Nazianzus, *Discours 20–23*, ed. Justin Mossay (Paris: Editions du Cerf, 1980)
  Autobiographical poems, trans. and ed. Carolinne White (Cambridge: Cambridge University Press, 1996)

Haar, Michel, 'Michel Henry entre Phénoménologie et Métaphysique', *Philosophie* 14 (1987), pp. 30–54

Hamacher, Werner, *Pleroma – reading in Hegel: the genesis and structure of a dialectical hermeneutics in Hegel*, trans. Nicholas Walker and Simon Jarvis (London: Athlone, 1998)

Hanmer, Meredith, *The Auncient Ecclesiasticall Histories of the First Six Hundred Years after Christ* (London, 1585)

Hartman, Geoffrey H., *Wordsworth's poetry 1787–1814* (New Haven and London: Yale University Press, 1964)

Hegel, G. W. F., *Phänomenologie des Geistes*, ed. Johannes Hoffmeister (Hamburg: Felix Meiner, 1952)
  Science of logic, trans. A. V. Miller (London: George Allen and Unwin, 1969)
  Werke (20 vols., Frankfurt am Main: Suhrkamp, 1969)
  'The spirit of Christianity and its fate', in *Early theological writings*, trans. T. M. Knox (Philadelphia: University of Pennsylvania Press, 1975), pp. 182–301
  Phenomenology of spirit, trans. A. V. Miller (Oxford: Oxford University Press, 1977)

Heidegger, Martin, *Being and time*, trans. John Macquarrie and Edward Robinson (Oxford: Blackwell, 1962)
  Sein und Zeit (16th edn, Tübingen: Max Niemeyer Verlag, 1986)

Über den Humanismus (Frankfurt am Main: Vittorio Klostermann, 1991)

Einführung in die phänomenologische Forschung, Gesamtausgabe 17 (Frankfurt am Main: Vittorio Klostermann, 1994)

Nietzsche, Gesamtausgabe 6.2 (2 vols., Frankfurt am Main: Vittorio Klostermann, 1997)

Henry, Michel *Marx* (2 vols., Paris: Garnier, 1976)

L'essence de la manifestation (2nd edn, Paris: Presses Universitaires de France, 1990)

Genealogy of psychoanalysis, trans. Douglas Brick (Stanford, Calif.: Stanford University Press, 1993)

Hertz, Neil, 'Lurid figures', in *Reading de Man Reading*, ed. Lindsay Waters and Wlad Godzich (Minneapolis: University of Minnesota Press, 1989), Theory and History of Literature, 59, pp. 82–104

Hillis Miller, J., 'The stone and the shell: the problem of poetic form in Wordsworth's Dream of the Arab', in *Mouvements Premiers: Etudes critiques offertes à Georges Poulet* (Paris: Librairie Jose Corti, 1972), pp. 125–47

Hobbes, Thomas, *A True Ecclesiastical History, from Moses to the Time of Martin Luther, in Verse* (London, 1722)

Leviathan, ed. Richard Tuck (Cambridge: Cambridge University Press, 1991)

Horkheimer, Max, 'Schopenhauer today (1961)', in *Critique of instrumental reason: lectures and essays since the end of World War II*, trans. Matthew J. O'Connell and others (New York: Seabury Press, 1974), pp. 63–83

Horkheimer, Max, et al., 'Diskussionsprotokolle', in Horkheimer, *Gesammelte Schriften* (15 vols., Frankfurt am Main: Fischer, 1985–), vol. XII: *Nachgelassene Schriften 1931–49*, pp. 563–70

Jacobus, Mary, *Romanticism, writing, and sexual difference: essays on* The Prelude (Oxford: Clarendon Press, 1989)

Jama, Sophie, *La nuit de songes de René Descartes* (Paris: Aubier, 1998)

Jarvis, Simon, 'The "unhappy consciousness" and conscious unhappiness: on Adorno's critique of Hegel and the idea of an Hegelian critique of Adorno', in *Hegel's phenomenology of spirit: a re-appraisal*, ed. G. K. Browning (Amsterdam: Kluwer Academic Publishers, 1997), pp. 57–72

'Prosody as cognition', *Critical Quarterly* 40.3 (Autumn 1998), pp. 1–14

Adorno: a critical introduction (Cambridge: Polity Press 1998)

'The gift in theory', *Dionysius* 17 (December 1999), pp. 201–22

'Problems in the phenomenology of the gift', *Angelaki: Journal of the Theoretical Humanities* 6.2 (August 2001), pp. 67–77

'An undeleter for criticism', *diacritics*, special issue on 'Rethinking beauty', 32.1 (Spring 2002), pp. 3–18

'Adorno, Marx, materialism', in *The Cambridge companion to Adorno*, ed. Tom Huhn (Cambridge: Cambridge University Press, 2004), pp. 79–100

'What is speculative thinking?', *Revue Internationale de Philosophie* 227 (2004), pp. 69–83

Jolley, Nicholas, 'Malebranche on the soul', in *The Cambridge companion to Malebranche*, ed. Steven Nadler (Cambridge: Cambridge University Press, 2000)

Kant, Immanuel, *Critique of pure reason*, trans. Norman Kemp Smith (London: Macmillan, 1933)

   Kritik der Urteilskraft, ed. Gerhard Lehmann (Stuttgart: Philipp Reclam Jun., 1963)

   Critique of judgement, trans. Werner S. Pluhar (Indianapolis: Hackett, 1987)

   'Critique of practical reason', in *Practical philosophy*, ed. and trans. Mary J. Gregor (Cambridge: Cambridge University Press, 1996), pp. 137–271

   Critique of pure reason, ed. and trans. Paul Guyer and Allen Wood (Cambridge: Cambridge University Press, 1998)

Kaufman, Robert, 'Red Kant, or the persistence of the third critique in Adorno and Jameson', *Critical Inquiry* 26.4 (Summer 2000), pp. 682–724

   'Negatively capable dialectics: Keats, Vendler, Adorno and the theory of the avant-garde', *Critical Inquiry* 27.2 (Winter 2001), pp. 354–84

   'Everybody hates Kant: Blakean formalism and the symmetries of Laura Moriarty', *Modern Language Quarterly*, 61.1 (March 2001), pp. 131–55

Kennedy, Emmet, *A philosophe in the age of revolution: Destutt de Tracy and the origins of 'Ideology'* (Philadelphia: American Philosophical Society, 1978)

Kirk, G. S., J. E. Raven and M. Schofield, *The presocratic philosophers* (2nd edn, Cambridge: Cambridge University Press, 1983)

Kisiel, Theodore, *The genesis of Heidegger's 'Being and time'* (Berkeley, Los Angeles and London: University of California Press, 1993)

Klancher, Jon P., *The making of English reading audiences, 1790–1830* (Madison, Wis.: University of Wisconsin Press, 1987)

Lamb, Charles, 'A complaint of the decay of beggars in the metropolis', in *Elia and the Last Essays of Elia*, ed. J. Bate (Oxford: Oxford University Press, 1987), pp. 130–7

Lamb, Jonathan, 'Hartley and Wordsworth: philosophical language and figures of the sublime', *Modern Language Notes* 97.5 (1982), pp. 1964–85

Leask, Nigel, 'Pantisocracy and the politics of the "Preface" to *Lyrical ballads*', in *Reflections of revolution*, ed. Allison Yarrington and Kelvin Everest (London: Routledge, 1993), pp. 39–57

Le Goff, Jacques, *Your money or your life: economy and religion in the Middle Ages*, trans. Patricia Raum (New York: Zone Books, 1990)

Levinson, Marjorie, *Wordsworth's great period poems* (Cambridge: Cambridge University Press, 1986)

Lévi-Strauss, Claude, *The elementary structures of kinship*, trans. James Harle Bell, John Richard von Sturmer and Rodney Needham (Boston: Beacon Press, 1969)

Locke, John, *An essay concerning human understanding*, ed. P. H. Nidditch (Oxford: Clarendon Press, 1974)

Lonsdale, Roger, ed., *Gray, Collins and Goldsmith: the complete poems* (London: Longman, 1969) ed., *New Oxford book of eighteenth-century verse* (Oxford: Oxford University Press, 1984)

Loux, Michael J., *Metaphysics: contemporary readings* (London: Routledge, 2001)

Lowman, Moses, *A Dissertation on the Civil Government of the Hebrews* (London, 1740)

Lowth, Robert, *Isaiah. A New Translation* (London, 1779)

Lucan, *The Civil War*, ed. and trans. J. D. Duff (London: Heinemann, 1969)

Malebranche, Nicolas, *The search after truth*, trans. Thomas M. Lennon and Paul J. Olscamp (Cambridge: Cambridge University Press, 1997)

Mapp, Nigel, 'History and the sacred in de Man and Benjamin', in *Between the psyche and the polis: refiguring history in literature and theory*, ed. Michael Rossington and Anne Whitehead (Aldershot: Ashgate, 2000), pp. 38–58

Marion, Jean-Luc 'Générosité et phénoménologie. Remarques sur l'interprétation du *cogito* cartésien par Michel Henry', *Les Etudes Philosophiques* 51.1 (1988), pp. 51–72

    Étant donné: essai d'une phénoménologie de la donation (2nd, corrected edn, Paris: Presses Universitaires de France, 1998)

    'Does thought dream? The three dreams, or the awakening of the philosopher', in *Cartesian questions: method and metaphysics* (Chicago: University of Chicago Press, 1999)

Maritain, Jacques, *Le songe de Descartes* (Paris: Editions R. A. Corréa, 1932)

    The dream of Descartes, together with some other essays, trans. Mabelle L. Andison (New York: Philosophical Library, 1944)

Marx, Karl, 'Kritik des Gothaer Programms', in Marx and Friedrich Engels, *Werke* (42 vols. in 44, Berlin: Dietz, 1960–83), vol. XIX, pp. 15–32

    'Die Deutsche Ideologie', in *Frühschriften. Zweiter Band*, ed. Hans-Joachim Lieber and Peter Furth (Stüttgart: Cotta-Verlag, 1971)

Marx, Karl, and Friedrich Engels, 'Die Deutsche Ideologie', in *Werke*, vol. III (Berlin: Dietz, 1962), pp. 9–530.

    The holy family; or, critique of critical criticism, in *Collected works*, vol. IV (London: Lawrence and Wishart, 1975)

    Capital, volume 1, trans. Ben Fowkes (Harmondsworth: Penguin Books, 1976)

    Theories of surplus value, trans. Emile Burns (3 vols., London: Lawrence and Wishart, 1978)

McCracken, Charles J., *Malebranche and British philosophy* (Oxford: Clarendon Press, 1983)

Mellor, Anne K., *Romanticism and gender* (New York and London: Routledge, 1993

Menn, Stephen, *Descartes and Augustine* (Cambridge: Cambridge University Press, 1998)

Milner, Joseph, *The History of the Church of Christ* (4 vols., Cambridge, 1795–1809)

Milton, John, *Complete shorter poems*, ed. John Carey (London: Longman, 1971)

Momigliano, Arnaldo, 'Marcel Mauss and the quest for the person in Greek biography and autobiography', in *The category of the person* ed. Michael Carrithers, Steven Collins and Steven Lukes (Cambridge: Cambridge University Press, 1986), pp. 83–92

More, Henry, *Divine Dialogues* (2 vols., London, 1668)
    'An antidote against idolatry' in *The Theological works* (London, 1707)

The New Jerusalem Bible (London: Darton, Longman and Todd, 1990)

O'Donnell, Brennan, *The passion of meter: a study of Wordsworth's metrical art* (Kent, Ohio, and London: Kent State University Press, 1995)

Owen, James, *The History of Images and Image-Worship. Shewing, The Original and Progress of Idolatry among Pagans, Jews, and Christians: with A Refutation of the Second Council of Nice, and of other Advocates for Idolatry* (London, 1709)

Paine, Thomas *The Age of Reason. Part the Second. Being an Investigation of True and Fabulous Theology* (London, 1795)
    Political writings, ed. Bruce Kuklick (Cambridge: Cambridge University Press, 1989)

Paley, William, *Reasons for Contentment; addressed to the labouring part of the British public* (London, 1793)

Parry, Jonathan, 'The gift, the Indian gift, and the "Indian gift"', *Man*, NS 21 (1986), pp. 453–73

Pfau, Thomas, *Wordsworth's profession: form, class, and the logic of early Romantic cultural production* (Stanford, Calif.: Stanford University Press 1997)

Plotz, John, 'The necessary veil: Wordsworth's "Residence in London"', in *The crowd: British literature and public politics* (Berkeley, Calif.: University of California Press, 2000), pp. 15–42

Pope, Alexander, *The Dunciad*, ed. J. Sutherland (London: Methuen, 1943)

Potts, Abbie Findlay, ed., *The ecclesiastical sonnets of William Wordsworth: a critical edition* (New Haven: Yale University Press, 1922)

Poulet, Georges, 'The dream of Descartes', in *Studies in human time*, trans. Elliott Coleman (Baltimore: Johns Hopkins University Press, 1956), pp. 50–73

Priestley, Joseph, *An History of the Corruptions of Christianity* (2 vols., Birmingham, 1782)
    An Answer to Mr. Paine's Age of Reason (London, 1795)

Prior, Matthew, *Poems on Several Occasions* (London, 1709)
    The literary works, ed. H. Bunker Wright and Monroe K. Spears (2 vols., Oxford: Clarendon Press, 1971)

Prynne, J. H., *Poems* (Newcastle upon Tyne: Bloodaxe, 1999)

Pyle, Forrest, *The ideology of imagination: subject and society in the discourse of Romanticism* (Stanford, Calif.: Stanford University Press, 1995)

Quine, W. V. O., 'On what there is', *Review of Metaphysics* 2 (1948), pp. 21–48

Rodis-Lewis, Geneviève, 'Le premier registre de Descartes', *Archives de Philosophie* 54.1 (1991), pp. 353–77; 54.2 (1991), pp. 639–57

Rose, Gillian, *Hegel contra sociology* (London: Athlone, 1981)

'From speculative to dialectical thinking', in *Judaism and modernity: philosophical essays* (Oxford: Blackwell, 1993), pp. 3–63.

Ryle, Gilbert, *The concept of mind* (Chicago: University of Chicago Press, 1984)

Schiller, Friedrich, *On the aesthetic education of man: in a series of letters*, ed. and trans. Elizabeth M. Wilkinson and L. A. Willoughby (Oxford: Clarendon Press, 1967)

Schlegel, Friedrich, 'Athenäums-Fragmente', in *Werke in einem Band*, ed. Wolfdietrich Rasch (Vienna: Carl Hanser, 1971), pp. 25–88

Schmitz, Hermann, *Anaximander und die Anfänge der griechischen Philosophie* (Bonn: Bouvier, 1988)

Shaver, Chester L., and Alice C. Shaver, *Wordsworth's library: a catalogue* (New York: Octagon Books, 1979)

Simpson, David, *Wordsworth and the figurings of the real* (London: Macmillan, 1982)

Wordsworth's historical imagination: the poetry of displacement (London: Methuen, 1987)

Smith, Adam, *An Enquiry into the Nature and Causes of the Wealth of Nations* (2 vols., London, 1776)

An Inquiry into the Nature and Causes of the Wealth of Nations, ed. Edwin Cannan (2 vols. in 1, Chicago: University of Chicago Press, 1976)

Smyser, Jane Worthington, 'Wordsworth's dream of poetry and science: *The Prelude, V*', *Publications of the Modern Language Association* 71.1 (March 1956), pp. 269–75

Stock, R. D., ed., *Samuel Johnson's literary criticism* (Lincoln, Neb.: University of Nebraska Press, 1974)

Strathern, Marilyn, 'No nature, no culture: the Hagen case', in *Nature, Culture and Gender*, ed. Strathern and Carol MacCormack (Cambridge: Cambridge University Press, 1980), pp. 174–222

Stukeley, William, *Stonehenge. a Temple Restor'd to the British Druids* (London, 1740)

Sutherland, Kathryn, 'Revised relations? Material text, immaterial text, and the electronic environment', *Text. Transactions of the Society for Textual Scholarship* 11 (1998), pp. 16–39

Sutherland, Keston, 'J. H. Prynne and philology', unpublished Ph.D. thesis, University of Cambridge, 2004

Swift, Jonathan, *A tale of a tub and other works*, ed. Angus Ross and David Woolley (Oxford: Oxford University Press, 1986)

Sykes Davies, Hugh, *Wordsworth and the worth of words*, ed. John Kerrigan and Jonathan Wordsworth (Cambridge: Cambridge University Press, 1986)

Theunissen, Michael, *Sein und Schein. Die kritische Funktion der Hegelschen Logik* (Frankfurt am Main: Suhrkamp, 1980)

Thomas, Gordon Kent, ed., *Wordsworth's Convention of Cintra: A Facsimile of the 1809 Tract* (Provo, Utah: Brigham Young University Press, 1983)

Thompson, E. P., *Customs in common* (London: Penguin, 1993)

Toland, John, *Letters to Serena* (London, 1704)

Tort, Patrick, *La Constellation de Thot* (Paris: Aubier-Montagne, 1981)
    Marx et le problème de l'idéologie (Paris: PUF, 1986)
Turgot, Anne Robert Jacques, 'Reflections on the formation and distribution of wealth', in *Turgot on progress, sociology and economics*, ed. and trans. Ronald L. Meek (Cambridge: Cambridge University Press, 1973), pp. 119–82
Volney, Constantin, *Travels through Syria and Egypt in the Years 1783, 1784 and 1785* (2 vols., London, 1788)
    The Ruins: or a Survey of the Revolutions of Empires (2nd edn, London, 1795)
    Law of Nature, or Catechism of French Citizens (London, 1796)
Warminski, Andrzej, 'Facing language: Wordsworth's first poetic Spirits', in 'Wordsworth and the production of poetry', ed. Warminski and Cynthia Chase, special issue of *diacritics* 17.4 (Winter 1987), pp. 18–31
Watson, Richard, *An Apology for the Bible, in a series of letters addressed to Thomas Paine* (London, 1796)
Weiner, Annette, *Inalienable possessions: the paradox of keeping-while-giving* (Berkeley, Los Angeles and London: University of California Press, 1992)
Wennerstrom, Ann, *The music of everyday speech: prosody and discourse analysis* (Oxford: Oxford University Press, 2001)
West, Thomas, *The Antiquities of Furness* (London, 1774)
Wilkinson, John, 'Cadence', *Reality Studios* 9 (1987)
Wilkinson, Joshua Lucock, *The Wanderer: or anecdotes and incidents, the result and occurrence of a ramble on foot, through France, Germany and Italy, in 1791 and 1793* (2 vols., London, 1798)
Williams, Daniel H., 'Constantine, Nicaea, and the "fall" of the Church', in *Christian origins: theology, rhetoric and community*, ed. Lewis Ayres and Gareth Jones (London and New York: Routledge, 1998)
Wordsworth, William, *The Excursion, being a portion of The Recluse, a Poem* (London, 1814)
    The poems, ed. John O. Hayden (2 vols., London: Penguin: 1977)
    Selected prose, ed. John O. Hayden (London: Penguin Books, 1988)
Wrangham, Francis, *Rome is Fallen! A Sermon; preached at the Visitation held at Scarborough, June 5, 1798* (York, 1798)
    A Poem on the Restoration of Learning in the East (Cambridge, 1805)
Wu, Duncan, 'Editing intentions', *Essays in Criticism* 41.1 (January 1991), pp. 1–10
Wyatt, John, *Wordsworth and the geologists* (Cambridge: Cambridge University Press, 1995)

Index

Abraham, 41
Adorno, Theodor W., 102, 155, 186, 227, 228, 231
  on Hölderlin's late style, 207
'aesthetic ideology', concept of, 13, 74–8, 83, 126, 173, 191
Ahlers, Rolf, 242
Algeria, 103
Althusser, Louis, 69–73, 74
Ambrose, 98
American Indians, 16
Anaximander, 19–20
Antiparos, grotto of, 145
Antony, St, 125, 186
Archimedes, 15
Arianism, 120–1
Ariosto, Lodovico, 48, 151
  Orlando Furioso, 151
'Arminian' enlightenment, 111
Arnold, Paul, 246–7
Athanasius, 121–2
Athens, classical, 126
aufheben, 249
Augustine, 62, 64–5, 121, 165, 206–7
Augustinianism, modern sub-, 196
Ausonius, 175

'bad infinity', 133–7, 149
Bacon, Francis, 53, 82, 83
Bahti, Timothy, 246–7
Baillet, Aarien, 176, 177
Basil the Great, 112-113, 118, 119–31
bathos, 8, 25
Bauer, Bruno, 57, 72
Bayle, Pierre, 115–16, 118
Beaupuy, Michel, 151, 175
Bedouin, the, 184, 190–1
Beierwaltes, Werner, 206–7
Benjamin, Walter, 133, 137
Berkeley, George, 164, 179

Bernhardt-Kabisch, Ernst, 184
Bewell, Alan, 22, 224, 244
Bialostosky, Don H., 244
Bingham, Joseph, 115–16, 123–4, 128
Blake, William, 41, 163–5
Blanchot, Maurice, 88–91
Blayney, Benjamin, 40, 50
bliss, 201, 204
Blount, Charles, 66
Bourdieu, Pierre, 93–7, 103–4
Bourdin, Pierre, 160
Boyle, Robert, 66–8, 79
Bromwich, David, 1–3, 23, 156, 243
Brown, John, *Dissertation on Poetry and Music*, 16
Büchner, Georg, *Lenz*, 179
Burke, Edmund, 99, 112–13
Butler, James, 37

Calvert, Raisley, 101
Calvinism, as 'Superlapsarianism', 66
Cambridge Intelligencer, 54
Canaanites, destruction of, 43, 44
Castoriadis, Cornelius, 96
Cave, William, 118, 127
Cavell, Stanley, 3, 204
Celan, Paul, 193
  'The Meridian', 179–80, 189
Cervantes, Miguel de, 48
  Don Quixote, 60, 150–1, 166, 175, 189, 190, 214
Chandler, James, 53
Chanut, Hector-Pierre, 174
Chase, Cynthia, 244
Chrétien, Jean-Louis, 246–7, 249
Cole, John H., 247
Coleridge, Henry Nelson, 229
Coleridge, Samuel Taylor, 2, 4, 23, 24, 28, 35, 42, 48, 54, 120, 137, 166–9, 175, 229, 244
  Lectures on Revealed Religion, 44–5

CAMBRIDGE STUDIES IN ROMANTICISM

General Editors
MARILYN BUTLER, *University of Oxford*
JAMES CHANDLER, *University of Chicago*